FRIENDS MADE, MOMENTS SHARED, MEMORIES FOR LIFE

AN ORAL HISTORY OF VMSB 343 UNITED STATES MARINE CORPS IN WORLD WAR II

by

MEMBERS OF THE VMSB 343 REUNION ASSOCIATION

Walter G. LeTendre, Compiling Editor
Ferner L. Burkholder, Contributing Editor
Wm. F. S. Lemieux, Technical Editor

Nadine LeTendre, Cover Design Artist

Published by Lemieux International, Ltd.

ISBN: 0-9667269-4-4

Library of Congress Cataloging-in-Publication Data

Friends made, moments shared, memories for life : an oral history of VMSB 343
United States marine Corps in World War II / by members of the VMSB 343
Reunion Association ; Ferner L. Burkholder, editor, Walter G. LeTendre,
compiling editor, Wm. F. S. Lemieux, technical editor.
    p.cm.
    ISBN 0-9667269-1-X— I SBN 0-9667269-4-4 (pbk.)
    1. World War, 1939-1945—Aerial operations, American. 2. World War, 1939-
1945—Campaigns—Pacific Area. 3. United States. Marine Scout Bombing
Squadron, 343rd. 4. Soldiers—United States—Interviews. 5. Pacific Area—
History, Military—20th century. 6. World War, 1939-1945—Personal narratives,
American. I. Burkholder, Ferner L., 1923- II. Letendre, Walter G., 1923- III.
Lemieux, Wm. F. S., 1938- IV. VMSB 343 Reunion Association.

D785.U63 F75 2000
940.54'25—dc21
                                                                  00-030973

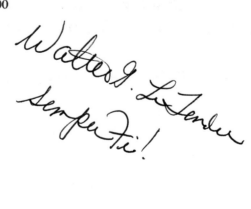

*This book is dedicated to the memory of
Master Sergeant Ferner Lohr Burkholder,
and all the other members of our squadron
who have passed on before us to join that
Great General in the sky.*

*"Bucky" Burkholder, as he was known,
was the first historian for VMSB 343 Reunion
Association, and with the assistance of his
wife, Vida, got us going in the right direction.*

*Our good buddy, Burkholder,
served twenty-two years in the Marine Corps,
including tours of duty on the U.S.S. Saratoga,
and in Tarawa, Iwo Jima, Okinawa, and on Midway.*

"Bucky" is dearly missed by all of us.

Acknowledgments

The members of the Reunion Association of VMSB 343 are deeply grateful to all those who so generously dedicated their time and effort to the compiling and production of this book. Without their persistence, ingenuity, and the ongoing support of their families it would not have been brought to completion.

We are especially indebted to our historian, Walter "Joe" LeTendre, who volunteered to continue the work of "Burkie" Burkholder in collecting these memories, news clips, pictures, and photos, and organizing them into the story and history of VMSB 343. We also extend a warm and personal thank you to his son, Daniel E. LeTendre who created the book's title, and to his granddaughter, Nadine LeTendre, whose professional artistry and design grace our cover. A very special thank you to Ralph Heidenreich for his role in tracking down members, stories, and memorabilia for our book and handling the funds to produce it.

A profound thank you to our typesetter, Barbara Olive, who turned an enormous pile of typed and handwritten letters into a book, to William. F. S. Lemieux whose editing helped express the thoughts and feelings of everyone in our association, and to our copy editor, David Subat, who tidied up our punctuation and grammar.

We can't begin to list everyone who contributed to the making of this book, or every person who took the time to share personal insights and memorabilia with us, but we offer our heartfelt thanks to each and every one of you.

TABLE OF CONTENTS

EDITOR'S NOTE

WWI was the war to end all wars, but it didn't! Within twenty years, America faced the greatest danger she had faced since the Revolutionary War. In Europe, Germany had re-armed, Italy had a dictator, and the fascists had defeated a Democratic Government in Spain. England and France were bankrupted by depression, and had to cut military spending. America had dismissed the great army of World War I, and had failed to re-arm.

Faced at last in 1941 with the bombing of Pearl Harbor by the Japanese, an Asian tyranny, at last America flexed her industrial muscle and struck back.

The biographies of Patton, Eisenhower, Marshal, Nimitz and McArthur, tell the great story of America's rise to defeat this enemy and to dominate the 20th Century.

However, the greatest story remains largely untold. It is the story of the American people, ordinary people, who joined together to put their lives on hold and defeated an enemy intent on destroying their freedom.

At age sixty-one, I belong to the last generation which fully remembers World War II. It was a fact of life as I grew up. It colored every aspect of my growing up, creating memories that have remained with me throughout my life. My father was a soldier scheduled to land in the first wave on Japan. My uncle, my father's brother, was a shore patrol officer. The third brother worked for the Soo Line and lived in North Dakota. His job was to keep the trains going East and West. My Aunt Ruth, a nurse and also my godmother, cared for the wounded as they came back from Europe. My mother took over part of my father's job at the store he managed, since there were no men to do the work. As a result I spent a lot of my time at my grandparents' home.

Among the most poignant memories that strike my consciousness are those of my Cousin Helen, whose husband's plane disappeared over the Pacific. I remember her running into my grandparents' home screaming, "Aunt Lil! He went down! He went down!" In her arms she was holding the son her husband had never seen. My grandmother put her arms around Helen and rocked her softly on the sofa. I remember my grandmother looked at me, tears coming down her cheeks, and said, "Billy, go in the dining room and sit with grandpa. "Just then Uncle Walt, our city's fire chief, and Aunt Francis, my grandmother's sister rushed in. Jimmy Lee, the baby in Helen's arms, the son who would never see his father, started to squall.

A few months later I was sitting at home on a Saturday afternoon with mom. I remember that it was sunny but cold, very cold. A car pulled up outside. There had been a battle called "The Bulge". They were sorry to tell my mother that her brother had died. According to accounts he had taken out a flame thrower, saving the men under his command. He had been burned alive. My dad had gone to the Philippines, or some other isle in the Pacific a few days earlier. Mom picked up the telephone, called my grandparents and said we would be walking over. She said something about my needing my grandfather.

I remember a little garden in the backyard called a "Victory Garden". It had twisted carrots, onions, a few radishes and some lettuce. I probably drowned most of it out with my all too frequent watering. I remember grandpa bringing home a piece of round steak. My grandmother cut it in half and cut one of the halves in half. The big piece went on my plate. There were daily morning Masses, well attended; standing-room-only benedictions on Sunday night. There was laughter, as when Helen brought Jamie Lee, Sr. over to be married because he was shipping out. There were tears, when Jamie Lee was taken from our lives. There was generosity as with the steak, and an entire nation's dedication as with the poor "Victory Garden". Most of all there was a time of unity and strength for which we are the living memorial. The real strength of the nation in World War II was that people came together to defeat a common enemy. They came together as Americans.

U.S. Marine Corps Dive Bombing Squadron, VMSB-343 was composed of such Americans. They were marines in the tradition of Semper Fi, molded as part of a generation bred to loyalty and honor.

In 1987, survivors of this squadron formed an organization dedicated to the heroism and memory of fallen comrades. Shortly thereafter, they realized that their individual memories and experiences were an important part of the great story of WWII.

They were right. No General, no Admiral, no President, can fight a war without the will of a nation and the complete support of the fighting warriors in the field. This book is a monument to the valor, will, and experiences of VMSB-343 and those that have come to love them. It is not, however, only the story of VMSB-343. It is also a window into the lives of every American who lived and fought in this war.

When Walter LeTendre asked me to complete the editing he and Fern Burkholder had begun in this book I was honored, and more than a little intrigued. It touched ghosts of the past in my own life and memories seldom discussed. At first I thought I would strengthen every sentence, but as I dug into the manuscript it dawned on me that this book, like my family story, was a recounting of human experiences held alive in hearts and memories. Its strength lay in the fact that it told the story of American men and women as they fought, lived and created the second half of the century. If in any way their language had rough spots, their story did not. In the end I only changed those sentences which were unclear or confusing for a reader. The book is organized into eight chronological sections, though one or two segments were placed out of time line because they advanced the story. An example is Walter's wife's describing how she met Walter, which implies their future journey to the altar.

In some instances events are recounted by more than one person, each from their own perspective. The truth of all the stories in the book is demonstrated by the remarkable similarity in the accounts of different writers.

There are two kinds of memory. The first is memory that comes near to being relived when brought forward; scent, flavor, mind, all jumble into a momentary reliving of the event. The other kind of memory is a technical memory for days, weeks, and facts. It has little of life because it is only stored information. The memories in this book are of the former. They are part of the defining experiences of the writers. One might say this book was never written, rather it was experienced. In editing it I have tried to allow the reader to touch that experience. VMSB-343 created this story, a page in the history of America. Without these stories the epic tales of a Manchester, the great biographies of the leaders, the presidential decisions that guided the nation, have no meaning.

VMSB-343 and tens of thousands of other such groups, along with their civilian supporters were and are the true muscle of "the greatest generation" that won the war for democracy, snatching freedom from the jaws of tyrants at great cost. I would like to thank all the members of VMSB-343 for allowing me the privilege of editing their story.

William F. Lemieux

PREFACE

GHOSTS AND SURVIVORS

Return to the Battle of MIDWAY

by Thomas B. Allen
Photographs by David Doubilet

For the warriors who survived it, the Battle of Midway lives on, etched in their memories as searing moments that carried death but gave them life. The epic World War II duel between aircraft carriers of the United States and Japan ended with five of those carriers sunk. They lie over three miles deep in the Pacific, gone but still remembered by the men who stood on slanting decks as their ships began to die.

On June 4, 1942, 18-year-old Bill Surgi crouched on a catwalk on the port side of the *Yorktown,* feeding .30-caliber bullets to a machine gun lashed to a rail. Surgi saw three torpedoes drop from Japanese bombers that were skimming the sea through a hail of gunfire. He looked up and saw a Japanese airman in a white scarf waving or shaking his fist. He watched one torpedo, "bright and shiny," speeding toward him. Then came two blasts, hurling Surgi to the deck of the catwalk.

Fifty-six years later Surgi and three other war veterans—one American, two Japanese—sailed with Robert D. Ballard, the underwater explorer who found the *Titanic*, as he searched for the lost ships of Midway. I was also aboard, learning about Midway from these old foes turned latter-day shipmates. Their remembered moments led me to other survivors, to other moments that formed a mosaic of men who were there.

Aboard Ballard's search ship, every time the U.S. Navy robot submersible went down to seek his ship, Bill Surgi took up his watch station at a monitor showing images transmitted from far below us. Bill wore a white Navy hat, dungarees, and a blue shirt with a petty officer 1st-class insignia on the sleeve. In his lap he held the helmet—"my tin hat"—that he had clutched when, with his left arm broken, he had tried to stay afloat in the oily waters near the abandoned *Yorktown*. An officer had ordered him to let go of the helmet, but he had stubbornly held on. While he watched the monitor, he held the helmet, vowing not to put it on until he saw his ship again.

Then came the day when the image of the *Yorktown* appeared on the monitor, green and ghostly. Lights played across the hull. And there, black against the camera's spotlights, was the hole made by the Japanese aerial torpedoes.

"She looks good for the shape she's in," Bill said softly. And he put on his helmet.

Taisuke Maruyama, a 19-year-old flying from the carrier *Hiryu*, commanded the plane Bill Surgi had seen torpedoing the *Yorktown*. As Maruyama's plane began its torpedo run, bullets ripped into it, wounding the gunner. "Gas was coming out like a vapor," Maruyama tells me as we sip tea alongside a Japanese garden. "It was like being in a spiderweb of bullets. I thought, I don't want to die before dropping my torpedo." He ordered his pilot to release it. The *Yorktown* loomed before them. The pilot zoomed across the carrier, the propeller almost touching the flight deck. Maruyama, seated between the pilot and the gunner, slid back the canopy and swung a camera around to photograph the torpedo's explosion.

Three of the four survivors sailing on Ballard's search ship had also fought in the air. Harry Ferrier had flown as a radioman-gunner in a torpedo plane defending Midway. It was the first time the 17-year-old had seen combat.

Yuji Akamatsu and Haruo Yoshino had flown from the aircraft carrier *Kaga*. Both men were veterans of battle. On December 7, 1941, in the Japanese attack on Pearl Harbor, Yoshino had torpedoed the battleship *Oklahoma,* and Akumatsu had attacked the battleship *Arizona*. Now, six months later, they were part of a

Japanese invasion armada heading for the U.S. naval base on Midway, two small islands that form a coral atoll in the North Pacific, about 1,300 miles northwest of Hawaii.

That armada was the main prong of a colossal offensive aimed at destroying American power in the Pacific. Japanese strike forces, spread across 2,000 miles of ocean, were to invade Midway and two islands in the Aleutians, the bleak archipelago curving westward from the Alaska mainland. Japanese strategists expected to draw the U.S. Pacific Fleet from Pearl Harbor and into a decisive battle. Adm. Isoruku Yamamoto, commander in chief of the Japanese Combined Fleet and architect of the Pearl Harbor attack, believed that his plan would smash the enemy fleet, forcing the Americans to a negotiated peace.

Spearheading the Japanese operation were four aircraft carriers: the *Akagi, Kaga, Hiryu, and Soryu.* Surrounding them was a screen of 11 destroyers, two battleships, and three cruisers. The other forces included transports for the 5,000 troops who would invade Midway. Secret documents recently made available show that U.S. commanders had reason to believe the Japanese were contemplating poison gas for the invasion. This would have been a fateful decision, for the United States would have retaliated, and a horrible new weapon would have entered the war.

As the Japanese fleet steamed toward Midway on June 2, Yamamoto hoped the advantage of surprise was still on his side. But in fact three U.S. carriers-the *Yorktown, Hornet,* and *Enterprise*— with their destroyers and cruisers, were waiting to pounce on an enemy they knew was coming because of the incredible performance of U.S. code breakers.

Since long before the Pearl Harbor attack, U.S. cryptanalysts had been chipping away at the Imperial Navy's most secret communications. The frontline code breakers worked in a basement room at the naval district headquarters building in Pearl Harbor, a dank, dark place known as "the dungeon". It is still there, empty and forgotten.

Ruling the room in 1942 was a genius of code breaking, Comdr. Joseph J. Rochefort. Rarely sleeping or eating, he paced the windowless room in his shabby red smoking jacket and carpet slippers, downing cups of coffee and coming up with answers to riddles. "He never took anything for granted," remembers Gilven M. Slonim, one of the cryptanalysts. "Only if it could be proven was it intelligence."

REPORT TO THE U.S.S.ENTERPRISE: "ENEMY FLEET UNITS ON A COURSE FOR MIDWAY. LAUNCH BOMBING 6."

At age 88 Richard Best recalls the day he commanded Bombing 6, a squadron of Dauntless dive-bombers. He spotted the Japanese carrier *Akagi* and aimed at the flight deck's red rising sun. His bomb hit home. Other Dauntlesses set a cruiser afire. A faulty oxygen system seared Best's lungs, and after Midway he never flew again. But, he says "I quit at the top."

In the spring of 1942 the code breakers cracked intercepted Japanese messages referring to an attack on AF, a place that Rochefort deduced to be Midway. When superiors in Washington would not accept his theory, Rochefort employed a ruse. He told Midway to transmit to Pearl Harbor radio messages about a water problem, both in clear test and in low-level code that he knew the Japanese could read. On May 22 Japanese naval intelligence, in a message heard by U.S. interceptors, reported a water problem on AF. So AF was Midway.

Reporting to Adm. Chester W. Nimitz, commander in chief of the Pacific Fleet, Rochefort predicted that the Japanese would attack the Aleutians on June 3 and Midway the next day. Although members of his staff and jittery officers in Washington warned Nimitz that the code breakers were falling for a Japanese deception operation, Nimitz used Rochefort's report as the linchpin for U.S. strategy.

To fight the four Japanese carriers and their fleet, Nimitz had two seaworthy carriers—the *Enterprise* and the *Hornet*—and the battered *Yorktown.* She had arrived in Pearl Harbor on May 27, a stream of leaking oil spreading for miles behind her. A bomb had struck her in the Battle of the Coral Sea on May 8, holing her flight deck and exploding deep within the ship. Crewmen like Bill Surgi expected that she would be sent to the U.S. West Coast for repairs.

But Nimitz ordered her readied for battle in three days. Some 1,500 yard workers clambered aboard, patched her flight deck, welded steel plates on her hull, and shored up her collapsed bulkheads with timber.

The *Enterprise* and the *Hornet* left Pearl Harbor on May 28. Two days later came the *Yorktown*. Arrayed with their support ships in two task forces, the carriers rendezvoused on June 2 at a spot about 390 miles northeast of Midway designated "Point Luck." The name was fitting, for the outnumbered American forces would need large measures of luck to win the day. Their chances of success would be much higher if they could find the Japanese before the Japanese found them.

As it happened, June 3 was their lucky day. That morning "Ens. Jack Reid, piloting a PBY Catalina flying boat, was flying a search fan out of Midway. At 9 o'clock, 30 miles beyond his 700-mile search range, Reid saw what first looked like "dirty spots on the windshield." After a second look he shouted, "I believe we have hit the jackkpot!" Reid dived, putting the PBY just above the wave tops, and began counting enemy ships and sending coded messages. Hours later, as he landed in the Midway lagoon, one sputtering engine quit; as he moored at a buoy, the other engine also ran out of gas.

That same day two Japanese carriers in Alaska waters launched planes that bombed Dutch Harbor in the Aleutians, just as Rochefort had predicted. His other forecast came true at dawn on June 4 when the Japanese strike force launched 108 aircraft to bomb Midway.

The planes that attacked Midway ran into heavy antiaircraft fire and fought fierce dogfights against slow, outclassed U.S. fighters. Swarms of fast, agile Japanese Zeros massacred the Americans. Of the 25 Marine fighters that rose to defend Midway, only 8 survived, and only 2 of those would ever fly again. Fourteen of the pilots were killed and four wounded.

Fifty-one other Midway planes, among them six TBF Avenger torpedo bombers, set out to attack the Japanese fleet. Each Avenger was manned by a pilot and two gunners. As the planes neared their target, more than 20 Zeros jumped them. Within seconds a Zero's cannon shells and machine-gun bullets tore into one of the planes, killing turret gunner Jay Manning. The pilot, Ens. Bert Earnest, did not immediately know that Manning was dead. But Harry Ferrier, in the tunnel-like lower gun station, did. He felt something dripping and looked up and forward to see, through a red haze, a sight he would always hate to remember.

Other shells knocked out the hydraulic system and elevator wires. The tail wheel dropped, slowing down the already slow-moving bomber. A shell fragment hit Earnest's right cheek. A bullet grazed Ferrier's scalp, knocking him out. As the plane dived toward the sea, Earnest saw a cruiser and dropped his torpedo. The plane lurched upward, and Earnest managed to get control. "There was blood all over the plane," he recalls. "I thought I was long gone." He had no compass, but eventually he saw the big black smoke rising from Midway and headed for that, his bomb bay doors hanging open and 70-odd holes in his plane.

He skidded in for a landing, "I waited for the other people to come back," Earnest says. "But no one came back." Every other Avenger was shot down, and all the other men were killed.

On Bob Ballard's ship Ferrier showed the baseball cap he had worn to his first battle. The cap had a hole in it. "If I were an inch taller," he says, "I would be dead."

One day Ferrier realized that our ship was on the exact reverse heading of the course his torpedo bomber group had taken from Midway. He stood alone at the bow rail, looking down at the water where the Avengers' men had died.

The fierce opposition from Midway blunted the Japanese attack, so the leader of the raid, Lt. Joichi Tomonaga of the *Hiryu*, radioed his commander: "There is need for a second attack wave." But Japanese ordnance men were already loading aircraft with torpedoes and armor-piercing bombs for the next phase of the operation: a strike on the U.S.carriers Yamamoto hoped to lure to their deaths. Another attack on Midway meant rearming planes with ground-attack bombs, so the men were ordered to exchange the torpedoes and armor-piercing bombs for ground-attack bombs. At almost the same moment the *Hornet* and the *Enterprise* began to launch their aircraft for a strike on the Japanese carriers. The *Yorktown* planes followed soon after. The mission would take many of the warplanes to the edge of their range. Fliers knew the risk facing them; they might not have enough fuel for a round-trip.

Twenty-three minutes after Tomonaga's call for a second attack on Midway, a Japanese scout plane reported seeing "what appears to be ten enemy surface ships." At that last moment, on the *Enterprise,* code breaker Slonim translated "teki, teki, teki—enemy, enemy, enemy" from the intercepted message and instantly deduced that the U.S. carriers had been spotted. "My heart sank," he remembers. "This meant that they were going to do to us what we wanted to do to them."

On the Japanese carriers, officers ordered another switch—back to torpedoes and armor-piercing bombs. The carriers' decks were crowded with rearming, refueling planes when 15 TBD Devastator torpedo bombers from the *Hornet's* Torpedo Squadron 8 appeared. But before the Americans could attack the vulnerable carriers, an inferno of gunfire wiped out the squadron. The only survivor of 30 men was Ens. Gearge H. Gay. His riddled plane cartwheeled into the water with the radioman-gunner dying and Gay wounded. He crawled out and clung to a seat cushion, reluctant to inflate his highly visible yellow life raft.

Iyozo Fujita, flying a Zero from the *Soryu* saw a torpedo heading toward his carrier. "I waggled my wings to signal the ship," he remembers. "They didn't pay any attention. Fortunately it did not hit."

Fujita kept attacking the torpedo planes until *Soryu* gunfire hit his plane. Pinned down by the g force on his flaming Zero, he flipped out backward. "I went out like a tumbler," he says. His chute did not open. He shook the parachute bag, and it opened. "I had about a half-second before I hit the sea.' Like Gay, Fujita would bob in the ocean throughout the battle, one man watching a victory, the other a defeat.

Devastator torpedo bombers kept coming—14 from the *Enterprise*, another 12 from the *Yorktown*. Enemy fighters shot them to pieces. Some airmen who ditched would survive. Two were rescued after 17 days in a life raft. Three picked up by Japanese destroyers were interrogated and executed, two by being thrown overboard with weights tied to their feet.

Of the 41 Devastators that had flown unescorted by fighters against the Japanese carriers, only 4 survived. No torpedo hit an enemy ship.

But the Devastators had not gone down in vain. Lumbering in at low levels, they kept the Zeros and antiaircraft crews busy while, far overhead, dive bombers arrived, unnoticed and unopposed.

Lt. Comdr. Clarence Wade McClusky, air group commander of the *Enterprise,* had led 32 SBD Dauntless dive-bombers to where the Japanese fleet was supposed to be, only to look down at an empty ocean. His fuel was running out when he spotted a long wake made by a Japanese destroyer speeding north-northeast after attacking a U.S. submarine. McClusky surmised that the warship was heading toward the Japanese carriers and decided to follow it. About 25 minutes later McClusky's fliers were over the fleet. At 10:22, with a squadron behind him, he dived on the *Kaga.* Another squadron, led by Lt. Richard Best, tipped over, aiming at the *Akagi.* Then 17 SBDs from the *Yorktown* arrived and dived on the *Soryu* as she was turning into the wind to launch planes.

Four bombs hit the *Kaga,* setting off gasoline fed fires among the planes on deck. Two bombs hit the *Akagi,* one striking the amidships elevator, which crumpled into the hangar deck. Fires and explosions spread among 60-odd aircraft, most of them fueled and armed. Three bombs struck the *Soryu,* touching off explosions and fires on the flight and hangar decks. In scarcely six minutes the three carriers were fatally ablaze and listing.

Haruo Yoshino, returning from a scouting mission, had seen U.S. torpedo planes close to the *Kaga.* "I landed and went to the pilot room," he says. "Then"—he points upward, referring to the dive-bomber attack. "I thought it was a trick."

When the first bombs hit, he was on the flight deck. "Smoke was coming up from the hangar deck," he recalls. "Torpedoes were exploding, and bombs. I jumped into the sea."

Yuji Akamatsu was eating breakfast aboard the *Kaga* when he heard the air-raid alarm. He went out on deck. A bomb hit nearby, knocking him unconscious. By the time he roused, "there were many explosions and fires," he says. "We could not put them out. We had to escape. I closed my eyes and jumped".

The fourth Japanese carrier—the *Hiryu*—had only hours to live. American dive-bombers would fatally wound her later that afternoon. But now from her deck, heading for the *Yorktown,* flew a vengeful force of 18 Val dive-bombers and 6 Zero escorts. U.S.

fighters protecting the *Yorktown* got ten Vals; a wall of antiaircraft fire stopped two more. Four U.S. fighters dived on the last of the *Hiryu* bombers. The lead U.S. pilot squeezed his trigger. An electrical failure stilled his guns. As he pulled away in frustration, the other three U.S. planes followed his lead. The surviving Japanese dive-bombers flew on, three coming in from astern the *Yorktown*, the others off to starboard.

"All hell broke out," Pete Montalvo recallsl He was on a 1.1-inch gun mount astern of the smokestacks on the starboard side. Dozens of guns ripped one of the planes into three pieces. But its bomb hurtled on, tumbling through the air. "It blew up about ten feet behind me," Montalvo says. "I remember feeling a wall of flame engulfing me. I ripped my helmet off and blood was covering my face and eyes. I called out for my mother. I looked around and saw one of my shipmates. He had no legs. The two sailors on the seats of the gun mount . . .there was nothing from their waist up."

The bomb tore open the flight deck. Red-hot shrapnel touched off fires in the *Yorktown's* hangar deck. An officer quenched the flames by switching on the sprinklers and water curtains. A second bomb pierced the flight deck and exploded above the fire room, knocking out five of the ship's boilers. The carrier, which had been twisting evasively at 30 knots, abruptly slowed to 6. Another bomb hit an elevator, plunged deep into the ship, and exploded.

Shipmates carried Montalvo to sick bay, five decks down. Lying in a lower bunk on the port side, he felt the concussion of the two torpedoes that hit during the next attack from the *Hiryu*. One of those torpedoes had been fired by Taisuke Maruyama, whose bomber Bill Surgi had seen as it flew off. Within two hours both men were in the water after obeying orders to abandon their ships.

Able-bodied men got Montalvo and the other wounded out of sick bay, dragging some across a listing deck too steep for carrying stretchers. Montalvo had only one good hand; he could not go down a knotted line to the oily sea. A shipmate told him to stand on his shoulders and hold on with his left hand. Somehow he got into the water, one of about 2,270 men later picked up by destroyers.

On the abandoned *Yorktown* some bodies still lay in sick bay. The dead were to go down with the ship. But two of the men left behind were still alive.

George K. Weise had been firing a .50-caliber machine gun at the plane that dropped the second bomb. The explosion slammed his head into the gunsight, fracturing his skull. Half-conscious, his right side paralyzed, he lay in sick bay under eerie blue battle lights. He heard the order to abandon ship.

Hours later, in darkness and stillness, he heard Norman Pichette, another seaman, calling from a nearby bunk. They knew they had been given up for dead on a dying ship.

"What can we do?" Pichette asked. Weise, unable to move, told Pichette to get help.

Shortly after dawn on June 5, Pichette wrapped a sheet around his bleeding stomach wound and made his way up to the listing port side of the hangar deck, where he found a machine gun, its barrel aiming at the sea. With ebbing strength he fired the gun, alerting sailors on the nearby destroyer *Hughes*. A rescue boat took the unconscious Pichette back to the destroyer. He came to, living long enough to tell his rescuers about the other forgotten sailor. The boat returned for Weise.

"I remember being on a mess table on the *Hughes,*" Weise says. "I got a blood transfusion from a doctor. It was his blood."

Now began an effort to save the *Yorktown*. A tug arrived and started towing the carrier to Pearl Harbor. The destroyer *Hammann* tied up alongside the *Yorktown*. A 170-man salvage team went aboard, jettisoning aircraft, cutting loose an anchor, and trying to trim her by pumping seawater into empty fuel tanks.

"*Yorktown* was dark and dead and silent," one of the salvagers said later. But she was rallying. Counterflooding had reduced her list, and the weight reduction had raised her higher in the water, making towing easier.

Lt. Cmdr. Yahachi Tanabe, captain of submarine 1-168, could hardly believe his luck as he peered through his periscope. The last time he had risen to periscope depth he had seen six destroyers guarding his quarry. Now, almost by chance, he had risen so near the *Yorktown* he would have to back away to fire torpedoes. Submerged about 500 yards from the carrier, he listened to the silence above him and wondered if the sonar operators were all at lunch. He maneuvered into position and fired four torpedoes, then swerved around and began his successful escape.

One torpedo struck the *Hammann*, ripping her in half. Two passed under the destroyer and hit the *Yorktown*. As the *Hammann* sank, her depth charges began exploding at preset depths; the concussions killed many men in the water. An officer on the *Yorktown* watched them disappear—the way a "windshield wiper erases the droplets from your windshield." Of the *Hammann*'s 241 officers and crew, 81 died.

The *Yorktown* finally sank, with battle flags flying, shortly past dawn on June 7. By then U.S. carrier planes had claimed another ship: the cruiser *Mikuma*, sunk while withdrawing from the battle that would be the turning point in the Pacific war. Although that war would go on for three more years, the Japanese Navy would never again launch an offensive.

The battle cost 362 American lives, including those killed defending Midway. Japan lost 3,057 men. For the United States, Midway was a magnificent victory—a "glorious page in our history," as Admiral Nimitz said. But the words that a U.S. Navy officer wrote to his wife came closer to what the survivors on both sides felt: "Let no one tell you or let you believe that this war is other than a grim, terrible business."

Reprinted with permission of the National Geographic Society

INTRODUCTION

by Lt. Col. Walter E. "Bill" Gregory

It is the start of a new millennium. Wars in former Yugoslavia and Africa fill nightime news – programs with short thirty-second sound bytes. Throughout the world, the USA stands guard as the lone superpower after surviving a long bitter Cold War with the USSR. The war that shaped our present world, that divided it into two and fostered the forty-year face off called the Cold War, dims into the memories of the elders.

Because it is not discussed, it is all but forgotten by the young. If thought of at all, the great war is treated as a test question in the third-last chapter of a U.S. History Book. It is true the deep feelings, both happy and sad, pressed into the hearts of men and women of an older generation, are sometimes glimpsed on TV specials on the History Channel – a brief backward glance as the world speeds on.

A survivor of these awesome times is led to ask, "Is this all that shall be remembered of that terrible struggle for mankind's survival?"

For any who understand, the only reasonable answer is "God forbid". The freedom we so often take for granted was purchased at too great a price in lives and human experience to be relegated to such cold tombs of memory. We cannot afford to let the heroic generation which saved our country pass into the recess of history without recording their great deeds and wonderful heroism as a foundation to inspire the future.

A generation might be described as a group of people with experiences, beliefs, and attitudes held in common. It is created by defining events that forge the many communal happenings of a lifetime into a definable and lasting character, both individually and as a community. The personnel assigned to Marine Scout Bombing Squadron 343 of World War II are well within such a "defining event".

These Semper Fi types came of age during the Great depression, fought in World War II, and then came back to build modern America. They continued to stand proud for her during the long years of the Cold War. Tom Brokaw, NBC Nightly News anchor, labels them in his book of the same title, "The Greatest Generation".

They were the generation caught between two sets of tyrants who fought first one with a war, and then the other with the resolve that comes of building families and sharing common values with their children. Most were ordinary citizens, a few were recognized heroes, and some are remembered as famous. According to Brokaw: ..."they were all raised on this fundamental diet of honesty, duty, loyalty, honor, and personal responsibility ... those were the pillars of their lives."

The members of 343, except for a couple of warrant officers, were born between the close of World War I and 1925. The middling age was probably twenty. They lived dead center of the most famous of all depressions. These future Marines couldn't grasp the problems their parents and grandparents were having. To them it was simply a way of life. Except for an unexpected death, there were fathers living in the households, with households made up of people that attempted to support each other. It was part of a common set of values, the foundation of a work ethic and the basis of an unspoken motto, "You get what you earn." It was in such homes that the warriors-to-be grasped a clear meaning of what their country was, and found reason to trust and share with their fellow man.

In 1937 Nazi Germany began expanding with little or no

resistance. By 1939 Nazi Germany had set a wildfire that was about to envelop Europe, North Africa, much of Russia, and the Balkans. Only England and its Commonwealth stood against them. Concurrently, Japan controlled Korea, Manchuria, and vital parts of China. The world was rapidly becoming a tyrant's oyster. Only then did the USA, with its World War I equipment and bases, begin expanding its military capability. Recruiting activity, with conscription in the forefront, finally brought the world of war to the American mind.

The U.S. Marine Corps used the Mississippi River to divide recruit training areas. Those east of the Mississippi were assigned to Parris Island. This included most of the lads destined for duty with VMSB-343. On arrival, each recruit brought with him regional and cultural differences which the Marines needed to pound into a unity that was American.

As training centers, Parris Island and its companion center in San Diego were without peers. It was true when the members of 343 were in basic training and it is true now. Even now this is where the ethos of a Marine is born in each recruit. This is where lifetime friendships blossom. This is where Semper Fi makes its entrance.

The graduates of "boot camp" are next assigned to selected technical training units for specialization. Once qualified for a specific duty assignment and awarded a MOS (military occupation specialty), each individual Marine is usually assigned to a tactical command. Here they prepare for field and combat duty. This is the period which this book will cover. Although it is written as a remembrance of these moments by many contributors, in the background a history of the command's movement and accomplishment may be found.

In the late Summer of 1945, the personnel, both officers and enlisted, were detached from 343 and returned to Pearl Harbor by a Navy Transport. VMSB-343 continued to exist at Midway with a commanding officer and a small staff. Shortly thereafter VMSB-343 was transferred to China where it was returned to operational strength. In the meantime, as the transport was entering Pearl Harbor, all hell broke loose. There were rocket, cannon, automatic weapons and small arms fire --- just like the Fourth of July. The Japanese had just surrendered --- the war was over. Of special interest, the 343 personnel now arriving at Pearl Harbor were scheduled for duty at Okinawa as part of the forces designated for the invasion of Japan. They were immediately rescheduled for travel to the East!

Back to Tom Brokaw ...Concerning the returning veterans he said, "One element that was so striking, they had given up so much of their lives, in some cases as much as five years, and they didn't hesitate once the war was over. They just kept right on going. They came right out of the war and they went right to work or went right to college. They learned at an early age the meaning of sacrifice and discipline, and they were able to apply that to the building of the country in a way that was useful for America. And they kept their values."

During the D-Day commemoration ceremonies in 1994, President Clinton spoke at one ceremony, and as the camera found the aged and weathered faces of the veterans, he said, "Never let us forget that when they were young, they saved the world."

SECTION I

MARINE SCOUT BOMBING SQUADRON 343 IN WORLD WAR II

VICTORY AND OCCUPATION

&

THE ORIGIN OF "GREGORY'S GORILLAS"

VMSB - 343

Top - Capt. Simpson, Lt. Inman, W.O. Blevins, Lts. Ernest, Hicks, Deines, Jungbluth, Magill.
Center Left - Lts. Smith, Nash, Barry, Scruggs, Crutcher, Wase, Vehon, Davis, Laney.
Center Right - Lts. Israel, Covington, Edwards, Kalmoe, Lange, Stevenson, Spurlock, Holloway, Donovan, Capt. Brogan.

Bottom Left - W.O. Curtis, Capts. Janson, Glen, Maj. Schlendering, Dr. Hawks, Lts. McDermott, Roe, DeVries.

Bottom Right - Lts. Haughton, Peterson, Studt, Alarik, W.O. Burke, Lts. Skotvold, Henry, Watkinson, Maj. Gregory, Lt. Shellito

PILOTS

1

COMMISSIONING of VMSB 343 August l, 1943

Major Walter E. Gregory to Walter LeTendre

These several words are concerned with the commissioning of Marine Scout Bombing Squadron 343 aka VMSB 343, and other things. If this happening were not supported by facts now lost in some archive, it would be a winner in any liars' contest.

It was August l, 1943. I, Captain Walter E. Gregory USMCR, had reported to the Third Marine Air Wing only weeks before. The 3rd MAW was located at the Marine Corps Air Station, Cherry Point, North Carolina. I spent my first night under this command at some remote, isolated, rural place called Atlantic Field. I reported on the following morning to the Commanding Officer of VMSB 342. 342's CO was Walt Keen the Model Marine. Having been a captain for almost one year, I was the squadron's senior "Two Bar". I assumed the duties of executive officer and, of course, checked out in the SBD-4 aircraft. To my credit, I never ran the obstacle course (a physical training activity) with Keen --- August 1, 1943 and the U.S. Marine Corps saved me.

Immediately following my return from a morning flight on the first day of August, I was notified to report to the Commanding Officer of the Air Group (MAG-34) at 1400 hours. I flew to Cherry Point and reported to the MAG's Skipper. The Colonel (writer's memory has lost his name), after a brief introduction, focused my attention to his desk. From within the several offices of Headquarters, USMC, three separate pieces of correspondence had reached his desk within hours of each other. The subject matter contained in these three directives was as follows: Promote Walter E. Gregory to Major USMCR; Promote Walter E. Gregory to Major USMC, and Execute the commissioning of VMSB 343.

The sequence of events that followed was:

1. The correspondence which authorized my promotion to Major USMC, included a notation to disregard my promotion to

5

USMCR.

2. I was then reduced from Captain USMCR to Second Lieutenant USMCR, which was my permanent rank.

3. I was then discharged/separated (your choice) from the Marine Reserve segment of USMC --- at that moment, and for several more, I was a civilian! Was I tempted? I'll never tell.

4. Thereafter I was sworn in as Second Lieutenant USMC.

5. Then I was appointed to the temporary rank of Major USMC.

6. Then the Colonel directed me to take command of VMSB 343, which (on paper) had been commissioned at an earlier hour.

As I was leaving the MAG 34 office, the Colonel handed me a pair of gold leaves which he had worn only eighteen months before. At the flight line, the NCO in Charge advised me that a Marine needed a ride to Atlantic Field -- would I take her. Her? Oh yes, one of those skirt wearing Marines. On occasion I would observe one of those Marines who were authorized to wear a skirt. I replied that I would. Then the Sergeant asked me if I would help her strap on the parachute (a parachute is placed on the seat -- a person first sits on it, then straps it on). I instructed the Sergeant to have one of the ground crew perform this need. The Sergeant quietly replied that the passenger would feel more comfortable if the pilot would come to her aid. What was a commanding officer to do? I then turned around and about fifteen feet away stood a corporal in a skirt type uniform -- there stood a most attractive young lady.

As I flew back to Atlantic Field, I reviewed my afternoon. When I arrived at Cherry Point, I was a Captain USMCR. Now I was returning to Atlantic Field in the Grade of Major USMC and as the Commanding Officer of VMSB 343. Oh yes, there was a very attractive corporal in the radio-gunner's seat.

As I was making my final approach to Atlantic Field, I suddenly wondered who would help the lady unstrap.

THE ORIGIN OF "GREGORY'S GORILLAS"

by Vic Kalfus -- September 1943

"BoBo" Beauford and Vic Kalfus were driving stakes in the ground for tents at Atlantic Field and officers looked out along with Major Gregory and observed us driving the stakes, and commented, "Look at those two Gorillas out there." And Gregory says, "That's going to be our logo".

"Gregory's Gorillas" were born.

VMSB—343 USMC

VMSB 343 in World War II

Commissioned 1 August 1943 at MCAAF, Atlantic, NC
Transferred to Greenville, NC in December 1943 and trained there
until 15 July 1944, when Squadron was alerted for oversees duty.

Sailed from Miramar, CA 31 August for Ewa. A 1,100 mile
overwater hop to Midway made 27 October 1944. Operated at
Eastern Island as part of Hawaiian Sea Frontier. Transferred to
Sand Island in April 1945 where it was when war ended.

Commanding Officers:
  Maj. Walter E. Gregory 1 August 1943 to 2 August 1945
  Maj. Harold G. Schlendering 3 August 1945 to 17 Aug.1945
  Maj. Perry H. Aliff 18 August 1945 to 30 August 1945
  Maj. Jack Cosley 31 August 1945 to date of surrender

Copied from:
HISTORY OF MARINE CORPS AVIATION IN WWII
By: Robert Sherrod

MARINE SCOUT BOMBING SQUADRON 343

Victory and Occupation

Marine Scout Bombing Squadron 343, nicknamed "Gregory's Gorillas," was commissioned 1 August 1943 at Marine Corps Auxiliary Air Field, Atlantic NC, under the command of Major Walter E. Gregory, USMC.

Early in December 1943 orders arrived for transfer to Greenville NC, where an airfield had been recently completed. Training continued at this base until 15 July 1944 when the squadron was alerted for overseas duty and transferred to MCAD, Miramar, California. After a short delay, the squadron shipped out on board the USS Altamaha on 31 August 1944 and arrived at Ewa, Hawaii, early in September and was assigned to MAG-32.

Twenty-four new SB2C-3 Curtiss Hell Divers were assigned to the unit, and the pilots began familiarization flights in the new planes. During October, orders were received and a 1,100 mile flight over the water to the Midway Islands was made. Upon arrival, the squadron was transferred to MAG-23.

At Eastern Island, Midway Group, the squadron began operating in a defensive area of the Hawaiian Sea Frontier. At dawn and at dusk, two planes made a search close to the islands hoping to intercept enemy submarines which were continually lurking offshore. Six aircraft continually stood by as a striking force against a possible enemy attack. However, the nearest things to action were the occasional enemy submarine contacts.

In April 1945, the squadron moved from Eastern Island to the nearby Sand Island, but its mission remained unchanged.

Between 7-11 August, the squadron was reformed. The first echelon of the squadron, acting on verbal orders, embarked on board the USS Arneb (AKA-56) on 22 September 1945 for China. This echelon was commanded by Capt. J. L. Irvin, USMCR, and consisted of 25 officers and 203 men. On 27 September 1945, VSMB-343 was transferred to the 1st MAW. The flight echelon, consisting of 24 officers and 24 men, embarked on board the USS NASSAU (CVE-16) on 25 September. The third echelon consisting of 12 officers and 70 men did not sail until 5 October when they went on board the USS WYANDOT (AKA-92).

The first echelon disembarked at Tsingtao on 12 October 1945 and proceeded to the Tsingtao airstrip. The flight echelon catapulted from the Nassau on 20 October and flew to the airstrip. The third echelon finally landed on 29 October and proceeded immediately to join the remainder of the squadron.

Taken from the Military Journals of VMSB 343

CHRONOLOGY, MARINE FIGHTER ATTACK

SQUADRON 343

1 Aug 1943   Activated as Marine Scout Bombing Squadron-343, Mag-34, at Marine Corps Auxilliary Air Facility. Atlantic, North Carolina.

Dec 1943   Moved to Ncaap, Greenville, North Carolina.

21 Jul 1944   Moved to Miramar, California, joined Marine Fleet Air West Coast. Alerted for overseas duty upon completion of training operations and preparations for combat duty.

31 Aug 1944   Sailed for Ewa on board the USS Altamaha.

5 Sep 1944   Arrived Ewa. Joined MAG-12, 3d MAW.

19 Oct 1944   Assigned to MAG-23

27 Oct 1944   Moved to Naval Operation Base, Eastern Island, Midway.

12 Apr 1945   Moved to Sand Island.

6 Aug 1945   Assigned to Headquarters Squadron-3.

22 Sep 1945-
5 Oct 1945   Squadron embarked on board the USS Arneb and the USS Wyandot forTsingtao, China. Assigned to 1st MAW.

12 Oct 1945   Arrived Tsingtao, China.

17 May 1946 Assigned to Station Maintenance Squadron-32

18 May 1946 Embarked on board the USS General J. C.
Breckinridge for return to the U. S.

2 Jun 1946 Arrived in U. S. Joined Marine Air West Coast.

10 Jun 1946 Deactivated.

1 Oct 1960 Reactivated as Marine Attack Squadron-343,
Marine Air Group-15, 3d MAW, FMF, MCAS,
El Toro, Santa Ana, California.

30 Apr 1961 Deactivated.

STREAMERS, MARINE FIGHTER ATTACK SQUADRON 343

World War II Victory Streamer

China Service Streamer (China, Oct 1945 - May 1946)

National Defense Service Streamer

VMSB-343. Comm 1Jul43 at MCAAF, Atlantic.
Transf to Greenville in Dec43 and trained there
until 15Jul44, when Sq was alerted for overseas
duty. Sailed from Miramar 31Aug44 for Ewa.
An 1,100-mile overwater hop to Midway made
27Oct44. Operated at Eastern I as part of Hawaiian
Sea Frontier. Transf to Sand 1 in Apr45 where it
was when war ended. CO's: Maj Walter E. Gregory
1Aug43 to 24Aug45; Maj Harold G Schlendering
3-17Aug45; Maj Perry H Aliff 18-30Aug45;
Maj Jack Conley 31Aug45 to date of surrender.

Fleet Marine Force Status–30 April 1945 [1]

Units and Locations	Strength			
	USMC		USN	
	Off	Enl	Off	Enl
Outside U.S.A.				
Hawaiian Area				
Oahu				
Headquarters and Service Battalion, FMFPac	244	1,265	42	29
Signal Battalion, FMFPac	72	415	49	0
Tactical and Gunfire-Air Observation Training Center (Provisional), FMFPac	35	12	0	0
Transient Center, FMFPac	260	8,106	40	284
45th Replacement Draft, FMFPac	36	1,012	0	0
62d Replacement Draft, FMFPac	47	1,050	0	0
Headquarters Company, Supply Service, FMFPac	103	352	0	3
6th Base Depot, Supply Service, FMFPac	134	2,865	9	62
41st Depot Company, Supply Service, FMFPac	4	160	0	0
Marine Air Support Control Units, Amphibious Forces, Pacific Fleet	95	272	0	4
Headquarters Squadron, AirFMFPac	87	232	7	0
Air Warning Squadron-11, 3d MAW	26	312	0	7
Headquarters Squadron-3, 3d MAW	102	797	10	30
Marine Observation Squadron-4, 3d MAW	11	34	0	0
Marine Observation Squadron-5, 3d MAW	11	27	0	0
Service Squadron-14, 3d MAW	15	379	0	0
Marine Transport Squadron-953, 3d MAW	91	451	1	8
Marine Utility Squadron-1, 3d MAW	18	86	0	0
Marine Utility Squadron-3, 3d MAW	19	70	0	0
Headquarters Squadron-44, MASG-44	22	141	5	15
Service Squadron-44, MASG-44	18	461	0	0
Marine Fighter Squadron-215, MASG-44	93	301	1	4
Marine Torpedo-Bomber Squadron-332, MASG-44	22	326	1	4
Marine Scout-Bomber Squadron-333, MASG-44	48	290	1	7
Area Sub-Total	1,613	19,416	166	457

See footnote at end of table.

Units and Locations	Strength			
	USMC		USN	
	Off	Enl	Off	Enl
Hawaii				
5th Marine Division	847	14,855	129	938
11th Amphibian Tractor Battalion, FMFPac	27	508	2	8
5th Amphibian Truck Company, FMFPac	7	187	0	0
5th Joint Assault Signal Company, FMFPac	33	404	14·	0
2d Marine Detachment (Provisional), FMFPac	11	254	0	4
3d Rocket Detachment (Provisional), FMFPac	3	52	0	0
Corps Evacuation Hospital I, FMFPac	0	1	27	225
6th Separate Laundry Platoon, FMFPac	1	57	0	0
8th Field Depot, Supply Service, FMFPac	99	1,580	5	31
1st Service and Supply Battalion, Supply Service, FMFPac	30	639	2	13
27th Replacement Draft, FMFPac	27	213	2	12
31st Replacement Draft, FMFPac	3	28	1	1
Area Sub-Total	1,088	18,778	182	1,232
Kaui				
1st Marine Detachment (Provisional), FMFPac	14	276	3	11
3d Service and Supply Battalion, Supply Service, FMFPac	27	563	0	9
Area Sub-Total	41	839	3	20
Maui				
Headquarters and Service Battalion, VAC	107	699	11	60
Medical Battalion, VAC	1	97	29	230
Motor Transport Battalion, VAC	6	110	0	0
Signal Battalion, VAC	65	738	3	14
2d Bomb Disposal Company, VAC	12	71	0	0
Air Delivery Section, Headquarters and Service Battalion, VAC	3	83	0	0
4th Marine Division	836	15,317	126	1,043
1st FMFPac Amphibian Tractor Group Headquarters (Provisional)	4	4	0	0
3d Amphibian Tractor Battalion FMFPac	47	551	2	11
5th Amphibian Tractor Battalion, FMFPac	31	511	3	28
10th Amphibian Tractor Battalion, FMFPac	33	523	3	29
2d Armored Amphibian Tractor Battalion, FMFPac	37	812	4	34
3d Military Police Battalion (Provisional), FMFPac	19	336	0	0
12th Motor Transport Battalion (Provisional), FMFPac	28	518	1	1
4th Amphibian Truck Company (Provisional), FMFPac	6	181	0	0
1st Joint Assault Signal Company, FMFPac	33	395	13	0
2d Separate Topographical Company, FMFPac	6	78	0	0
2d Separate Laundry Platoon, FMFPac	1	64	0	0
8th Separate Laundry Platoon, FMFPac	1	62	0	0

Units and Locations	Strength			
	USMC		USN	
	Off	Enl	Off	Enl
1st Separate Radio Intelligence Platoon, FMFPac	1	49	0	0
5th Separate Radio Intelligence Platoon, FMFPac	1	49	0	0
3d Marine Detachment (Provisional), FMFPac	10	272	0	3
1st Rocket Detachment (Provisional), FMFPac	1	57	0	0
2d Service and Supply Battalion, Supply Service, FMFPac	34	1,031	2	10
55th Replacement Draft, FMFPac	36	1,256	0	0
59th Replacement Draft, FMFPac	35	1,251	0	0
Area Sub-Total	1,394	25,115	197	1,470
Midway				
6th Defense Battalion	29	710	3	21
Headquarters Squadron 23, MAG–23	25	173	6	14
Service Squadron 23, MAG–23	22	602	0	0
Marine Fighter Squadron 324, MAG–23	55	225	1	8
Marine Scout-Bomber Squadron 343, MAG–23	31	291	1	8
Area Sub-Total	162	2,001	11	51
Southwest Pacific				
Lingayen				
Headquarters Squadron 24, MAG–24	36	119	8	22
Service Squadron 24, MAG–24	19	481	0	0
Marine Scout-Bomber Squadron 133, MAG–24	48	285	1	8
Marine Scout-Bomber Squadron 241, MAG–24	55	281	1	8
Area Sub-Total	158	1,166	10	38
Luzon				
Marine Scout-Bomber Squadron 244, MAG–24	47	298	1	8
Mindanao				
Air Warning Squadron 3, 1st MAW	18	249	0	6
Air Warning Squadron 4, 1st MAW	17	243	0	6
Headquarters Squadron 12, MAG–12	27	148	13	24
Service Squadron 12, MAG–12	23	469	0	0
Marine Fighter Squadron 115, MAG–12	54	229	1	8
Marine Fighter Squadron 211, MAG–12	52	216	1	8
Marine Fighter Squadron 218, MAG–12	64	188	2	8
Marine Fighter Squadron 313, MAG–12	50	247	1	8
Headquarters Squadron 32, MAG–32	28	134	9	20

KIRISIMA (*Japan*, 1915). One of the KONGO class. DISPLACEMENT: 29,330 tons. DIMENSIONS: 704' x 95' x 27' 6" draft. COMPLEMENT: Over 1,300. HORSEPOWER AND SPEED: 64,000, 26 knots. ■ ARMOR: 8" Belt, 6¾" Decks, 6" Battery, 10" Barbettes, 10" C.T. ■ GUNS: 8—14 inch, 45 cal.; 16—6 inch, 50 cal.; 8—5 inch A.A.; numerous smaller A.A. ■ AIRCRAFT: 3. OTHER SHIPS IN CLASS: *Kongo* (1913), *Hiei* (1914), *Haruna* (1915). NOTE: One and possibly two of class sunk.

KONGO (*Japan*, 1912). One of the KONGO class. DISPLACEMENT: 29,330 tons. DIMENSIONS: 704' x 92' x 27' 6" draft. COMPLEMENT: 980. HORSEPOWER AND SPEED: 64,000, 26 knots. ■ ARMOR: 8" Belt, 6" Battery, 10" Barbettes, 9" Gunhouses, 10"-6" Conning Tower. ■ GUNS: 8—14 inch, 45 cal.; 16—6 inch, 50 cal.; 8—5 inch A.A.; 4—landing; 4—M.G. Torpedo tubes: 4—21 inch. ■ AIRCRAFT: 3. Catapult: 1. OTHER SHIPS IN CLASS: *Hiei, Haruna, Kirisima.*

KAKO [Heavy Cruiser] *(Japan, 1926)*. Of KAKO class. DISPLACEMENT: 7,250 tons. DIMENSIONS: 595' x 50' 9" x 14' 9" draft. COMPLEMENT: 770. HORSEPOWER AND SPEED: 95,000, 33 knots. ▪ ARMOR: 2" Side, 2" Deck, 1½" Turrets. ▪ GUNS: 6–8 inch; 6–4.7 inch A.A.; 8–47 mm; several M.G. A.A. Torpedo tubes: 12–21 inch. ▪ AIRCRAFT: 2. Catapult: 1. OTHER SHIPS IN CLASS: *Aoba, Hurutaka, Kinugasa* (all 1926-1927). NOTE: Two to three ships of class sunk.

NATORI [Light Cruiser] *(Japan, 1922)*. Of NATORI class. DISPLACEMENT: 5,175 tons. DIMENSIONS: 535' x 46' 9" x 15' 10½" draft. COMPLEMENT: 650, est. HORSEPOWER AND SPEED: 70,000, 33 knots. ▪ ARMOR: 2" Side, 2" Deck, 1" Gun Shields, 2" Conning Tower. ▪ GUNS: 7–5.5 inch, 50 cal.; 2–3 inch (now increased); numerous smaller A.A.; 2–M.G. Torpedo tubes: 8–21 inch. ▪ AIRCRAFT: 1. Catapult: 1. OTHER SHIPS IN CLASS: *Isuzu, Nagara, Yura, Kinu, Abukuma* (all 1922-1925). NOTE: *Abukuma* reported modernized 1940 and rearmed as A.A. cruiser. Three to five ships of class believed sunk.

MILITARY TABLE OF ORGANIZATION

If a military structure has a commanding officer aka CO, it will have a Table of Organization aka TO. Should there be no commanding officer, a military structure, no matter its size, will not operate under a TO. This is true now, it was true during World War II, during the time of the Roman Legions, and well before.

A standard TO has been in existence to satisfy an array of commands. The same format is used whether it is a company, a squadron or a division. The basic TO follows:

COMMANDING OFFICER
S-1 Administration
S-2 Intelligence
S-3 Operation
S-4 Logistics

These four offices are responsible to the commanding officer for the total activity of the command. Any observed activity will be under one of these four. For example, medical, adjutant, chaplain, legal, mail, mess, etc. are within the oversight of S-1. S-2 activity is rather most routine during peaceful moments. It is just the reverse when troubles come forth. S-3 is responsible for tactical training and combat execution, controlling all immediate supporting elements. S-4 controls procurement and issuing of all material and equipment, whether expendable or accountable.

Further, the TO identifies the number of individuals authorized within a specific command, designating each individual's assignment and paygrade within that assignment.

With the previous bit of information to refresh memories, it is now time to introduce the Third Squadron of the Fourth Group of Third Wing of the Marine Corps, which is better known as VMSB-

343. It had stays at Atlantic Field, Midway, and China. At each of these military airfields, such things as mess facilities, barracks, recreation facilities, post exchanges, medical facilities, and refueling points for both aircraft and vehicles were provided by another command. The squadron also had a stay at Greenville, North Carolina. On this assignment, the outfit was on its own in a totally civilian environment. Greenville is a charming city with a university where the female students outnumbered the male students by a one hundred to one ratio.

The command arrived at Greenville in the Fall of 1943. It was provided a closed WPA training facility which, with a bit of squeeze, could house the outfit. A real plus was an excellent mess hall which was completely equipped and waiting to be put to use. A surprise came with this camp site. The University of East Carolina was located on adjacent property and allegedly there was a hole in the fence that separated the two properties. The command was also provided an excellent airfield which was not in use. But, of course, it was located at the opposite end of the city from the camp.

On its arrival at Greenville, 343 was at TO strength in pilots and radio-gunners, however a bit under strength elsewhere, but manageable. This estimate was based on the providing of an adequate support unit to handle assignments not found in the squadron's TO. It was obvious that this most critical need had been overlooked. For example, the airfield and the camp were several miles apart, with each requiring its own security detail. Approximately two-thirds of the command would be living at the camp and working at the airfield. Food had to be moved from the camp to the airfield.

Suddenly four or five standard military trucks arrived and a motor transport section was immediately established --- a 343 motor transport section. From that moment on, a special personnel roster began developing, changing day-to-day to accommodate additional needs. For example, the non-rated officers making this move consisted of a flight surgeon, an administration officer, a supply officer and an engineering officer, a total of four. This rapidly increased to a flight surgeon, an administration officer, a supply officer, an engineering officer, a motor transport officer, a mess officer, an intelligence officer, a chaplain and a dentist, a total of nine. A legal officer was available upon request. The enlisted personnel roster, although at a less noticeable pace, followed a similar pattern.

Back to the airfield --- sans everything --- well, almost everything. There was a small, empty control tower mounted over a small, empty hangar and, gratefully acknowledged, a head. When the squadron's twenty-four SBD-4 aircraft began arriving, a youngster with a green and red signal light brought them in. Each was immediately refueled. 343 was now in the refueling business, refueling trucks and aircraft. Fuel came from approximately seventy miles away. Indeed, the official TO for a scout-bomber squadron had surrendered to the needs of this command. Whatever was required always made its appearance.

Concerning the established TO for a tactical scout-bomber squadron, VMSB-343 had strayed further from these closely followed guidelines than any other squadron in the Marine Corps. It was truly a physically independent unit. It was warmly received by Greenville. If there was a hole in the fence, it was never repaired.

Submitted by members of VMSB 343 Reunion Association

REQUIREMENTS FOR BECOMING
A COMMANDING OFFICER

JANUARY 1, 1942

"BUBBLES"

by Walter E. (Bill) Gregory

It was January 1, 1942. Major T. C. Green's VMO 1 (later redesignated VMSB 151) with its SBC-4 "Hell Diver" aircraft was assigned antisubmarine duty out of North Island (San Diego). Captain John Stage, aka "Big John", was SOP (Senior Officer Present) of a four plane detachment located at NAS Long Beach. Other pilots in the detachment included Second Lieutenant Walter Gregory, aka "Junior", Master Sergeant Paul Martin and Technical Sergeant Virgil Martin, aka "Red".

On the first morning of 1942, I, the one called "Junior", with my 398.1 hours of flight time, was scheduled to lead a three plane section on a convoy escort mission. No radio or other communications between air and surface elements had been developed. In fact, there was no information as to size of the convoy or where it was from or going. Our mission was simply to provide air coverage. Oh yes, my three plane section included "Red" Martin, whose log showed well over 2,000 flight hours, and Paul Paquin, whose log was in excess of 3,000 flight hours. But "Junior" was senior.

Each of our three biplanes carried a 500 pound general purpose bomb with delayed fuse, and, of course, forward mounted 30 caliber machine guns for shooting holes in our own propellers. One other point of importance warrants comment. Besides canvas helmets, we wore white scarves which sometimes trailed in the slipstream---just like James Cagney and Wallace Beery trailed them in their movies.

The convoy was located just northeast of Catalina Island, headed in the general direction of the Los Angeles Harbor. It consisted of several commercial ships, a destroyer or two and several naval boats with capability to launch depth charges aka "subchasers".

We hadn't been on station too long before I noticed the "subchasers" covering the stern of the convoy had increased their speed, rapidly closing on the convoy. Almost concurrently they began firing depth charges aka "ash cans" in considerable numbers. This would get any second Lieutenant's attention. Immediately thereafter, Paul, who was forward of the convoy, radioed that there was a disturbance several miles directly ahead of the convoy. This second lieutenant was now about as alert as a second lieutenant can become.

I joined Paul and immediately observed a circle of churning water forward of the convoy. This churning mass was between 100 and 150 feet in diameter. My aeronautical chart showed this area to be clear. Those "ash can" throwing "subchasers" must have caused a submarine to execute a quick departure from harm's way, which, in turn, caused the sub to strike and impel itself on a sandbar or other underwater object. I began climbing at full power in preparation for a bombing run ---climbing at a good 400 feet a minute. Concurrently I radioed NAS Long Beach and reported my observations. I got an immediate "stand-by". Within minutes NAS contacted me. The NAS Commanding Officer had me repeat my "target". I complied. As I pulled up in a left turn, I looked over my left shoulder and saw the white scarf in the breeze and the target. I had pinwheeled that churning water and the bomb had executed its purpose. The churning had increased and the water in that entire area was bubbling.

Everything became peaceful with the constant throb of the SBC's powerplant and the whine of the wind as it passed around the struts and wires associated with a biplane. Such things as "subchasers", "ash cans", status of the convoy etc., became vague. Realizing I had gotten a direct hit on a "sub" had taken over.

A call from NAS awakened me. I was instructed to return to base and to leave the other two members of my flight with the convoy. I headed toward the air station wondering what my accomplishment might bring forth. --- maybe an air medal!

When I came to a stop at the flight line, I was met by 'Big John'. His first remark was, "'Junior', return to North Island now." I dismounted the SBC-4 and headed for the hangar. 'Big John' asked, "Where are you going?" I replied I was going to the BOQ to pack. To this he replied, "Your gear has been packed --- here it is." I once again headed for the hangar. 'Big John' once again asked, "Where are you going?" I replied to operations for a flight clearance. "Here it is", stated 'Big John' and he handed it to me. By now my aircraft was fueled so I headed south.

The flight south was uneventful. When I reported to the squadron office I found a quiet atmosphere, in fact, quite quiet. And so went the afternoon. That evening the squadron's pilots went to the O'Club for dinner. We sat together at one large table. It was a pleasant gathering, yet somewhat subdued. At the conclusion of dinner, the skipper requested everyone to remain seated and had a number of bottles of Sparkling Burgundy delivered to the table. After glasses were filled and in the hands of every member, Major T. C. Green proposed a toast. Holding a stem glass, he looked at me and said, "'Junior', congratulations on your direct hit." He hesitated for proper timing, then added, "A direct hit on the Los Angeles Sewer!"

I have often wondered what would have happened if that fragile, sensitive, unpredictable radio had failed to involve the CO, NAS Long Beach.

U.S. MARINE
CORPS
AIRCRAFT
1914-1959

Curtiss SB2C-1 in 1943 camouflage: white stripes on the fin helped the landing signal officer to estimate the angle of approach. (*Curtiss-Wright photo*)

Curtiss SB2C Helldiver

The long series of Curtiss combat aeroplanes built for the US Navy and Marine Corps between the two world wars was brought to a highly successful conclusion with the company's first monoplane bomber and the last to carry the name Helldiver. Ordered on May 15, 1939, while the earlier Helldiver biplane was still in quantity production (see page 141), the new type was a low-wing monoplane with the same general layout as the Brewster SB2A Buccaneer, with which it was in competition. It was a two-seat scout-bomber powered by the big Wright R-2600 Double Cyclone engine, and had an internal bomb-bay in the fuselage.

The prototype XSB2C-1, with a 1,700 hp R-2600-8, made its first flight on December 18, 1940, but was destroyed a few days later. Large-scale production had already been ordered on November 29, 1940, but a large number of modifications were specified for the production model. The size of the fin and rudder was enlarged, fuel capacity was increased and self-sealing added, and the fixed armament was doubled to four 0·50-in guns in the wings, compared with the prototype's two cowling guns. Curtiss established a new factory for SB2C production at Columbus, Ohio, and the first production model did not fly until June 1942. After the first 200 SB2C-1s, fixed armament was again changed to two 20-mm cannon, in the SB2C-1C version; in addition the Helldiver had two 0·30-in guns in the rear cockpit, and an internal bomb load of 1,000 lb.

Production at the new Columbus factory was protracted, and, although deliveries to VS-9 began in December 1942, 11 more months elapsed before the type had been brought up to operational effectiveness and was ready for action. The first operational sortie was made on November 11, 1943, when VB-17 attacked Rabaul. Production of the SB2C-1 totalled 978; one of these was converted to the single XSB2C-2 floatplane, another became the XSB2C-5 and two became XSB2C-6s. The SB2C-3, which began to appear in 1944, had the R-2600-20 engine with a four-blade propeller, while the SB2C-4 had wing fittings for eight 5-in rockets or up to 1,000 lb of bombs and, in the SB2C-4E version, carried a small radar set. Production by Curtiss totalled 1,112 SB2C-3s and 2,045 SB2C-4s. Finally came 970 SB2C-5s, starting in February 1945, with increased fuel capacity. Two XSB2C-6 prototypes had R-2800-28 engines and longer fuselages.

Added capacity for Helldiver production was provided at two Canadian factories; Fairchild produced a total of 300, designated XSBF-1, SBF-1 SBF-3 and SBF-4E, while Canadian Car and Foundry built 894 designated SBW-1, SBW-3, SBW-4, SBW-4E and SBW-5, these models being respectively equivalent to their Curtiss-built counterparts.

Throughout 1944 the Navy's new Helldivers mounted an ever-growing offensive against Japanese targets in the Pacific, taking over from Douglas SBDs. So vital did they prove in this task that all production of the type

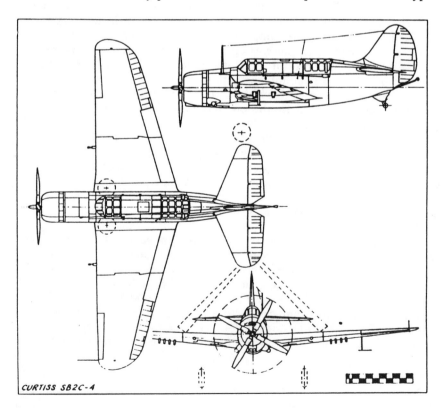

CURTISS SB2C-4

was retained by the US Navy with the exception of 26 Canadian-built aircraft supplied to Britain under lend lease arrangements and designated SBW-1B for this purpose. The Marine Corps took on strength a large portion of the 900 Helldivers built by Curtiss for the USAAF as A-25As, and these were designated SB2C-1A after transfer.

Late versions of the Helldiver remained in US Navy service several years after the end of World War II, and others were supplied to foreign countries.

TECHNICAL DATA (SB2C-4)

Manufacturer: Curtiss-Wright Corporation, Airplane Division, Columbus, Ohio; Canadian Car & Foundry Co, Ltd, Montreal; and Fairchild Aircraft Ltd, Longueuil, PQ, Canada.
Type: Carrier-based scout-bomber.
Accommodation: Pilot and observer.
Power plant: One 1,900 hp Wright R-2600-20.
Dimensions: Span, 49 ft 9 in; length, 36 ft 8 in; height, 13 ft 2 in; wing area, 422 sq ft.
Weights: Empty, 10,547 lb; gross, 16,616 lb.
Performance: Max speed, 295 mph at 16,700 ft; cruising speed, 158 mph; initial climb, 1,800 ft/min; service ceiling, 29,100 ft; range, 1,165 st miles with 1,000 lb bomb-load.
Armament: Two fixed forward-firing 20 mm cannon in wings; two 0·30-in machine guns in rear cockpit. Up to 1,000 lb bombs internal and 1,000 lb external.
Serial numbers:

XSB2C-1: 1758.	SB2C-5: 83128–83751; 89120–89465.
SB2C-1: 00001–00200.	XSB2C-6: 18620–18621.
SB2C-1A: 75218–75588; 76780–76818.	SBF-1: 31636–31685.
SB2C-1C: 00201–00370; 01008–01208;	SBF-3: 31686–31835.
18192–18598.	SBF-4E: 31836–31935.
XSB2C-2: 00005.	SBW-1: 21192–21231; 60010–60035.
SB2C-3: 18599–19710.	SBW-3: 21233–21645.
SB2C-4: 19711–21191; 64993–65286;	SBW-4E: 21646–21741; 60036–60209.
82858–83127.	SBW-5: 60210–60295.
XSB2C-5: 18308.	

Curtiss SBW-4E, built by Canadian Car & Foundry, with Naval Reserve markings in 1946.
(*Gordon S. Williams*)

Curtiss SB2C-5 U. S. Navy
Improved version recognizable by the pilots ribless side windows.
VMSB-343 lost six out of twelve in a 1945 storm at Laichow, China.

Douglas R4D-5 (39074) Peter M. Bowers
With cargo doors open on a Chinese airfield. Center facing wall
bucket seats made simultaneous cargo loading possible in the R4D.

Douglas R4D-3 (06996) William T. Larkins
Rare C-53 passenger version. 28 only were built, three are believed
to have been used by the Marine Corps. P & W R-1830-92 engines.

Wright
R-2600-20
Cyclone

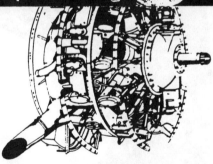

The Marines received most of the USAAF's castoff A-25As, but these all remained stateside in non-combat roles. In 1944, they received newer Beasts which were rapidly deployed in the Pacific. Here, two SB2C-3s of VMSB-343, Gregory's Gorillas, patrol near Midway during late 1944. This unit had the dubious distinction of suffering the last operational losses of Helldivers in US markings when six of its Beasts went down in a snowstorm over Tientsin, China, on 8 December 1945. (USMC via Jim Sullivan)

A great many SB2C-3s survived to take on training duties in the immediate postwar period. Here an SBW-3, built by CC&F, is seen at Morrison Field, FL, in 1946. The removal of the lower gear door was common on land-based Helldivers. (Hal Andrews via Jim Sullivan)

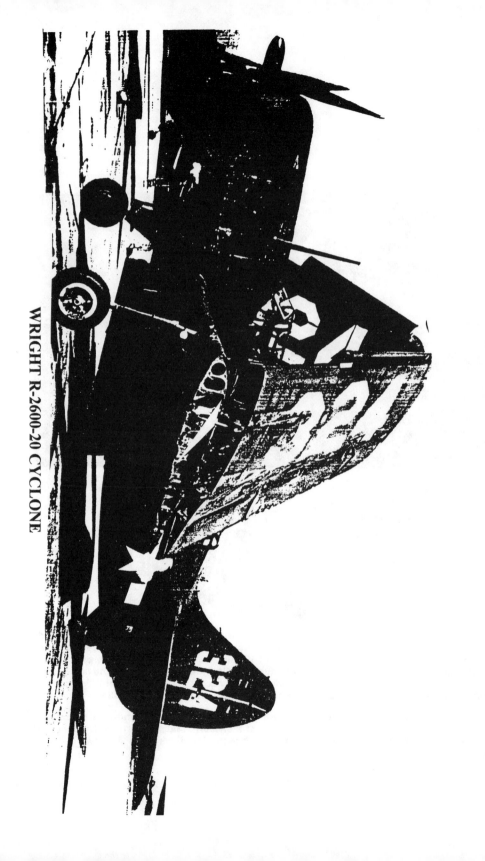

WRIGHT R-2600-20 CYCLONE

U. S. FLEET MARINE FORCE

MARINE AIRCRAFT WINGS, PACIFIC
Hq Sqdn   1 R5O-5, 1 SNJ-4

FIRST MARINE AIR WING
Hq Sqdn 1	2 SNJ, 1 PV-1, 1 PBY-5A, 1 JRB
VMD-154	6 PB4Y-1, 1 SNJ
VMF-211	33 F4U-1
VMF-212	10 F4U-1
VMJ-252	1 J2F-5, 3 R4D-1, 2 R4D, 1 R4D-5
VMSB-243	15 SBD-4
VMSB-244	11 SBD-3, 7 SBD-4
VMF(N)-531	15 PV-1

MARINE AIR GROUP ELEVEN
Hq Sqdn 11	2 TBF-1, 6 F4U-1, 1 JRF, 2 SNJ
Svc Sqdn 11	1 J2F-5, 6 SBD-4, 1 SBD-5, 1 JRF, 1 J2F-5, 1 SNJ
VMF-112	24 F4U-1
VMF-123	24 F4U-1, 1 J2F-5, 1 NE
VMF-124	20 F4U-1
VMF-215	20 F4U-1
VMSB-132	25 SBD-4, 1 SBD-5
VMSB-235	31 SBD-4, 1 SBD-5
VMTB-232	25 TBF-1
VMTB-233	20 TBF-1

MARINE AIR GROUP TWELVE
Hq Sqdn 12	1 J2F-5, 1 F4F-7, 1 NE
VMTB-143	27 TBF-1
VMSB-234	23 SBD-4

MARINE AIR GROUP TWENTY-ONE
Hq Sqdn 21	1 F4F-4, 1 J2F-5, 1 J2F-2
VMF-214	20 F4U-1
VMF-221	20 F4U-1, 1 F4F-3

MARINE AIR GROUP TWENTY-FIVE
Hq Sqdn 25	2 R4D, 1 F4F-7, 1 SNJ
VMJ-152	12 R4D
VMJ-153	12 R4D
VMJ-253	10 R4D

SECOND MARINE AIR WING
Hq Sqdn 2   1 JRB

MARINE AIR GROUP FOURTEEN
   Hq Sqdn 14   18 SBD-3, 9 SBD-4
   VMF-121   19 F4U-1
   VMSB-141   25 SBD-4

THIRD MARINE AIR WING
Hq Sqdn 3   3 J2F-5, 1 JRF-1A, 1 R4D-1, 1 SNJ-4
MARINE AIR GROUP THIRTY-ONE
   Hq Sqdn 31   11 F4U-1, 1 SBD-5, 1 SNJ-4
                       (Cherry Point & Quantico)
   VMF-311   19 F4U-1, 2 SNJ-4 (Parris Island)
   VMF-321   22 F4U-1, 1 SNJ-4 (Oak Grove)
   VMSB-331   20 SBD-5 (Bogue Field)
   VMSB-341   20 SBD-5 (Atlantic Field)
   VMF-312   11 F4U-1, 1 SNJ-4 (Parris Island)
   VMF-322   10 F4U-1 (Oak Grove)
   VMF-323   9 F4U-1, 7 SNJ-4 (Formed 1 August at
                       MCAS Cherry Point)

MARINE AIR GROUP THIRTY-THREE
   Hq Sqdn 33   1 SBD-4 (Cherry Point)
   VMSB-332   4 SBD-4, 9 SBD-5 (Cherry Point)
   VMSB-333   3 SBD-4, 1 SNJ-4 (Formed 1 August at
                       MCAS Cherry Point)
   VMSB-334   3 SBD-4 (Formed 1 August, Cherry Point)

MARINE AIR GROUP THIRTY-FOUR
   Hq Sqdn 34   3 SBD-4 (Cherry Point)
   VMSB-342   4 SBD-4, 5 SBD-5, 1 J2F-1, 4 SNV-1
                       (Atlantic Field)
   VMSB-343   3 SBD-4, 4 SBD-5 (Formed 1 August at
                       Atlantic Field)

MARINE AIR GROUP THIRTY-FIVE
   Hq Sqdn 35   1 SBD-4 (Cherry Point)
   VMJ-352   6 R4D-5, 1 R5O-6 (Cherry Point)
   VMD-354   1 F4U-1 (Cherry Point)
   VMO-351   1 F4U-1, 3 SNJ-4 (Cherry Point)

MARINE NIGHT FIGHTER GROUP FIFTY-THREE
   VMF(N)-532   12 F4U-2, 5 SB2A-4, 5 SNJ-4
                    (MCAS Cherry Point)

MARINE BOMBER GROUP SIXTY-ONE
   Hq Sqdn 61   24 PBJ (Formed 13 July at MCAS Quantico)
   VMB-413   12 PBJ (Cherry Point)

FOURTH MARINE BASE DEFENSE AIR WING
   Hq Sqdn 4   21 SBD-4, 39 SBD-5, 1 F6F-3, 1 J4F
   VMF-224   33 F4U-1

Air, Fleet Marine Force, Pacific

Ewa - Hdqtrs. Sq.: MAG-15 - Hdqtrs. Sq. MAG-15 - Hdqtrs. Sq. 15,
  SMS-15, VMR-352 and VMR-953. MASG-44 - Hdqtrs. Sq. 44, SMS-
  44, and Prov. CAUS-1 (a).
Midway - VMF-322.
USS PUDGET SOUND - Marine CASD-6, VMF-321 and VMTB-454.
USS SAIDOR - Marine CASD-4, VMF-213, and VMTB-623.
USS POINT CRUZ - Marine CASD-8, VMF-217, and VMTB-464.
USS RENDOVA - Marine CASD-7, VMF-216, and VMTB-624.
USS BADOENG STRAIT - Marine CASD-5.

1st Marine Air Wing

Tientsin - Hdqtrs. Sq.-1 and VMO-3.
Tsingtao - MWSS-1.

MAG-12 - Peking

Hdqtrs. Sq.-12   VMF-211
SMS-12   VMF-218
VMF-115

MAG-24 - Peking

Hdqtrs. Sq.-24   VMF (N)-533
SMS-24   VMF (N)-541
AMS-7

MAG-25 - Tsingtao

Hdqtrs. Sq.-25   VMR-152
SMS-25   VMR-153

MAG-32 - Tsingtao

Hdqtrs. Sq.-32   VMTB-134
SMS-32   VMSB-224
VMO-6   VMSB-343
AWS-11

2nd Marine Air Wing

Hdqtrs. Sq.-2, MWSS-2, and VMD-254, all located on Okinawa.
MOG-1 - Hdqtrs. Sq., and VMO-5, at Sasebo; and VMO-2 on Nagasaki.

MAG-14 - Okinawa

Hdqtrs. Sq.-14   VMF-222
SMS-14   VMF-223
VMF-212

MAG-31 - Yokosuka

Hdqtrs. Sq. -31   VMF-441
SMS-31   VMF (N)-542
VMF-224   VMR-952
VMF-311

MAG-33 - Okinawa

Hdqtrs. Sq.-33   VMF-323
SMS-33   VMF (N)-543
VMF-312

MADC-2

Hdqtrs. Sq., AWS-6, and AWS-8, at Okinawa; and AWS-1 at Ie Shima.

4th Marine Air Wing

MARINE CORPS AVIATION

by George Bobb

On December 1, 1920, Flight F, 3rd Air Squadron was formed at Quantico, Virginia. The Flight Commander, Second Lieutenant Walter V. Brown, was killed in a crash near Colonial Beach, Virginia while enroute to a bombing exercise. On May 5, 1992, the air field at Quantico was named Brown Field in his memory.

On August 24, 1922, Flight F, 3rd Air Squadron was redesignated VF Squadron 1 and along with a sister squadron became the First Aviation Group. On September 1, 1926, VF-1 was redesignated VO Squadron 4, East Coast Expeditionary Force, Marine Base, Quantico. Then on May 11, 1927, prior to their departure aboard the USS Medusa, bound for Nicaragua on May 23, 1927 to support the ground forces who were carrying out America's Intervention Policy by suppressing a revolution. The Squadron was redesignated VO-7M and rejoined the East Coast Expeditionary Force at Quantico on June 15, 1933.

On December 8, 1933, the Fleet Marine Force (FMF) was established, causing a complete reorganization of Marine Aviation. Aircraft Squadrons, East Coast Expeditionary Force became Aircraft One, Fleet Marine Force while Aircraft Squadrons, West Coast Expeditionary Force became Aircraft Two, Fleet Marine Force.

On February 13, 1935, the Commander-in-Chief, United States Fleet assigned Aircraft Two to Aircraft Battle Forces, United States Fleet. The West Coast Squadrons, engaged in United States Fleet Problem XVI were operating from the USS Langley, April 29 through June 12, 1935, and in 1936 they shifted operations to the Lexington and Saratoga. In January of 1937, all Aircraft One Squadrons (including VO-7M, redesignated VMS-1 on July 1, 1937) flew from Quantico to San Diego to participate in Fleet maneuvers.

During the years 1938 through early 1941, VMS-1 was home based at Brown Field, Quantico and equipped with Great Lakes Dive Bombers (BG-1 Biplanes). In January of 1938, the Squadron went to Guantanamo Bay, Cuba for maneuvers. The BG's were flown down the East Coast to the Naval Air Station, Opa Locka, Florida, from which point the over water flight to Cuba was initiated. Six weeks later the aircraft returned to Quantico via the same route.

In January, 1939, the Navy General Board drafted the Mission of Marine Aviation: Marine Aviation is to be equipped, organized and trained primarily to support the Fleet Marine Force in landing operations; to support troop activity in the field (close air support); and be available as replacement squadrons for carrier operations.

From this point in time, FMF squadrons on both coasts engaged in Field Landing Practice (FCLP or "bounce drill"), periodic carrier qualifications and Fleet exercises aboard the Lexington (CV-2), Saratoga (CV-3), Ranger (CV-4), Yorktown (CV-5), Enterprise (CV-6), Wasp (CV-7) and Hornet (CV-8).

By March of 1940, the BG's of VMS-1 were getting pretty tired and required a lot of maintenance. All aircraft were downed at various times for scheduled engine checks, engine changes, and other mechanical problems. Some were sent for complete overhaul to Quantico's Overhaul and Repair Facility which included engine, airframe, fabric, propeller, radio and instrument shops. The facility had the complete capability of stripping any aircraft on the field down to the bare frame, overhauling and rebuilding the components, and reassembling them into what could be considered a new aircraft. The writer, George Bobb, was assigned to the Overhaul and Repair Facility in March of 1940 and worked there until June 1940 at which time he transferred into Radio section of VMS-1.

In spite of the shortages of aircraft, VMS-1 carried out the mission assigned to Marine Aviation. Along with basic squadron tactics -- formation flying, night flying, dive bombing, fixed and free gunnery, communications and navigation problems -- the squadron conducted bounce drills, periodic flights to Norfolk for qualification aboard the USS Ranger, and participated in combined Fleet Marine Force/Atlantic Fleet exercises.

During the third week of July 1940, Marine Air Group One flew to Norfolk to board the Wasp for transportation to Cuba. The squadrons VMF - flying Grumman F3F's, VMO - flying Curtis SBC's and Douglas SBD's, and VMS-1 - flying their BG's, flew out to the carrier and attempted to land. The first three aircraft to come aboard (F3F-3s) made good landings, catching the second or third arresting cable only to have their tail hooks fail, sending them plunging into the first barrier (two steel cables suspended across the deck between two steel posts that could be raised or lowered). All three aircraft were severely damaged and one pilot required hospitalization. Flight operations were halted. The remaining aircraft returned to Norfolk and an inspection of the flight deck was initiated. It was found that the aft elevator guard rail (normally flush with the deck when the elevator is in the up position) was sticking out above the deck. The tail hooks were striking the rail and cracking, resulting in hook failure upon engaging the arresting cable. While this condition was corrected, the Wasp developed engine problems and the trip to Guantanamo was aborted. The Wasp went to the Boston Navy Yard for repairs and Air Group One returned to Quantico.

In September 1940, the Air Group once again set out for Guatanamo. Ground personnel, along with equipment, went by train directly to the Wasp at pier side N.O.B. Norfolk. After loading their individual squadron equipment, the ground personnel boarded the carrier for the trip. The aircraft were flown aboard off the Virginia coast.

Arriving in Guantanamo Bay, the squadrons off-loaded and set up "Tent City", adjacent to a dirt strip that served as a runway. The field was established on the Windward Side of the bay entrance, where it stands today on top of McCalla Hill, overlooking Fisherman's point where the Marines landed in 1898 to establish a base of operations against the Spanish.

A PIECE OF HISTORY

When George Bobb headed for Parris Island in December of 1939, the Corps was small, tough, and comparatively unsophisticated. Assignment to aviation duty in those days didn't include orders to Memphis and comprehensive instructions in aviation fundamentals, but a trip up the coast to Quantico, and assignment to Base Aviation Detachment One (BAD-1). As he waited for the squadrons to return from the Caribbean, Pvt. Bobb honed his kills on mess duty followed by a tour on the "Bull Gang." Turner Field, as it was known then, was under construction, and after each rain, the "Bull Gang" had the task of clearing mud from the drainage ditches that bordered the landing area and placing it back in the field. Under the scornful eye of one Master Sergeant Joe Budroe, Bobb's first days on "aviation duty" were devoted to activities more closely related to his infantry brethren.

Eventually transferred to the Aircraft Overhaul Shop, George Bobb was given the job of tearing down aircraft slated for rework. On May 13, 1940, as he stripped canvas from a Great Lakes BG-1, he decided he would save the emblem that had adorned the aircraft's starboard side. The carefully painted emblem is probably one of the few surviving original pieces of the BG-1 in existence, and is an unusual representation of the Marine Corps emblem.

George Bobb went on to become a radioman/gunner and radar operator and a designated Combat Aircrewman, logging almost 900 hours in BG-1's, SB2U's, SBD's, SB2C's, and the TBF. As a combat aircrewman in VMS-1, VMSB-131, and VMSB-343, his service spans FMF maneuvers in Cuba, participation in the North Atlantic Neutrality Patrols from USS Ranger, and combat duty in the South Pacific at Henderson Field, Guadalcanal from November 1942 until the Spring of 1943, during which time he was awarded two Air Medals and the Navy Commendation Medal. He finished his war service at Midway, where he flew ASW patrols and

22

submarine escort cover missions.

Notable among his achievements was an attack on the Japanese battleship HIEL, off Savo Island on 13 November 1942. Despite heavy antiaircraft fire and enemy fighters, Bobb and his pilot, Captain George Dooley, made two torpedo runs in their TBF-1, and were credited with two hits. The following day, the pair attacked a Japanese heavy cruiser off New Georgia, scoring a hit. In that action their aircraft was badly damaged by antiaircraft fire. Two weeks later, Bobb and Captain William C. Hayter scored yet another torpedo hit on a light cruiser near New Georgia. Later, in April of '43, he took part in night attacks on Kahili Airfield on Bougainville.

MT/Sgt. George Bobb mustered out in December 1947, and went on to become an electronics test engineer in a defense related industry, retiring in 1988.

News article submitted by VMSB 343 Reunion Association

15-I/AWT/mgf
(12416)

HEADQUARTERS, MARINE FLEET AIR, WEST COAST,
U. S. NAVAL AIR STATION,
SAN DIEGO, 35, CALIFORNIA.

27 October 1944.

From: Commanding Officer.
To :   Commanding General, Third Marine Aircraft Wing.

Subject: Award, forwarding of, case of Sergeant
            George BOBB, USMC.

Enclosure: (A) One Commendation.
            (B) One Commendation ribbon.

1.   Enclosures (A) and (B) are forwarded herewith.

2.   Records of this office indicate subject named man
transferred to your command on 31 August 1944.

                                    H. M. SANDERSON.

53/P15:JAD-tph   First Endorsement   14 November, 1944.
HEADQUARTERS, THIRD MARINE AIRCRAFT WING, FMF, C/O FPO, SAN FRANCISCO, CALIFORNIA.

From: The Commanding General.
To :   Master Technical Sergeant George BOBB, (279324),
            U. S. Marine Corps.

Via :   The Commanding Officer, Marine Aircraft Group Twenty Three.

1.   Forwarded with congratulations.

                                    W. G. FARRELL.

```
-----------------------------------------------------------
KV53(23)/P15/djc      Second Endorsement      20 November 1944.
  Headquarters, MAG-23, 3MAW, c/o FPO., San Francisco, Calif.

Serial No. 1211-44

From:        The Commanding Officer
To  :        The Commanding Officer, Marine Scout  Bombing
                Squadron-343

Subject:     Award, forwarding of, case of Sergeant
             George BOBB, USMC.

  1.         Forwarded with congratulations.
```

L. B. STEDMAN, Jr.

```
-----------------------------------------------------------
KV53(23)/P15/kdg       Third Endorsement      22 November, 1944.
  Squadron VMSB-343, MAG-23, 3MAW, c/o FPO, San Francisco, California.

Serial No. 1211-44

From:        The Commanding Officer
To  :        Sergeant George BOBB, USMC, 279324.

  1.         Delivered with congratulations.
```

WALTER E. GREGORY

United States Pacific Fleet
Flagship of the Commander-in-Chief

The Commander in Chief, United States Pacific Fleet takes pleasure in commending

SERGEANT GEORGE BOBB, UNITED STATES MARINE CORPS

for service as set forth in the following

CITATION:

"For meritorious and efficient performance of duty as an aerial gunner attached to a bombing squadron during an engagement with the enemy in the Solomon Islands area on December 3, 1942. While participating in a strike against a strong Japanese task force, Sergeant BOBB capably assisted his plane commander in carrying out an aggressive and successful attack. As a result of this well coordinated strike, two enemy cruisers were sunk and two others were damaged. His skill and courage in the face of intense anti-aircraft fire and heavy enemy fighter plane opposition contributed materially to the success of the mission and were in keeping with the highest traditions of the naval service."

C. W. NIMITZ,
Admiral, U. S. Navy.

Commendation Ribbon Authorized

SOUTH PACIFIC AREA AND FORCE
Headquarters of the Commander.

Serial 1331   19 May 1945

From: The Commander South Pacific Area and Force.
To   :   The Commanding General, Aircraft, Fleet Marine Force,
          Pacific.

Subject: Awards - forwarding of.

Enclosure: (A) Twenty-one Temporary Citations.
           (B) One Gold Star.
           (C) Two Distinguished Flying Crosses.
           (D) Eighteen Air Medals.

     1.   The Commander South Pacific Area and Force has made
the following awards to the below listed officers and men, formerly
of Marine Scout Bombing Squadron One Hundred and Thirty-One, in
recognition of their meritorious achievement:

GOLD STAR IN LIEU OF A SECOND
DISTINGUISHED FLYING CROSS

ROUSH, Martin B., 1st Lt., USMCR.

DISTINGUISHED FLYING CROSS

MAGUIRE, James B. Jr., Capt., USMCR.
WARREN, Joe L., 1st Lt., USMCR.

AIR MEDAL

BENDER, Charles F. Jr., S/Sgt., USMC.
BOBB, George, S/Sgt., USMC.
BOLEN, William E., Sgt., USMC.
CHAPLOW, Neal R., S/Sgt., USMC.
COLEMAN, Eldon "B", Corp., USMC.
EMBRY, Henry S., Corp., USMCR.
GORCHOFF, Joseph M., Pfc., USMCR.
HINKLE, Harry F., T/Sgt., USMCR.
ISTIK, George R., Pvt., USMCR.

UNITED STATES MARINE CORPS
HEADQUARTERS, AIRCRAFT, FLEET MARINE FORCE, PACIFIC,
% FLEET POST OFFICE, SAN FRANCISCO, CALIFORNIA.

6 June, 1945.

1st Endorsement on:
ComSoPac ltr, ser 1331,
dated, 19 May, 1945.

From: Commanding General.
To :   Commanding Officer, Marine Scout Bombing Squadron-343.
Via :   (1) Commanding General, Third Marine Aircraft Wing.
            (2) Commanding Officer, Marine Aircraft Group-23.

Subject: Awards - forwarding of.

   1.   Forwarded, with pleasure, in the case of Staff Sergeant George
BOBB, USMC.

   2.   Please make the presentation an occasion of ceremony.

                                        JAMES T. MOORE.

Copy to: CMC.

KV53/P15:JH-jfe   Second Endorsement   9 June, 1945.
HEADQUARTERS, THIRD MARINE AIRCRAFT WING, FMF, c/o FPO, SAN FRANCISCO, CALIF.

Serial No. 11209

From: The Commanding Officer.
To :   The Commanding Officer, Marine Scout Bombing Squadron 343.
Via :   The Commanding Officer, Marine Aircraft Group 23.

   1.   Forwarded with congratulations.

                                        B. F. JOHNSON.

KV53(23)/P15/wpo   Third Endorsement   16 June, 1945.
Serial No. 641-45
Headquarters, MAG-23, 3MAW, FMF, c/o FPO, San Francisco, Calif.

From: The Commanding Officer.
To :   The Commanding Officer, Marine Scout Bombing
            Squadron 343.

Subject: Awards, forwarding of, case of Master Technical
            Sergeant George BOBB, (279324), USMC.

   1.   Forwarded with congratulations. Please comply
with paragraph (2) of the first endorsement.

      CERTIFIED A TRUE COPY
      JAMES G. BURKE,
      WC., USMCR.   L. B. STEDMAN, Jr.

In the name of the President of the United States, the Commander South Pacific Area and Force takes pleasure in awarding the AIR MEDAL to

STAFF SERGEANT GEORGE BOBB, UNITED STATES MARINE
CORPS

for service as set forth in the following

CITATION:

"For meritorious achievement while participating in aerial flight as a Radio Gunner attached to a Marine scout bombing squadron operating in the British Solomon Islands area from November 13, 1942 to April 29, 1943. During this period, Staff Sergeant BOBB took part in numerous bombing and strafing attacks against Japanese airfields, shipping and shore installations, frequently encountering intense anti-aircraft fire and fighter plane opposition. Through his skilful teamwork and accurate strafing of all targets assigned, he contributed materially to the success of our offensive aerial operations in the initial phase of the Solomon Islands Campaign. His conduct throughout was in keeping with the highest traditions of the United States Naval Service."

W. L. CALHOUN,
Vice Admiral, U. S. Navy.

YELLOW PERIL

by James H. Magill

It was a very nice day, December 17, 1992. Jack Pollinger and I were scheduled to fly our flying club airplane down to Indiantown, Florida. Jack had been a "Crop Duster" in the area and knew most of the local pilots and their airplanes. There was a Stearman airplane at the Indiantown airport and Jack thought he knew the owner. Maybe he would let me fly his "Stearman" for a reasonable consideration.

Should you not know the "Stearman", it is a Bi-Wing 220 horsepower, two place tandem cockpit trainer airplane, built by Stearman in 1933, later bought out by Boeing who produced several thousands of these trainers for the Navy and Army Air Corps. It was affectionately known as "The Yellow Peril".

Now back to my story.....we did find our "Stearman" and the owner agreed to let me fly it, but of course he would have to go along to make sure I wouldn't damage his plane. Not to elaborate, we took off and had a super flight. He was convinced that I sort of knew what I was doing. We did all the good stuff, stalls, rolls, loops, etc. Did I mention this is an open cockpit airplane? For me it was a truly wonderful experience to get "upside down" again without being all wrapped up in a tight fitting "G" suit, air conditioned cockpit, complete with hard hat, oxygen mask with torso harness, and leg restraints.

Oh yes! Free as a bird (well, maybe as an old crow). After shooting a couple of landings, our flight was over, and we returned the plane back to the parking ramp. After paying for my flight, I checked my watch and it was 2:00 P.M. December 17th, give or take a few minutes, it was the fiftieth anniversary of my first solo flight, which was made in a "Yellow Peril", based at N.A.S. Anastocia, DC. And now, for the rest of the story.

It was a chilly bright afternoon in northern Virginia, just south of Washington, DC, bordered to the east by U.S. 1, known as Hyble Valley Airfield. It had been a private airfield prior to the war. This week, I had ground school in the morning and flight training in the afternoon. It was December 17, 1942 and aviation Cadet Magill was on the flight schedule for the first and third flight periods for solo.

This was the day I had dreamed about, the climax of all my training and my greatest achievement...my first solo flight! It was the practice of the local Navy to allow Navy crewmen to fly with cadets who had primary and secondary C.P.T. (Civilian Pilot Training), in order to qualify for flight pay. On arrival at Hyble Valley A.A.S., I verified my flight schedule and reported to the flight equipment shop to draw winter flight equipment and my parachute. At the equipment desk I specified a solo flight helmet, one without the speaking tubes that were used by the instructors to talk to their back seat students.

As I was drawing my equipment, one of the men from the flight equipment department remarked, "Solo flight, eh?"

"You bet was my reply."

"Can I go along?" he asked.

"Could care less if you have permission", I said. So with that I proceeded to get wrapped up in my flight gear, sign off the yellow sheet, and with parachute over my shoulder, marched out to my "Big Yellow Peril", N2S Buno 30116.

Guess what? There was the equipment man dressed and ready for flight. As I did my pre-flight of the plane, he assured me he had permission to go along. I said, "Time is wasting, so let's go"--and that is the way it was, 1300 hours, December 17th, 1942.

Doing everything by the book, just like my instructor had taught us, "S" turns on the taxi strip, watch out for everything and be alert. At the end of the taxiway, turn into the wind, stick back, checklist complete. Green light to take the runway, lock tail wheel and "GO". Next thing you know, you are flying solo. What a thrill..you are on your way! All of a sudden I remember I have this air-crewman in the front seat with his seat lowered. I had almost forgotten about him. So I'll just stay in the traffic pattern and shoot a couple of landings to prove to him that he needn't worry that I can get the airplane back on the ground.

Departing the airport and local traffic, I headed South toward Mt. Vernon, Virginia, where there were many beautiful farms and rolling hills, doing climbing turns, gaining altitude, keeping the ball in the center, and watching for other aircraft as I was expected to do. Now my passenger in the front seat, who said he had permission to fly with me, raised the front seat to the top of the up travel of the seat. Doing this obstructed my view from the back and was annoying me, to say the least. Since there was no way to communicate except by hand signals, I signaled him to lower his seat and he only gave me a big grin into the rear view mirror, which provides eye contact between the cockpits. By this time, I'm really annoyed and I am looking at the broad shoulders of my passenger and see nothing but a big grin! Getting really frustrated by the distraction and looking at my instruments to be sure I'm not screwing things up, as I checked my speed and altitude I can see through the fuselage the raised seat in the front cockpit. I am now about 3700 feet, air speed 60 knots, and all would be well if my passenger would just lower his damn seat.

Suddenly I see his seat belts drop to the side of his seat. I look up into my mirror as he reaches up and grabs the hand holds built in the top wing. Wondering what the hell he was doing, I see this guy swing one leg out of the cockpit on to the wing, turning his body out of the cockpit - then jumps off the wing and gone from the plane. I circled around to make sure he didn't land in the Potomac River, and he waves a big thumbs up hand signal that he was OK.

By now, I've been flying about 30 minutes and have 45 minutes remaining. I thought to myself, "Out of my way! I've got a lot of flying to do before I'm scheduled back on the flight line."

In the mean time, I'm wondering why this guy bailed out. The plane was doing great and I need to do some more practice and get back in time to do four or five touch and goes before my time was up. I was one happy pilot doing all this stuff and I remember singing to myself, "I'm an old cow hand from the Rio Grande."

It had been a wonderful day and I had almost forgotten about the guy who bailed out of the airplane. After a few touch and goes, I got the plane back on time as scheduled.

I'm now parked and everything is quiet. As my feet touched the ground, I had an abrupt return to reality. I had returned without my passenger. One big Navy Chief greeted me, and his words in effect were, "Hey stupid, the Commanding Officer wants to see you immediately!" I was marched to the C.O.'s offices and no one looked very happy.

"What the hell is going on?" asked the C.O. "Why did you throw this crewman out of your plane and what was he doing there, and why didn't you return to base after he bailed out?" Needless to say, the crewman had stated that I had thrown him out of the plane. As I recall, I had a somewhat flimsy excuse, like he told me he had permission and NO, I did not throw him out...I wouldn't have had any idea how to do such a maneuver. After chewing me out for an hour, I was dismissed.

Where was my instructor? I really needed this guy, but he had the day off. Anyway, what do I do now? Just maybe, I might still be on the schedule. Wow, I really was. I still had on my flight gear and very quickly got out to the flight line and into my plane and had my second solo flight. I am pleased to report that my second flight was complete without any more mishaps. And so ended the day of my first solo flights. Would it be my last with the Navy or not?

The following day, 18 December 1942, I arrived on schedule. It was ground-school, lunch and board the bus for Hyble Valley airfield for more flying (I hoped). Upon arrival I was greeted by my flight instructor (not unlike a Marine D.I.) with a "What the hell have you been up to!" As he listened to my story of the previous day —with frowns of disbelief and maybe a slight smile – he said he had managed to keep me on the flight schedule for my third solo flight – "So don't screw it up and we'll get you out of here". After three solo flights you were transferred to another airfield for the remainder of 'primary' flight training.

Having completed training at Hyble Valley, I thought just maybe I had dodged a bullet. Not so; my Christmas present from the Navy was 49 hours and 49 demerits (Commanding Officers punishment). Fifty of either was cause for termination of flight training. As for the flight equipment sailor, he was declared unsafe to work around aircraft, and was assigned to barracks police. There was speculation that he had wagered his paycheck on the jump, provided that he could get a flight. However, this was never proven. He was later assigned to sea duty and was killed in action during the North-African campaign.

Thanks to my "Higher Power" I completed my "Yellow Peril" flight training by April '43, then went on to N.A.S. Pensacola, Florida for advanced flight training. I completed training with no screw-ups and was designated a Naval Aviator and commissioned a Second Lieutenant, United States Marine Corps Reserve.

My first assignment was to VMSB 343 at Atlantic Field, North Carolina. My first flight in VMSB 343 was 4 September '43. My last flight with the squadron was 5 August '45. Cpl. Lambert flew over 700 hours in my back seat as a radio-gunner. Regrettably, we did not keep in touch after the war.

No, 17 December '42 would not be my last flight. On 22 March 1999 the Federal Aviation Administration would 'ground' this great grandfather (unjustifiably in his opinion).

SECTION II

BECOMING
A MARINE

IN

VMSB 343

A Marine in WWII

by Charles "Chuck" Luedtke

When, "From the Halls of Montazuma" was your childhood lullaby, what else would you grow up to be but a Marine? My Dad was a Marine in World War I so when World War II engulfed the country, I wanted to join the Marine Corps. My Mother was not in favor of my enlisting as my older brother, Gene, was already in service but she finely relented and I enlisted in November, 1942, in Rockford Illinois.

Traveling to Chicago for my physical, I spent the day shivering in my birthday suit only to find that my blood pressure was too high. The recruiter suggested that I return to the hotel and get some rest before trying again in the morning. With three friends from high school, including Joe Ligman, all enlisting together, there wasn't much resting that night as we went out to see the sights of Chicago. That seemed to do the trick as I passed the physical the next morning and was sworn in on December 2, 1942 in Chicago.

That same day we left Chicago by train for a five-day trip to San Diego. All young recruits from the Midwest found everything we passed an adventure. When the train stopped in Phoenix, we spotted a tree beside the tracks, loaded with oranges. We asked the woman if we could pick some and she said, "Have all you want but you may not like them." We didn't, as they were very sour ornamental oranges.

The San Diego and Arizona Eastern Railroad took us through the fantastic Corrizo Gorge and dipped down into Mexico several times before pulling into the main depot in San Diego. What an amazing sight greeted us! San Diego was all covered with netting over Consolidated (Convair now) where they made the B-24's. On top of the netting was a regular town mocked-up -- houses, streets and trees. Barrage balloons on cables were raised every night with lots of searchlights swinging across the sky whenever an aircraft was sighted.

In boot camp at MCRD we were assigned to two-man pup tents with a 5:30 a.m. reveille. After breakfast in the mess hall, we were issued uniforms and another physical was endured. The next day we were assigned to a training platoon and to eight-man tents.

Our tent was next to the D.I.s, whom we thought were gods! One warm Sunday afternoon we were lazing around with the sides up on all of the tents, hoping to capture a breeze. We could see our D.I. leaning back on his bed reading a book, when he called out, "Luedtke, bring me a cigarette". I didn't have one so another guy gave me a cigarette to take over to the D.I. This "friend" was married and had gotten a pass to visit his wife. He'd bought "loads" and put one in the cigarette he gave me but didn't tell me about it until we saw it blow up all over the D.I.

My "friend" and I were ordered to put on full uniform with rifles and report in three minutes. Then we were ordered to stand at attention in front of the D.I. for one hour. Both of us would start to laugh and have to start over. It took about three hours to complete the assignment.

Toward the end of training, we were trucked to Camp Mathews which was east of where the Torrey Pines Golf Course is now, to learn to use and clean rifles and fire for record. When asked to list preference for advanced training, I chose aviation. We were tested in the Starlight Bowl and barracked in the building beside the Ford Building in Balboa Park. I asked to be a pilot but they said I was too big to fit in the fighters.

One of our high school four-some didn't do well on his tests, so we all chose metalsmith training and were shipped by train to Jacksonville, Florida, to the Naval airstation for metalsmith school.

On Sundays we'd go to church in town and frequently people would invite us home for dinner. We'd often catch rides on the PBYs that cruised up and down the coast on sub search. Sometimes I'd sign in for the authorized mechanic when we went up to search for survivors or debris. I'd flip switches for pilots to change gas tanks, lower pontoons or floats (wing tips).

Completing the training at Jacksonville, we were sent to Cherry

Point, North Carolina where the high school four-some was finally split up when Joe Ligman and I were sent to Atlantic Field on August 1, 1943. There we joined a new squadron, just formed on Cape Hattaras. We only had a few planes so there was not much work. It was boring just sitting around so I offered to work with the material man, sorting and stacking shelves. When the Master Sergeant came through with the promotion list, he asked my name and put me in for Corporal.

We often drew guard duty at night, walking along the shore, mosquito net over helmets and carrying Thompson sub-machine guns. Stories of German subs off shore, with the possible landing of spies, kept us ready and alert. One dark midnight, a dog came out of the bush, looking six feet tall. The closer he came, the smaller he got until he became just a friendly puppy. With everything blacked out, the darkness was mighty lonely.

At the end of November, 1943 the squadron was moved to Greenville, North Carolina. Since it was a new military field, the first few nights we slept in a peanut warehouse. After that it was big, solid tents out at the airfield. When the planes arrived, we went to the C.C.C camp near ECTC (Eastern Carolina Teachers' College) and were trucked back to the field daily. Lots of new members arrived for the squadron as it grew and organized. Sundays again found us in town for church and movies in the evenings. A few times we went to the USO for cookies but mostly we just roamed around town. Some weekends we hiked to explore the surrounding woods.

Again we were shipped by train across country to San Diego and in August, 1944, we shipped out of North Island on the Altamaha, a baby flat-top. It took seven days and nights to reach Hawaii, and I slept on the deck each night. I remember being served beans for breakfast and eating eggs, chicken, sliced ham and hot dogs.

The arrival at Pearl Harbor was unforgettable with the bombed-out ships all around the harbor and lots of damage still visible. The water was full of jellyfish, very exotic to Midwesterners. We were off-loaded and trucked to Ewa Marine airbase.

As soon as I could get a pass, I called Peg's aunt, Elizabeth

Marks, who was head visiting nurse of the islands. I took a bus into town to the residential area where she lived in an apartment. It was most comfortable with a lanai, kitchenette, living room, bedroom and bath. After a visit we took a bus to a downtown area where we had dinner.

One Sunday I went with my buddies on a free tour of the island. The Dole pineapple plant was an eye-opener as we watched the machines cut off the tops and sides. Girls removed the eyes and then the pineapples were sliced and canned. We tourists got samples and enjoyed the bubbler at the entrance that ran pineapple juice.

When we went swimming nude at the beach in Hawaii, the Captain said, "No", so I bought one yard of material, cut it kitty corner, put the small points together and lapped 6 or 8 inches. The parachute man seamed it and hemmed the edges to make a bikini, put on like a diaper.

One day a Navy squadron of SB2C's and F4Us was having an "exercise" with the Army flying P38s as "defenders" and the Navy as "enemies". While we watched, a P38 pulled up into the squadron as a F4U dove from above to defend the planes. The P38 rammed into the side of an SB2C, resulting in a huge explosion. Several of the planes caught fire and went down into the sugar cane fields while airplane parts rained down on the airfield. One engine went through a building under construction and caused considerable damage. Another landed in a lumberyard on base and sent wood flying everywhere. The SB2C engine fell beside the runway. The pilot of the P38 parachuted to safety but was injured, while the pilot and gunner of the other plane were both killed.

After working on squadron planes for two months, we flew off for Midway. The plane ahead of us had a cargo door fly open. The crew roped it and pulled it back in. The flight of 1,000 miles took about six hours and only one plane had to make a stop at French Frigate Shoales. Approaching Midway, we dropped lower and lower but could see only water below. Finally we popped over a reef and there was Eastern Island - very small! You could walk around the whole island in half an hour and that included looking for shells.

Soon after arrival, a flight was coming in from a training mission and a Navy plane pulling a target for ground gunners got in the way. One plane avoided it but the other crashed into it and both pilots were killed.

Housed in barracks that slept 50, we were up at 6:00 a.m., shaved, showered, and off to the mess hall near the hangar for chow. I saw my first gooney bird on November 1, in front of the mess hall. Of course, it made a crash landing. These birds have a wing span of six feet with large but very light bones. Looking like an overgrown seagull, they lay eggs, usually just one, about the size of an emu egg.

Their nests are small, lined with feathers, on the ground all over the island. The mates take turns sitting on the nest. Standing face to face, they start a mating dance with bobbing heads and mooing like a cow. They shake their beaks and then repeat the sequence. The babies are fuzzy, furry, little upside down punching bags and are dark grey while adults are white. They feed their young by regurgitation of partially digested squid and fish.

In order to get airborne, the birds run into the wind. Baby birds run, pop up into the air and collapse and fall into bushes or even barbed wire. Their take off on the water is the same. The large birds are a great hazard to airplanes. If hit, they can gouge chunks out of plane wings.

Food on Midway was seldom fresh, with lots of strong mutton from Australia. I still find it hard to face lamb. Sometimes the kitchen crew would go out in boats, throw out a hand grenade and scoop up the dead fish, for a change on the menu. If we went fishing from the beach, we'd cook the fish for a real treat.

When days were blistering hot, we worked on the planes at night. As only one plane could be in the hangar at a time, the outside planes were too hot to touch.

For recreation we went fishing, shelling, bowling, to movies and played cards. We did lots of crafts such as stainless steel watchbands and plastic boxes. When we first arrived on Eastern there was lots of debris left over from the Battle of Midway, including some stainless steel urinals that we cut and made watch bands for anyone who wanted one. Plastic was used in the windows of airplanes and scraps were great for forming small boxes. We also cast aluminum ornaments for the hilts of knives issued by the Marine Corps. It was also shaped and carved for new handles for knives. On Midway we could swim nude or wear shorts and a tee to keep the coral dust out. One time a Norwegian ship came into port and the Captain took his wife in a jeep for a tour of the island. The men always walked to the showers with just a towel slung over the shoulder. He and she came by in the jeep and from then on the men had to walk to the showers with their towels around their waists.

My close friends on Midway were LeTendre, Vazac, and McInerry. Ligman lived out in the revetment while Al Averbeck was co-leader of the metalsmiths.

In September, 1945, I returned to Hawaii for one month where I left the squadron and worked installing seats in planes going to return released prisoners from Japan and other areas.

Shipping back to the States in late October, we landed in Seattle, went by train to San Diego and then to my home in Beloit, Wisconsin. After marrying Peg on November 11, we honeymooned in Florida and then lived in New Bern, North Carolina while I was stationed at Cherry Point. A discharge in February completed my tour of duty with the Marine Corps but not my life-long association with the Marines.

MARINE TRANSPORT SQUADRON NINE FIFTY THREE
MARINE AIRCRAFT GROUP FIFTEEN
THIRD MARINE AIRCRAFT WING, FLEET MARINE FORCE
c/o FLEET POST OFFICE, SAN FRANCISCO, CALIFORNIA

15 September 1945

MEMORANDUM TO: Whom it may concern.

This is to certify that <u>StfSgt C.F. LUEDTKE</u> is a member of this organization and is granted weekend liberty from 1200, 15 September 19 to 0730, 17 September 1945.

Address will be:
YMCA
Honolulu, T.H.

H. A. Anderson Jr.
H. A. ANDERSON, Jr.
1stLt., USMCR,
Adjutant.

MEAL TICKET   Nº 9986

E-1 Mess

U. S. MARINE CORPS AIR STATION
EWA, OAHU, T. H.

Squadron 953

4202—S/M Base. (128)—5-13-44—10M.

FOURTEENTH NAVAL DISTRICT

Ship or Activity.......... **VMSB 343**

TO WHOM IT MAY CONCERN:
This is to certify that

Luedtke, C.F. Sgt.

has been examined and found qualified to operate Navy owned trucks not exceeding 1½ tons rated capacity; truck with trailer ....; passenger bus ...; tractor-trailer passenger unit ...

James D. Deraper
(Transportation Officer)
Lt. (jg) CEC USNR

Luedtke, C.F.

is authorized to drive Navy owned trucks not exceeding 1½ tons rated capacity; truck with trailer ...; passenger bus ...; tractor-trailer passenger unit ...

Robert B. ____
(Commanding Officer)

By Direction

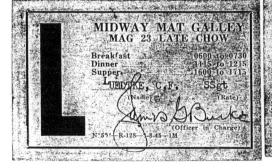

MIDWAY MAT GALLEY
MAG 23 LATE CHOW

Breakfast	0600 to 0730
Dinner	1115 to 1215
Supper	1600 to 1715

LUEDTKE, C.F.   SSgt
(Name)   (Rate)

James G. Burke
(Officer in Charge)

Nº5? — R-128 — 3-45—1M

JOINING THE MARINE CORPS

February 1, 1943

by Walter G. Letendre

I was inspired to write this article after receiving Chuck Luedtke's memories, and the memories it sparked in me.

On December 7, 1942 my cousin Robert "Bob" Letendre enlisted in the Marine Corps to avenge the 'Japs' for bombing Pearl Harbor on that day. Bob and I were closer than brothers, and had spent most of our teen-age life together, much of it swimming and fishing on Lake Muskego where his parents owned a home.

I thought to myself, if he can be a Marine, so can I. When my day off at the A & P store where I worked came, I took the streetcar downtown to the Marine Corps Recruiting Station and tried to enlist. I was disappointed to find out their quota of five for the day was already filled. I went back three more times and got the same answer each time--sorry.

On my next visit, on February 3, 1943, I was told there had been a policy change. From now on, in order to join the Marine Corps, a volunteer must first go to the Draft Board and pass their physical and exams. If you passed their test, you could then attempt to join the Marines.

I did what any red-blooded American boy of twenty would do. I rushed to the Draft Board at the Federal Building on East Wisconsin Avenue in Milwaukee and got in line with hundreds of others like myself.

Take off clothes.

Bend over and spread your cheeks.

Turn your head, cover your mouth, and cough
   as they checked your private parts.

Complete dental checkup.

Written exams

Wow, congratulations, you qualify high enough to enlist in the Marine Corps. Go over to that desk where the sailor is and sign up. Now I'm elated -- but not for long. I'm informed by the sailor that the Marine Corps quota of fifteen had just been filled, and I'm now in the Navy. I was stunned, and I blurted out, "I hate bell bottom pants with all those buttons in the front. I hate the Navy." While I was moaning and groaning, one of the Marines on the bench who had been accepted, walked up to the desk and said to the sailor in charge, "I understand those of us who are accepted into the Marine Corps must leave on a train at 6 p.m. tonight."

The sailor said, "Yes".

The Marine recruit said, "I can't do that, I've got business to attend to."

I jumped in and said, "I'll take his place!" and the two of us switched places. The fifteen of us were bussed over to Marine Recruiting and run through another battery of tests. By now it was 4 p.m. in the afternoon, and we were told to be at the train depot at 6 p.m. to head for San Diego. I took the streetcar home, rushed into the kitchen where my family was eating supper, and exclaimed, "I'm leaving at 6 o'clock, and I need a tooth brush, toothpaste, a razor and a spare handkerchief."

My mother said, "You're leaving tomorrow already?"

I answered, "No, I'm leaving in an hour, tonight." My Dad got the '36 Chevy out of the garage and drove us back to the Northwestern Railroad Depot, and got me there with fifteen minutes to spare. With hugs, and kisses, and tears I was off on my first train ride, a five day trip to "Dago".

When we got to San Diego, we were loaded onto Marine Corps busses and taken to the Marine Corps recruit depot. There a Corporal ordered us off the bus and told us to line up in two ranks. I was shocked to see how dumb all these Marines looked with their shaved heads. We were marched to the equipment warehouse, and on our way who do I see but my cousin, Bob, who immediately spotted me. We were issued dungarees, skivvies, (underwear), socks, boots, a cap, a pail, a scrub brush, a box of Rinso, a razor, shaving soap, a wool overcoat, and two blankets, and sheets. We were told the pail, brush, soap, and razor would be deducted from our pay! ($18.00 a month) We were told to load all our gear into our duffel bags, put the bag on our shoulder, and run to our assigned Quonset hut. We were told we were quarantined, and not to associate with the other Marine recruits.

Well, my cousin, Bob, followed us to our hut, and when the Corporal left, Bob began instructing me on how to properly make a bunk so a half dollar would bounce off the blanket. About then the Corporal came back, caught Bob, and I thought he was going to kill him. Bob thought he was a "salty Marine"--after all he had been in the 'Corps' for eight weeks.

In the following weeks we:

> had our head shaved--hey now we look salty like the
> other guys,
> drilled,
> received our shots,
> drilled,
> given combat training,
> drilled,
> trained in rifle and bayonet use,
> drilled,
> taught how to swim and jump off a 30' platform,
> drilled,
> taught how to live without Poggy Bait (candy) and Coke,
> and how to enjoy mess hall chow.

Upon graduation from boot camp, we were assigned to a month of mess hall duty, waiting on other Marine recruits.

From there I was assigned to aviation mechanics school at Navy Pier in Chicago for six months. Because of good grades, I was then assigned to a specialist school; at 87th and Anthony in Chicago to specialize in carburation.

Upon graduation I was assigned to Cherry Point Marine Corps Air Station, and then assigned to VMSB-343 in Greenville, North Carolina.

Being assigned to VMSB-343 turned out to be the best thing that happened to me, where lasting friendships were created which still exist to this day.

A PATRIOTIC TIME

by Shirley (Kittleson) LeTendre

The 1940's were very patriotic years. I was a mere teenager at the time, still attending high school. I hadn't met Wally yet, but apparently we both attended South Division High School at the same time--he a Senior, and I a Freshman. Everyone wanted to do their part in fighting the Germans and the Japanese. The Johnston Cookie Factory was looking for help, since all the men had gone off to war. They arranged through the highschool for us to work after school for 15 cents an hour packing hard candy for the servicemen. After school we would take the streetcar and ride the two miles to Milwaukee's Westside to the Johnston Cookie Factory. It was a huge red brick building, one block square and four stories high with huge windows all the way around. When we arrived we picked up our uniforms; a grey and white, stiff as a board dress, and a head cover with a band in front and cheese cloth hair netting, also starched.

This factory made cookies, graham crackers, soda crackers, chocolates, and hard candy. My job was to pack one-inch square hard candies wrapped in cellophane in boxes containing 24 pieces. These boxes of candy were destined for the servicemen, I believe through the Red Cross.

We were allowed to work four hours a day, and were always done by 9 o'clock, so we could get enough sleep for school. Most of my best friends in highschool worked there with me. Sneaking free chocolate was an added bonus. Nuts were also a treat. We never knew who was getting the candy, but we knew we were doing our part.

Of course, I didn't know, or hadn't met Walter as yet, although when I was a Freshman, he must have been a senior at the same highschool and he was a classmate of my sister, Louise.

How did we meet:

38

While Walter was overseas, his parents moved upstairs into the same flat my parents lived in downstairs. When he came home from overseas, I was standing on the front porch and noticed this handsome, sun-tanned Marine with the shiny shoes. Since I worked with his sister at Harnishfeger Corporation, we set him up. The rest is history.

CHARLIE

by Lt. Col. Walter E. "Bill" Gregory

On August 14, 1923, baby Franzo was born. He was delivered by a midwife. Midwife delivery was not unusual during this moment in history, neither was a report of birth required. When brother Johnny, then age twelve, first saw the new baby, he simply exclaimed, "It's a Charlie!", and "Charlie" he has been for the last seventy-five years. At his christening he was named after grandfather Carmino, except the "o" was replaced by an "e", thus Carmine Franzo. He continued to be Charlie to one and all. Later at his confirmation his parents wisely added "Charles". He was now known as Carmine Charles Franzo. At last "Charlie" had an origin.

In the Summer of 1939 he joined the Army and was attached to an Army support group. This particular support group supported the 69th Infantry, an Army National Guard regiment. Charlie's assigned location was at an Army armory which was located on 23rd Street, New York City. However much of his time was spent at Camp Kilmore, New Jersey, where various units of the 69th Infantry went for annual field training. With World War II underway, sometime in the Summer of 1942, the support group to which Charlie was attached was ordered to South America to assist in the training of selected forces of that area. In that Charlie had just completed his three year "hitch", and in that the U.S. Army didn't want troops under 21 years of age in South America, he was discharged.

Charlie once more found himself wandering the streets of the Big Apple, Only this time such activity grew old in a hurry, so he went to the local recruiting center. Conscription was in full bloom. He first visited the Army recruiting unit --- they didn't have time to recruit or reenlist --- they were processing draftees in record numbers. He went to the Navy--same story. He now wanted to reenlist --- period. The thought of being a draftee was becoming most upsetting. Hope was rapidly disappearing when he, by chance, saw the Marine Corps recruiting unit. They too were most busy processing draftees, but they always find time to reenlist a military man. No more wandering or wondering for Charlie --- he was immediately inbound to a place called Parris Island. This was in October, 1942. At this stage of his life he was nineteen years and two months old.

Parris Island completed, he was ordered to MCAS Cherry Point. He had experience driving trucks (U.S. Army), so he was assigned to and now waiting to attend a motor transport school. In the meantime he was temporarily assigned to CAG-23, which was supporting a field demonstration at the Marine Corps Schools at Quantico, Virginia. Ammunition was being expended at a rapid rate. Charlie drove a 6X6 truck, hauling ammunition which included loading and unloading his haul.

Now there was a Lieutenant William Steadman Witt, who was officer-in-charge of MAG-33 Marines pulling support duty. On one particular day Witt had a detail, which included Charlie, unloading ammunition from trucks from 0600 to well into the afternoon -- it was hot and shade did not exist. Around 1600 Witt notified Charlie that he would stand guard duty that night. Witt could not be swayed by Charlie's silver tongue.

With much of his boyhood on the streets of New York City and three years in the Army, Charlie was quite certain he knew his way around. For example, he arranged with Corp. Theal for Theal to pull his guard duty for five dollars. Back in those days five dollars was enough for a man to have a more than adequate liberty. Speaking of liberty, Charlie had the next two days off beginning at 0800 the next morning. He decided to start a bit early since his guard duty would indicate he had not left before his liberty period began. Off he went. Corp. Theal, good to his word, was out in the pitch black at Charlie's assigned post. Let it be said again that it was pitch black. Instead of having the Sergeant of the Guard make the rounds, Lt. Witt decided to check the guard. When he came to Charlie's post he was properly challenged and all went well until he asked for the guard's name. Instead of saying "Franzo" the corporal said "Theal".

When Charlie returned to Quantico, Witt was waiting for him. Witt had a list of charges. The standout charge was deserting his post in the time of war! Charlie was made a prisoner-at-large which he remained until the MAG-33 element returned to Cherry Point. Witt made certain Charlie never had an idle moment, except for food and sleep. Charlie was involved in all manner of unpleasant tasks.

Back at MCAS Cherry Point the officer-in-charge of the casual company to which Charlie was attached, reviewed the several charges submitted by Witt. He discussed the situation with Charlie and determined that Witt was a bit over-zealous. Charlie was given formal office hours, the verdict from which was forty days of hard labor.

Sometime in October of 1943, Lt. W. S. Witt reported to VMSB-343. Several weeks later, he hurried into the CO's office and in a most excited state said, "They are sending us all of their brig rats!" By unofficial contact, Witt had learned that seven transfers to the squadron were directly from the MCAS Brig. At that moment the CO was glad to increase the command by seven young Marines no matter where they came from.

On the designated day, seven new squadron members jumped off the rear of a 6X6 from Cherry Point. Before them stood Witt. There was no welcome aboard on his face. Each of six of the seven had a needed MOS and was quickly assigned to where needed. The seventh drove trucks and the squadron didn't have any trucks. Of course, the seventh was Charlie. Again, Witt was finding unpleasant tasks for Charlie. Whenever Charlie escaped Witt's attention, he would hang around the squadron office, making himself useful anyway he could. Now the officer assigned to oversee mail delivery was Lt. Snuffy Inman. Twice he lost his mail orderly to AWOL or other disciplinary problems. Each time, Charlie would immediately handle the assignment. Snuffy caused Charlie to be made the permanent mail orderly. It came to Lt. Inman's attention that Lt. Witt quite often disturbed Charlie without reasonable cause. Charlie's problem with Lt. Witt vanished. As mailman, Charlie had the opportunity to be in contact with all squadron personnel and they liked this lad from the streets of New York City.

Now the question in the forefront is, who are the other six "brig rats"?

THE SACRIFICIAL LAMB

by Ralph H. Heidenreich

In early 1940 in my hometown of Pittsburgh, Pennsylvania there were organized "BUNN" Associations as in many northern cities. These units were comprised of German immigrants in support of Adolph Hitler and the Third Reich. I remember these well. As a teenager this was exciting to watch as they would put on demonstrations. As we know now their total desire was support for Hitler and an effort to overthrow our government and win control with world dominance. German families loyal to the United States would have nothing to do with or associate themselves with this movement. Nonetheless, they as Germans found themselves in question as to their loyalty to the United States of America.

There I was a young American born in this country as was my mother and father, both offspring of German immigrants. We all wondered what was happening. No one could explain, so as a result fear engulfed these families. They were poor, hard-working people with the desire to achieve the "American Dream" - life without fear, freedom of religion and a feeling that all men are created equal. Their main thrust was to have a good job, educate their children, and create a better lifestyle for themselves and their families.

In pursuit of this dream, Emil Bartolizic, a friend of my brother, enlisted in the United States Marine Corps – a peace time Marine. After a number of years he came home wearing corporal stripes on his blue dress uniform and red blood stripes on his pants. What a sight to see!! It was then I knew I wanted to be a MARINE!!!!

I tried to enlist, but my parents would not sign. On the second try they agreed. The German Bunn in Pittsburgh, Pennsylvania became stronger and the European campaign of Germany was overrunning country after country. Everyone was alarmed. My parents, in fear, wanted to show their loyalty to our country. So I, as their offspring, with my desire to be a U.S. Marine, got them to sign my consent papers. They could display in the window of our home the banner that said, "We Have a Son in the Military" with a big star in the middle. My mother and father decided I could enter the Marine Corps, but my brother would wait until he was drafted. I never registered for the draft. I voluntarily enlisted in the Marine Corps. The Best Military Force the United States commands. My brother stayed behind, was drafted into the army, went through boot training, shipped overseas, went through North Africa, Sicily, and Italian campaigns, spending thirty-three months of his thirty-six months' tenure in the U.S. Army, overseas.

HOW WE FIRST MET

by Barbara McInerny

I've always envied the women who could say, "When I met my husband it was so romantic." But when it's your eighth grade graduation what are the chances of that?

Mac, as he was introduced, had come to the party as a favor to his friend. I knew the friend as he was in my sister's grade and one of the social group. At this time one of my classmates had a crush on him so she had invited him to the party. They were both two years older than most of us, and I'm sure that our party was the last place on earth Mac wanted to be that night. He refused to join in the games and informed us he didn't like girls. I thought he was rude and antisocial. Actually, a jerk.

My sister enlightened me the next day. He was the Mac that I would hear mentioned in their conversations. He was a sort of ringleader of the boys and lived in the big corner house enroute downtown. I had learned the hard way to avoid that corner. The group, when not playing ball or doing whatever boys were doing at that time, would meet on his third floor and think of fun things to do. Their number one favorite was to drop bags of water on people walking by. More than once I went home sputtering that I would like to kill that kid. Had I known that the night before I'm sure nothing would have followed.

After school was out for the summer I saw him a few times just in passing and never long enough for a conversation. Then he started coming to the house either with the gang or with my sister's boyfriend, also one of the group. But he never came alone. It wasn't long after they started to let me join the group on their social outings. We never paired off for anything. Tom still gave the impression he didn't like girls and I didn't think I liked him.

It was my dish night when my younger sister came into the kitchen and announced, "That McInerny boy is out there alone and wants to know if you're home." I don't know if it was shock, amazement, or just curiosity but I remember dropping the dish. I decided that night that he wasn't so bad and he decided he could stand girls. A few fights, even a couple of break ups, but always back together. For me it was a death do us part thing.

Barbara was the wife of Tom McInerny

THINGS I REMEMBER MOST ABOUT VMSB 343, MARINE DIVE BOMBER SQUADRON WORLD WAR II

(** real names not given)

by Ralph Heidenreich

VMSB 343 was commissioned August 1, 1943 at Cherry Point, North Carolina and moved to Atlantic Field that date. I was one of the original eighteen members who were sent to Atlantic Field, not knowing what our mission was, who we were assigned to or what was expected of us. We later learned our mission was support elements of a Marine Dive Bomber Squadron. Through extensive training, we became a valuable contribution to the war effort of WWII.

Later we learned we were designated to participate in the Normandy Invasion of Europe. We were assigned a mission to destroy a vital strategic emplacement which would affect the overall complexion of the invasion of Europe. "Top Brass" had other ideas about this in as much as they did **not** want Marines in the invasion of Europe. They wanted it all Army. Our orders were changed. We sent our pilots and support elements to Norfolk, Virginia to receive new SB2C's only to be reassigned back to Greenville, North Carolina July 8th or 9th of 1944.

Getting back to memories at Atlantic Field -the end of nowhere- the First/Sgt. was Steve Romanack, a career Marine who was every inch a Marine. He was later replaced by First/Sgt. Logan Lane, later replaced by Don Deems.

Taking Liberty (time off from duty) was a privilege - sometimes questioned, but nevertheless appreciated. I went to Morehead city with these "salty" Marines, and was exposed to what liberty was all about!! 1st Sgt. Romanack drove his Buick touring car, a convertible, wheels shining, top down--we were living!!!! Needless to say, I, as a Private First Class was in **big** company. I will not elaborate on the problems we found ourselves in that night. Suffice it to say we broke every law in the book and ended up facing the C.O. of Camp David (Army) after we violated their barricades on our way back to Atlantic Field. Camp David was between Morehead City and Atlantic Field. What a night!!!!

Then I remember "Jane Doe"**, the BAM (Broad Assed Marine) who vowed she would screw every marine stationed at Atlantic Field. She did this with dedication, for every night at the fish house lines were formed to get first in line.

I also remember trying to go to Atlantic to see a movie at the theater--so called. The only heat was from a coal stove down front on the right. Every so often the owner would come down, shake the burner and ashes. Smoke and dust was so thick one could not even see the movie screen!!

On December 1, 1943 we moved to Greenville, North Carolina. We moved and occupied on the outside of the airport on a stretch of land. We pitched our pup tents making sure they were all in line. First Sergeant Lane told us we were on review for all to see. Guess what? Next morning we were under an inch of snow. Consequently nobody came to see us, for snow in eastern North Carolina is a rarity and everyone stayed home.

I also remember the War Bond Drive when a station was placed in downtown Greenville for all citizens to participate. We Marines were also assembled in our mess hall and in order to leave, had to sign up for war bonds.

The kindness of Greenville citizens I remember vividly. We were the first contingent of the military to be stationed in Greenville, and the citizens opened their arms to us in welcome. We could be walking down the street on a Sunday, a window of a car was rolled down, a door opened, and an invite to have dinner at their homes was issued. What a tribute to Greenville and southern hospitality!!

I also remember quite vividly the day we left Greenville after being there several months--July 15, 1944. The reason I remember this date so well is that on July 13, 1944 Evelyn and I married. Nobody thought our marriage would last, but at this writing we have been together nearly fifty-five years!!! (I love her dearly!)

The trains were formed on 14th street in a switching circle. We boarded the trains for our travel to San Diego, California via South Carolina, Georgia, Alabama, Mississippi, Texas, New Mexico and finally California and San Diego. Seven days we were in those day coaches, in July in the heat of the summer. We traveled day and night, sweating, no showers, no bunks, only a day coach chair to sleep in. Our only food was from a field kitchen set up in a box car. But we were MARINES!!! We did not think it was tough. We bathed in helmets, shaved, and faced roll call ready for the call to duty.

We were relieved one day in Texarkana, Texas. We moved to a restaurant for our evening meal. We moved from our train to the restaurant in formation with everyone in step for we were Marines! What a great feeling! We were in clean atmosphere, good food, and no ashes falling on us or our food. You understand, all locomotives were coal fired in those days.

Off we go toward California, but first we had to completely cross Texas. Waco, Texas was a small crossroads which was Sgt. Charles "Bo Bo" Beauford's home town. We stopped here and some of the guys went out, gave nickels to the kids, instructing them to say, "Daddy! Daddy!!" when Bo Bo was in sight. We only had to take on water for the engines, but everyone enjoyed the kids hollering "Daddy" to someone they did not know.

After arriving at San Diego, one day a call came for T/Sgt. Heidenreich to report to Company Headquarters. I reported to Captain Russell Janson, our operations officer. He informed me, his operations NCO, that I would be 1st Sgt. for a detail to travel to El Toro Marine Air Facility at Santa Anna, California to complete our training. I was instructed to take only the radio/gunners, flight plane captains, and engineering personnel necessary to complete our training. At El Toro, Captain Janson informed me we would be airborne at 0700 and secure operations at 1630 "You are in charge of personnel, so command as you see fit", I was told. I knew after securing operations all the pilot officers were gone, so I challenged our support elements to clean our barracks before we left at 0600 so we could pass any inspection that might be called. This we all did without question. We never had a problem. At 1630 the flight line was closed, with everyone who chose going on liberty, keeping in mind we had to keep a security guard on the flight line guarding our assigned aircraft. What a pleasant two weeks we had, knowing this was our last hurrah. We knew we were moving overseas shortly.

We never saw the pilots, only when they walked onto the flight line to board their planes for take-off for their next training mission. All this was coordinated by Captain Janson and myself as operations NCO.

The weekend between the two weeks was another story. Captain Janson told me we would secure at 1630 Friday and resume operations at 0700 Monday. I questioned, "What shall I do with the men?" His reply was, "Sergeant, do what you feel is proper." I knew all the pilots were gone so I decided all of us would have liberty also, except for our security guards. As in life today, people always segregate themselves. We were no different. The senior NCO's went on pass together. We chose to check out San Francisco. None of us had ever been exposed to the city of the bay or cable cars. Well here we are, M/Sgt. Dick Bowles, M/Sgt. Stanley Harris, and T/Sgt. Ralph Heidenreich. Our first experience was a visit to a night club which simulated a ship by having giant plastic tubes of popcorn simulating the roll and yawn of a ship at sea. The effect was quite impressive. This is where M/Sgt. "Doe"** met "Bushel Tits". Now M/Sgt. "Doe" had stated quite frankly that he had lost nothing in the South Pacific and now was a bad time to go looking for it. He told us he was not going for his intention was to get a good case of the "clap" (venereal disease). He shacked up with "Bushel Tits" that weekend. After we returned to duty he kept watching for signs of infection. When we returned to San Diego two or three days later, he hollered from the latrine, "I've got it!!" He checked into sick bay. So much for M/Sgt. "Doe"--so you may think!!! Some days later as we embarked onto the USS Altamaha (a light aircraft carrier) for our overseas journey to Pearl Harbor, Hawaii, all answered "Present" except M/Sgt. "Doe". Boarding ship for overseas was a very disciplined maneuver. You approached the boarding ramp, your name was called like "Heidenreich?", you would answer "Ralph H." You were then permitted to board. Having accomplished all this I reported to Major Gregory that all were present and accounted for except M/Sgt. "Doe", who was in sick bay. The Major smiled and said, "He will be along!" The next thing, sirens were blowing, blue lights flashing, with an ambulance escorted by military police vehicle down the boarding dock, up to our loading ramp. Doors flew open, then there stood M/Sgt. "Doe" who was escorted shipboard by medics. He could not sit down for in those days the only medication for that kind of infection was sulfur which was injected through the butt with a long, long needle. M/Sgt. "Doe"s only comment was. "I tried, but all I have is a sore ass!!!"

On board ship, the USS Altamaha, we stood on the fantail observing all the ships in our convoy--forty or so weaving, changing course, etc, so not to be a fixed target for a Japanese torpedo. The only feeling all of us nineteen and twenty year olds had was seeing the mainland of the United States fading into the horizon, not knowing if ever we would see your homeland again. Needless to say there were many tears streaming down the cheeks of these young, brave Marines. Thanks, with the grace of God, we did return to our homes eighteen months later.

I remember going into Pearl Harbor. What a sight to see!! All the sunken ships of the sneak attack by Japan!! Scoffield Barracks, Henderson Field, etc. all lay in complete and total destruction. All around us were signs of the attack of Pearl Harbor on December 7, 1941. As we lay tied up to the dock, we were quarantined for 24 hours before we could disembark. We stood aboard, watching our ship's Navy personnel going on liberty for four hours. The sailors would leave ship, saluting the ship's colors as they left in their sparkling white uniforms, only to see them return four hours later-- caps gone, white's dirty and torn, a monkey hanging on one sailor's shoulder, all drunk, but having a great four hours of shore leave. All of us watched with envy, wishing we could have been in that liberty section.

I also remember Lt. Bill Barry stealing a Navy jeep, repainting it with Marine paint and decals. This jeep was his personal vehicle while he remained at Pearl Harbor as our Supply Officer, supporting the unit which was deployed to Midway Island, protecting our most forward submarine base in the South Pacific.

LEARNING TO SWIM IN THE MARINE CORPS

by Walter LeTendre

While growing up in Milwaukee, life was simple. I was about twelve years old, and during the summer my cousin Bobby LeTendre and I would ride our Schwinn Balloon Tire Bikes from the south end of town to Estabrook Park. The Milwaukee River ran through the Park and they had a beach where we would swim. The river was about 150 feet across, and by then I had learned to swim a little bit. On one of our visits my cousin, Bob, and I decided to swim across the river. Bob got across and was waiting for me. I got about two-thirds of the way across and stopped to rest. Where I had stopped was at a drop-off, and in my panic I kept trying to put my feet on the ledge which was too deep to reach. Instead of swimming I was groping and kept going down. My cousin noticed my plight and swam out and pulled me out, saving me from drowning. From that day forward I had a terrible fear of the water.

Enter the Marine Corps. In 1943 at the age of nineteen I joined the Marine Corps. They put me on a train in Milwaukee and shipped me to San Diego and Boot Camp. While in Boot Camp the Drill Instructor told us everyone has to learn to swim. Several times a week they would march us over to the swimming pool. They told us that since we would go overseas on Naval ships and land or storm beaches on LCT's, we had to know how to jump off a ship. They had towers that were 30 feet high, with an eight-foot square platform on top. We would climb to the top, and were told to walk off the platform, (do not look down) and hold your family jewels. Those of us who couldn't swim, had to walk off the tower anyway, feet first. If you refused you had to stand on the tower until you did. The record while I was there was twenty-eight hours. Once you walked off, if you couldn't swim, they reached out to you with twelve-foot long poles and pulled you out. That's what happened to me.

If you couldn't swim, every night in your free time, you would be marched to the pool, and they would try and teach you how to swim. In most cases it would be so cold at night that I would march to the pool in my wool overcoat. By the end of boot camp I still couldn't swim! After I completed Boot Camp, I qualified for the Marine Air Corps, and was assigned to the aviation mechanics school at Navy Pier in Chicago (one of the greatest liberty towns in the country). Here those of us who couldn't swim were told that we would not get liberty until we learned to swim.

Wow -- this is terrible -- no liberty in Chicago!!!

Navy pier was a Naval installation, and the Navy had a class for swimming instructions that was held in an athletic club north on Lake Drive. Since I wanted liberty, I enlisted in the swimming classes. So now, five days a week, I was being driven to swimming classes, and they were excellent. First they taught me how to float, and this gave me extreme confidence. Then they taught me how to take off my boots and tie them together and hang them around my neck. (If you were shipwrecked on a coral island you would need them to walk on the razor sharp coral.) Next they taught us how to take off our dungarees and jacket while in the water, and trap air in them, tie them off, and use them as floats. It works! Even an upside down helmet acts as a float. Once I mastered that, they taught me how to swim under water, backstroke, breaststroke, crawl, and side stroke. Now I loved to swim, and couldn't get enough of it. Naturally, after passing the swimming tests I got my liberty in Chicago and thoroughly enjoyed the best liberty town in the U.S.A.

When we shipped out of California, we went to Ewa, Oahu, T.H., prior to going to Midway Islands. With the Pacific Ocean all around me I had to swim. Waikiki Beach, which I though would be great, was full of large rocks, I believe to prevent miniature sub penetration by the Japanese. Further down the coastline towards Diamond Head was a huge Olympic size pool that was fed salt water directly from the ocean. Once I found that pool, that's where I spent all my liberties.

In late October or early November we shipped out for Midway Islands. Again I was surrounded by the Pacific Ocean. Eastern and Sand Islands are encircled by a coral reef, thus creating a huge swimming pool. The water was crystal clear, blue-green, and warm. When we weren't engaged in repairing our dive bombers we were free to enjoy the ocean. Midway is very small, very flat, has no trees, and no natives. We fashioned fishing spears, so that in addition to swimming we could spear-fish among the coral reefs, always on the lookout for sting rays, octopus, sharks, and eels. It was some of the most enjoyable swimming I've ever done.

I never lost my love of swimming, and our Wisconsin substitute for the Pacific turned out to be Lake Beaulah. We made hundreds of trips there with our kids, where they learned to swim.

Now that I'm seventy-five years old, one of my favorite swimming holes is my brother, Bozo's (Gene) and his wife Angie's pool in Sussex, Wisconsin. It's also crystal clear blue. After that I'll settle for Clearwater Beach, Florida.

Keep   on   swimming!

GUARD DUTY: ATLANTIC NORTH CAROLINA,

NOVEMBER 1943

by Ralph Heidenreich

I was stationed at Atlantic North Carolina with VMSB-343 and I was promoted 1 Aug. 1943 to PFC. I was one of the eighteen original members of the squadron. I found myself subjected to guard duty. Guard duty and such was not a big deal, but when you subject a city boy to walk his post between barbed wire barricades six feet from the surf, things take a different perspective. We were at war with Germany and in the middle of the German's attack on our shipping in the Atlantic. You can remember how the Germans tried to destroy our shipping off the East Coast; thus destroying our ability to supply our troops in the European theater of operations. German submarines were plentiful and they sank tons of shipping, but we also sank submarines. We were alerted in the middle of the night many times, full battle gear to search the woods for German saboteurs who possibly had infiltrated our shores.

Walking my post I saw a set of eyes approaching me. I called "Halt, who goes there?" as I was taught. Nothing happened - so again I called, "Halt, who goes there?" Again nothing happened, with the eyes coming closer to me all the time. I, from the very beginning, was locked and loaded, so I called the third time, "Halt who goes there". Hearing no answer I fired my weapon aiming directly at the eyes. Next I called Sgt. of the Guard Post #3.

When the Sgt. of the Guard arrived he and I, accompanied with others, found I had shot and killed a 1,350 pound German cow.

THE VIRGIN AND THE PATRIOT

by Lew D. "Buck" Buckner

On a cold fall day in 1943 an old red-headed boy named Charles Churchill and myself were loaded into the back of a six-by truck. We left Cherry Point, NC, and headed for Atlantic Field, NC. If we had been pregnant women, the babies would have been born girls, because those old trucks would shake the nuts off anything.

Upon arriving at Atlantic Field, we were assigned to VMSB-343. We had both been to Aircraft Maintenance School, but I was temporarily assigned to Material (Supply). I was put to work with a woman Marine who had also just arrived at Atlantic Field. Her name was Peggy Weir and the best I can remember Peggy was from Philadelphia.

Peggy kinda frightened the old country boy from Tennessee. I had never known a woman that had such a fascinating past, and didn't mind at all talking about it. She told me that she had worked in a house in Philly that had a red light on the front porch. Then she told me she had joined the Marines to do her part in keeping up the morale of the men. Her words to me were "I plan to screw every Marine on this base." Well I'm for sure she missed one because I left Atlantic Field still a virgin.

THE HAYSEED AND THE CITY SLICKER

by Lew D. "Buck" Buckner

Before I left Atlantic Field, I had been put on Lew McCrum's check crew with some others - most of them don't stick out in my mind except for one, Dalessio. He was kinda a loud Italian, which was also something new to an old country boy. He used to call me "Hayseed", but it didn't take long for me to find out he didn't know everything. One day I said something about digging peanuts, and he said you can't fool me, I happen to know they are picked off a bush. We also had an argument one time about where mules came from. This I considered myself an expert on having surveyed many acres of land using that compass under the mules tail. If I didn't learn anything else about farming, I did learn to hate mules and tobacco. To this day I have no use for either one of them.

One day McCrum sent Dalessio and myself to get something on the back side of the Air Field at Greenville. There was some swampy places with a filled in road across them. We were in one of those old Ford ordnance trucks where the seat on the right side didn't face the front. I do believe it was the first time Dalessio had ever driven anything. Well when we started going across on the filled in road, he just ran right off the fill on the right side. Then he jumped all over me because I wasn't watching my side. Guess I really was wrong for even getting on that thing with him driving.

GOING TO THE MOVIES

by Ralph H. Heidenreich

VMSB-343 commissioned 1 August 1943 was stationed at Atlantic Field, Atlantic, North Carolina. Atlantic is geographically located about forty miles due east of Morehead City, North Carolina. To say the least, we were at the jumping-off point into the Atlantic Ocean.

The town of Atlantic had a population of about 250 fishermen, their wives, and children. None the less they had a movie theater.

Being stationed at Atlantic Field, come dusk we were permitted liberty. So many of us rode to town on Pat and Charlie, these being our feet, for no one had wheels to ride on. After checking out the front gate Marine guards, we walked toward Atlantic, where we again had to pass through another guard station which was manned by Army MP's. After showing our ID's we went into town. The purpose of the Army MP station was to only admit legal persons, because at that time the East Coast of North Carolina was being infiltrated with German Saboteurs, landed by submarines.

Having passed the check-point we proceeded to town to buy a soft drink or whatever, for the town had only commercial fish houses and a movie theater. All streets as well as Main Street were dirt, so you can imagine what happened to our shined shoes. We soon were told that they had a movie house, so seeing no lights on the dirt downtown streets we converged to the dimly lit light bulb outside the movie theater.

Once inside, sitting on our straight back folding chair we were ready for the movie. No pop-corn, drinks, candy, or the usual concessions, just plain movies.

When the movie started everyone, as well as ourselves, applauded for we were ready to see something, anything, for there was nothing to see in Atlantic, North Carolina.

Once the movie started everything got quiet, then the operator of the theater decided he needed to shake the coal stove in the front right of the movie house. He shook the grates time and again until we couldn't see, not only the images on the screen, but the screen itself. After about ten minutes everything came back into focus. We left the movie theater, rode Pat and Charlie through the two MP gates and returned to Atlantic Field barracks after a night of Liberty at Atlantic, North Carolina.

THE MAN WHO KEPT OUR PLANES FLYING

by Ralph Heidenreich

Everyone attached to flight operations in VMSB-343 knew that in the engineering section there was one great driving force, that being Master Sergeant Lawrence E. Smith from Chicago, Illinois. The engineering section was commanded by Chief Warrant Officer Paul Curtis, a career Marine. He directed the section from years of knowledge and know how. Everyone who came in contact with Gunner Curtis recognized this immediately

We had two Master Sergeants, Bill Mead who was administrative and Lawrence Smith who was performance. Every day in the engineering sections or on the flight line one could see "Smitty" with sleeves rolled up above the elbows, arms covered with grease, and working on problems we had with our assigned aircraft. He worked smart and endlessly, keeping our planes ready on the flight line. We had twenty-four aircraft, and we seldom saw but one or two downed for mechanical reasons. Of course there was grounding for prescribed flight maintenance. When they said to the pilot, "Sir your plane is ready for take-off", they meant just that!! All the plane captains had the greatest respect for "Smitty's " knowledge of aircraft and what needed to be done to keep them airworthy.

What a great Marine, M/Sgt. Lawrence E. Smith. He daily exemplified "Semper Fi". He was always faithful and much more!!

PUTTING ON THE BOXING GLOVES

Atlantic Field - 1943

by John Shellito

The following events occurred while I was the officer of the day. As I was making my rounds in my jeep I came upon a large circle of Marines watching two of their buddies fighting. I broke through the crowd and addressed the two that had been fighting bare fisted. One of the marines was Vic Kalfus and the other was someone I can't remember.

I told my jeep driver to go back to the barracks and pick up two pair of boxing gloves, and bring them back to me. When he brought them back to me I told Vic and the other fighter to put on the boxing gloves. I then told them to go to it, with no stopping, no rests, just go to it until they drop. Well, the two of them bobbed and weaved and slugged each other until finally they couldn't even hold up their arms any more. They were totally exhausted, and I told them to shake hands and make up. Then I collected the gloves, dispersed the crowd and told them to go back to their barracks. I never ran into that problem again.

And now for the rest of the story:
In relating this story to Vic Kalfus, he told me what precipitated the fight. Vic said he was standing in the chow line waiting to eat, when this guy broke into the chow line. Vic told him to "Get in line like the rest of us." The other Marine said, "Why don't you make me?" They then walked out into the boonies, and started the fight that Shellito stumbled across.

RACCOON ISLAND

by Tom Gibbons

In the Fall of 1943 after finishing school at Jacksonville, a group of us were sent to Cherry Point to await assignment to a squadron. Each morning some of us would be nabbed for a "shift" detail like cleaning latrines or other chores. We'd get up in the morning and hide someplace until the details were assigned.

One morning, Bernie Gallagher and I got caught. We were assigned with a group of five and a staff sergeant to go by boat to Raccoon Island to build a target for practice for the SBD's. The boat was about a thirty footer with a large outboard motor with a staff sergeant at the tiller.

We loaded lumber, saws, hammers, and nails and set out about mid-morning.

Just after shoving off a storm came up and we pulled in to shore in a little town called, I think, Oriental. There was a store there that sold beer so we had a party until the storm passed.

As we approached the island we were greeted by a storm of hungry mosquitoes. After we unloaded, the boat left us and the Sergeant explained that he would return for us the next morning. We finished building the target late in the afternoon. When it got dark, we tried to get some sleep on our ponchos with little success. The mosquitoes were at us all night. We couldn't wait for the boat to arrive the next morning. Only the boat didn't arrive. About mid morning, we were still hoping for the arrival of the boat when we got the shock of our lives. We couldn't believe it when we saw the SBD's heading in our direction. One by one, they dove and dropped smoke bombs on our target. We ran like hell, as far as we could get from the target and tried to get the attention of the pilots. We screamed, waved, and shouted but couldn't get their attention. The boat didn't get there that day and we dreaded having to spend another night on the damned island. We got less sleep than the first night and the mosquitoes never let up.

On the next morning the boat arrived. We cursed and damned the Sergeant, but he shrugged and said it wasn't his fault. When we got back to the Point we did get an apology from the Lieutenant who sent us out. "Men", he said, "I apologize for the SNAFU but I'm going to make it up to you. Y'all can be the first on the chow line for lunch."

LIBERTY TRUCK TO HARKERS ISLAND

by Joseph C. "Jay" Higgins

When we were stationed at Atlantic, North Carolina we ran liberty trucks to Moorehead City, and occasionally to Harkers Island when they had dances.

One Saturday in November, it was cold and a light rain was falling. So Willie Clary and I fueled up the truck we were going to use for our run to Harkers Island. Two trucks were going to Moorehead City and about ten Marines were planning to go to the dance. After chow we got ready to leave, but there was just one problem----OUR TRUCK WAS GONE! We checked out everything, but all the trucks were gone or were being serviced. The only available vehicles were 600 gallon refuelers!! What were we going to do? Ten Marines ready to go on Liberty, 30 miles to town--and no truck. After some discussion, we decided to take a refueler.

As I recall, I drove the truck through the gate, past the guard station, and waited out on the highway. Every one else walked out the gate and we piled as many people in the cab as we could, about a total of six. Needless to say we were a little crowded.

We got to the dance, had a good time and returned to Atlantic Field around midnight. The return trip didn't seem as crowded. We must have lost some along the way!!!!!

THE MIRACULOUS BRIDGE

by V.S. "Vic" Kalfus

Atlantic Field

When the squad was first forming, I was one of the first Sgt.'s to arrive. The skipper ordered me to have my men construct a small bridge across a drainage ditch. We didn't have any materials so, as I remember, a contractor had just built a bridge at another location over the ditch. So we got together a night raiding party. We borrowed the contractor's bridge and painted it that night.

The next day the contractor told our skipper that someone took his bridge. The skipper called me in and wanted me to look into the matter. After the contractor left, the skipper went out and drove around the Base. When he returned he looked at me and said, you and your men did a good job on the bridge. I still think he knew where the bridge came from.

FITNESS REPORTS & MARGARET

by Major Walter E. Gregory

It was close to the end of VMSB-343's stay at MCAAS, Atlantic aka Atlantic Field. Although the squadron was still well below authorized strength, it had almost twice the number of pilots authorized in the Table of Organization. It was at this moment in time that the submission of annual fitness reports was at hand. I, Major Walter E. Gregory, USMC, had seventy-three officers to report on.

Concurrently, the U. S. Marine Corps, in its infinite wisdom, assigned the squadron a full time adjutant directly from the Quantico school system. Without question, his total classroom study relating to the duties of an adjutant was probably two weeks. His orders identified him as First Lieutenant William Stedman Witt, USMCR. When he reported in, he was accompanied by a bride of several weeks. Her given name was Margaret. She was a real Southern belle who had been sheltered from most of the less desirable conditions in life which confront each of us from time-to-time.

My first order to Lieutenant Witt was to personally handle the fitness report matter. For example, to review the front page of the fitness report form with each of the officers being reported on to assure correctness, and to make certain no officer was overlooked. The second page of the report was thereafter completed in longhand by the commanding officer.

Atlantic Field was located immediately adjacent to a village named Atlantic. Atlantic had been there for untold years with little change at any given time. It was at the end of a county roadway system and was without running water, street lights, sewer system, and related items. It consisted of a hundred or so individual homes, each of which were on large lots, with large evergreen bushes and

67

oak trees constituting the basic landscape. I had rented one such house which included a water pump in the kitchen (an upgrade) and a new outhouse which was about twenty-five feet from the house. Witt subsequently rented a large bedroom in the house which was directly to the rear of my house ---about seventy-five yards separated the two units.

On one particular evening in this time period, my flight returned to the airfield at sundown so I went directly home. I had just finished supper when there was a knock on the kitchen door. It was Witt. He had a flashlight as it was totally black outside. His visit was to update me on his progress on the fitness report assignment. I offered him a drink which he readily accepted as his landlady didn't permit drinking in her home. As we sipped our drinks, my wife, Peggy, came in from the front of the house. She greeted him and then asked him what Margaret was doing. He muttered "Margaret" quietly then yelled "MARGARET", and bolted out the kitchen door. There was no "by your leave", "goodnight", "I've got a problem" ---nothing.

Margaret, the Southern belle and bride, was afraid to go to the outhouse after dark. So Witt would escort her on such occasions, close the outhouse door latch, and slip thirty or so feet away to provide her with privacy. On this occasion as he was waiting thirty feet away, his thoughts wandered to fitness reports --- he hadn't briefed the Major today. Then and there he walked to my home directly from where he had been waiting for Margaret's signal to open the outhouse door.

Margaret Witt proved to be a caring and thoughtful young lady.

A HURRICANE SCARE - 1943

by James "Hap" Hazzard

Now for the trip down memory lane. There are several events that stand out in my memory. Most I am sure have been thoroughly discussed at the reunions. Not having been there to know I'll go ahead with my recollections.

"Tex" Hampton and I were among the first group of eight or ten enlisted personnel assigned to the squadron. We were fresh out of Aviation Machinist Mate school at Millington, Tennessee and, as is normal in the military, we were assigned to the material section. As this was a new squadron we were inundated with supplies. We had a very small warehouse so much of the material was stored in hospital tents. It was at this time we had a hurricane warning which required that the tents be collapsed on the material and lashed down. Trenches were dug for the aircraft unable to be flown to Cherry Point. We waited and waited for what seemed like days. The storm veered offshore and we had to undo all we had done in preparation. It was almost a letdown that the storm bypassed us.

TAKING CHARGE OF THE ACCIDENT

by James "Hap" Hazzard

While on shore patrol in the booming metropolis of Atlantic, North Carolina, another Marine, (again the name is gone) and I were walking along the road when the movie let out. A number of officers and their wives left the theater (barn) and were walking with us when a truck, without headlights due to a blackout, came from behind and hit the other Marine with the bed of the truck. It knocked him several yards ahead then stopped with the rear wheels on his feet and ankles. Since I was on duty, hence officially in charge I ordered the officers to look after the injured man and to call the base for an ambulance. Meantime I went to get the necessary information from the driver (a thirteen-year old boy). However, I was so shook-up that I couldn't write and had to have the boy, who was in better shape than I was, write the information for me. The injured man was transferred from VMSB 343.

SERGEANT OF THE GUARD

by James "Hap" Hazzard

"Tex" Hampton mentioned this event on the phone so I am sure that you and others will remember it. I was Sergeant of the Guard and observing the transfer of the side arm from the outgoing Officer of the Day to the incoming officer. The outgoing officer pulled the piece, withdrew the clip and inspected the chamber. He then handed the pistol and clip to the incoming officer who inserted the clip, pulled the bolt and fired the pistol between the legs of the outgoing officer. Fortunately he was a bad shot and missed everything. But oh what could have happened.

FOLLOWING ORDERS

by James "Hap" Hazzard

Then there was the time when a Group Headquarters Officer flew in from Cherry Point to check out in the SBD. He took off OK but on return he did something wrong or didn't do something right and ended up-side-down in the marshy area between the runways. Everyone on the flightline ran to the scene against orders (some said they were the pilot's orders).

LOSING A BUDDY

by James "Hap" Hazzard

At Greenville, I was returning from the flightline to the line shack when I saw another plane captain climbing into the rear seat of his plane. The plane had just undergone a major check or overhaul and he told me this was the last check flight before his plane returned to regular duty. I cranked the starter, pulled chocks and gave a thumbs-up. The plane never got off the ground. Somehow his plane rolled onto the runway in front of another plane taking off and the plane captain was killed. As I recall the plane captain was scheduled to go to officers candidate school in just a few days after the accident.

At Midway, there was the flight, including my plane, returning from patrol where the flight leader collided with the Grumman Goose towing a target for the Sixth Defense Battalion. Five or six people were killed.

At Ewa, on Oahu, when the Army Airforce and Navy were having maneuvers with our field as target, the leader of a flight of P-38's of the attacking force and the leader of a flight of F4U's (not certain) collided head on. Both pilots were killed and several Marines on the ground were seriously injured. A fellow I worked with for many years observed this mid-air collision from his ship off-shore, near Ewa.

Then there is the one on me that I don't think I've told anyone. After the days work at Ewa, I was told to march the enlisted personnel back to the barracks. In error, instead of saying right face the direction to the barracks, I said left face, the barracks being to my left. This of course reversed the column and those that were in front were very angry with me, thinking I was being a smart-ass. Not true! Dumb, maybe.

SCARED OF THE DARK

by Steve Greytak

Let me tell you of my experience of being scared of the dark.

Remember Harkers Island? Remember the occasional dances they had there? When the truck would take us from Atlantic Field to the island and then pick us up at ten or eleven o'clock to go back to the base. I went to one (and only one) of the dances. After the dance, I walked a girl home. She lived close by. By the time I got back, the truck was gone. All I could do was start walking and hope a car would come by and pick me up. Since there were no street lights, the only light was from the moon, which kept going behind clouds. I was born and raised on a farm, so I was used to the dark (outhouses and working before dawn and after dusk) - but this was different. I didn't know the road and had no idea what kind of animals were out there. I guess I was lucky in that respect. If I did know, I probably would have had a heart attack. The longer I walked the more scared I became. I knew I had to get back to the base by 7 a.m. or I would be AWOL - so I kept walking. I knew I was off the road when I walked on grass and I would have to feel my way back to the road. I got to the base at 6:45 a.m. - and would you believe it? As I got to the guard shack, a car drove up. The first one I saw all night. I would never like to have that experience again. I'm not ashamed to say, "I was scared".

SECTION III

GREENVILLE, NORTH CAROLINA

A TRIBUTE TO OUR FLIGHT TRAINING OFFICERS

by Ralph H. Heidenreich

After being commissioned on August 1, 1943 at Cherry Point, North Carolina, we moved to Atlantic Field, North Carolina, about thirty miles east of Morehead City. Our airfield was next to the Atlantic Ocean. We were a new squadron, consequently we were receiving pilots and aviation specialists daily. My first Operations Officer was Captain Bill Glenn. Being a Senior Pilot, he was assigned our training program for the squadron which had only half of our complement of SBD aircraft plus an SNJ aircraft which was also used for training in instrument flights.

After moving to Greenville Auxiliary Field in Greenville, North Carolina on December 1, 1943, things began to change rapidly. Before I get into the changes let me explain about the Auxiliary Fields the Marine Corps were using. North Carolina cities with an airfield were asked to relinquish their control over to the Marine Corps for auxiliary airfields to train the fighter and dive bomber squadrons. With this acquisition, training was enhanced for there was no way Cherry Point, North Carolina, the Third Marine Air Wing Headquarters, could accommodate all the subordinate units. We had auxiliary fields at Atlantic, New Bern, Greenville, Kinston, Edenton, and Elizabeth City, North Carolina.

Shortly after arriving at the Greenville airfield, the influx of pilots and personnel was overwhelming. Every day the same scenario, until we found our squadron over the TOE (Table of Organization and Equipment) with an excess of pilots and personnel. Before leaving Greenville through transfer, we finally reached our assigned TOE strength.

Early in January 1944, I believe Major Harold G. Schlendering who fought in the battle of Midway Island, Captain Russell Janson and Captain Archie D. "Hap" Simpson who fought in the battle of

Guadalcanal, came to our squadron. Much respect followed these Marine Pilots for they were part of turning the war favorably toward the United States. All three of these Officers were decorated flyers with Distinguished Flying Crosses and Air Medals. What a great addition to our unit.

When the Japanese attack on Midway, led by Admiral Chuichi Nagumo was launched on June 4, 1942, Second Lt. Harold G. Schlendering was a member of Squadron Commander Major Lofton R. "Joe" Henderson's VMSB 242's SBD2 Dauntless Dive Bombers. Henderson commanded eighteen SBD2's, but two of those were grounded because of engine trouble. Most of his pilots were green with very little time logged in SBD2's. The squadron flew out of Midway at 0620 just minutes ahead of the attack by Tomonaga's high-level bombers.

Henderson's squadron ran into Soryu's fighters just as they approached Nagumo's force. Second Lt. Harold G. Schlendering noted there were two types of fighters, some of which had fixed landing gear and some had retractable landing gear. Some had the traditional red and silver insignia and some were dirt brown in color with a purple insignia. The Japanese fighters were very organized and clever and they concentrated on Squadron Commander Henderson. Henderson's plane caught fire so Capt. Elmer G. Glidden took command. He led his squadron directly to a Japanese carrier, where they were savagely attacked by the Japanese fighters. In spite of the heavy anti-aircraft fire and the attacking fighters, VMSB 241 made several runs at the Japanese fleet, but made no direct hits. Eight of the sixteen Dauntless planes were lost, and those that made it back were unflyable. Schlendering almost didn't make it back to Midway. He lost engine power when he was still eight miles away, and he and his gunner PFC Edward O. Smith had to bail out. Schlendering swam to a reef that was five miles away. He was later rescued by P.T. Boat #20, which later rescued Pilot Merrill. Schlendering's gunner was never found.

Major Schlendering was assigned Executive Officer of VMSB 343, Captain Janson, Operations Officer, and Captain "Hap" Simpson our Training Officer with Captain Bill Glenn. These three Captains flew daily as section leader of flights of SBD3's and

SBD4's training our pilots. They worked endlessly training our young pilots using their combat experiences. During this, they trained our flying squadron to a level of readiness for combat. All personnel of the squadron felt this mutual admiration and respect for our three Captain Training Officers.

Captain Janson remained in the Marine Corps after the war and retired as Lt. Colonel. Captain "Hap" Simpson also remained, retired as a Colonel, but before retiring commanded an Air Group at Cherry Point, North Carolina.

All of the Pilot Officers I related to in this remembrance were MARINES who remained "Semper Fi" (always faithful).

MORE MARINES TO COME HERE

New Contingent To Begin Arriving Tomorrow

The first large contingent of Marines to be stationed here for training at the city-county airport will begin arriving tomorrow, according to Lieut. Col. R. C. Scollin who, accompanied by other officers, was here today making final arrangements for the coming of the approximately 225 men and 50 officers who will compose the squadron. The Marines will be quartered at the local NYA center pending erection of a camp at the airport.

The official party here today, in addition to Lieut. Col. Scollin, included Major W. E. Gregory, Lt. Robert A. Field, Lt. E. H. Brogan, Warrant Officer N. O. Rollins, Tech. Sergeant E. F. Koverman and Staff Sergeant Julius C. Kilgore.

The squadron to be located here is a part of the Third Marine Air Wing, of Cherry Point, and will be under the command of Major Gregory.

DEC. 3, 1944

Commissioners On Visit At Airfield

By CHESTER WALSH

The County Commissioners recessed their monthly meeting at the courthouse yesterday to visit the Marine Air Training Station and inspect the airport, the land for which was bought by the county and city of Greenville. They were impressed by the bristling activity of the Marine officers and enlisted men They expressed surprise that better housing facilities has not been provided for the two squadrons training there. The commissioners and county officials with them told Lieut. W. S. Witt, who conducted them over the airport, that they will be glad to do anything to help the Marines

Marine Air Wing At Greenville Airport

By CHESTER WALSH

"Those splendid women in charge of the Servicemen's Center at the Woman's Club deserve the praise and thanks of all our people for their patriotic work in looking after the welfare of men in the armed forces," said Mayor—Bruce Sugg. "Their generous good neighbor spirit has cheered thousands. They, with the help of others, have provided much for the comfort of servicemen and all of us should lend a hand in this work."

The Mayor complimented Mrs. John Horne, "Mom," as she is known to thousands of servicemen, for her Good Samaritan work at the Salvation Army Servicemen's Home the airport, came here a week streets. "The women at both places are doing some war work on the home front that is reflecting glory on our town, our county and our people," he said.

The Servicemen's Center at the Woman's Club (U. S. O.) is open daily at 5 o'clock in the afternoon since Major W. E. Gregory, commandant of the Marine Base at the airport, came here some days ago with a squadron of Marines for air training.

The Marines are quartered at the former NYA center near the city. Major Gregory has his headquarters there. All of the officers have procured temporary living quarters in various Greenville homes.

Lieut. Col. R. C. Scollin, commandant of the Third Marine Air Wing at Cherry Point, expressed appreciation of the assistance rendered by Mayor Sugg. Chamber of Commerce Secretary Willard T. Kyzer and June H. Rose, superintendent of city schools, who arranged for the Marines to use the NYA grounds and buildings, and others.

Preparations are being made to erect a tent city at the airport. When this is completed the squadron of about 225 non-commissioned officers and men will be transferred to the tent city and another squadron will move into the NYA center, it is understood.

Extending the third runway at the airport to 5,000 feet is being

Guadalcanal Hero At Pitt Tomorrow

The Greenville High School Band will feature the program at the Pitt Theatre tomorrow morning from 8:45 until 9:30 when a free motion picture "Seven Fighting Words" will be shown during a meeting of employers and employes to stimulate the sale of War Bonds, Manager T. Y. Walker stated today.

June H Rose will preside. Capt. Russell Jansen, Marine hero of the Guadalcanal campaign in the South Pacific, will be one of the speakers. W. H. Woolard, chairman of the War Finance Committee for this region, will tell about the War Bonds and the interest they pay, especially the "E" bonds.

Incidental to the showing of this free war picture at the Pitt tomorrow morning those in charge of the meeting will stress the selling and buying of War Bonds and the importance of doing so to back up the men on the battlefronts fighting to win this war as soon as possible.

Everybody is invited to see this free picture, "Seven Fighting Words."

JAN 25, 1944

Four-Engined Plane Attracts Attention

A Flying Fortress four-engined Marine plane, flying over Greenville this week, attracted considerable attention. The giant ship landed with ease on a 5,000-foot runway at the airfield and took off as easily as any of the planes in use here. Heavy formation plane maneuvers over Greenville recently have provided thrills for many who had never seen so many planes in action here before.

The county-city airport, leased by the navy as a training station for the Marines, is practically completed. Finishing touches are being applied here and there and final inspection is being made. The short stretch of road leading from the Bethel highway to the airfield has been paved and will shortly be ready for travel. City and county authorities have arranged for the removal of another house to provide more clearance for incoming and outgoing planes, Mayor Bruce Fugg stated today.

3/8/44

Flying Cross For Greenville Marine

By CHESTER WALSH

General Larkin, commandant of the Third Marine Wing, Cherry Point, Saturday awarded the Distinguished Flying Cross to First Lieut. Archie D. Simpson, stationed with the Marine squadron at the Greenville Marine Flying Base, for outstanding bravery and skill in combat in the Solomons in the South Pacific last summer. The presentation was made at Cherry Point in the presence of the entire wing.

The citation credited Lieut. Simpson with making a direct hit on a Japanese destroyer and sinking it and performance of duty in combat in accordance with the highest traditions of the service. He was awarded the Air Medal while in the South Pacific.

Lieutenant Simpson is a Virginian. He was a student at Shepherd College, Shepherdstown, W. Va., when he joined the Marines in the fall of 1941. He graduated as an officer at Pensacola, Fla., in the summer of 1942. He was at Guadalcanal six weeks and spent a year in the South Pacific. He returned to this country recently and was assigned to the Cherry Point Marine Air Base as an instructor. He is now attached to Major W. L. Gregory's squadron at the Greenville Marine air base as instructor.

DEC. 13, 1944

Officers' Wives To Entertain.

The wives of the officers of the Marine Air Training Station here will entertain the members of the Woman's Club at a tea at the home of Mrs. W. E. Gregory, 215 Woodlawn avenue, Wednesday afternoon from 3 until 5 o'clock.

They will entertain the Junior Woman's Club on Tuesday afternoon, Feb. 15, from 3 until 5 o'clock at Mrs. Gregory's home.

FEB. 7, 1944

Squadron Barracks, Mess Hall, Office Headquarters, Power Plant & Auxiliary Buildings. Location Greenville, N.C. (Old NYA Center for the Blind) December 1st 1943 to July 15, 1944.

Shops

Barracks

Mess Hall

Power Plant

SHERRARD MEMORIAL LIBRARY
R KAMMERER 1935

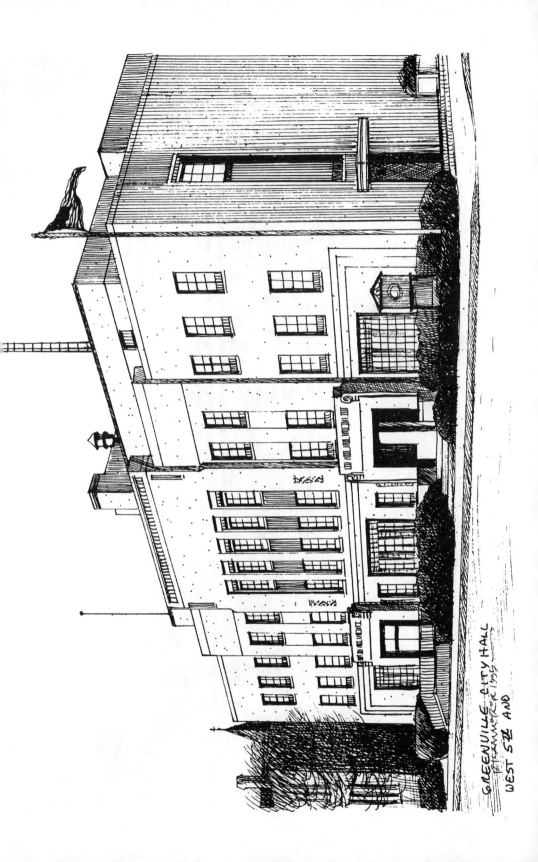

GREENVILLE CITY HALL
BY PFAFFINGER 1992

WEST SIDE AND

TAR RIVER BRIDGE GREENVILLE
P&R 1993

"FLYING CROSS FOR GREENVILLE MARINE"

by Chester Walsh, Reporter
The Daily Reflector
Greenville, North Carolina, March 13, 1944

General Larkin, Commandant of the Third Marine Air Wing, awarded the Distinguished Flying Cross to First Lt. Archie D. Simpson, stationed with VMSB343 at Greenville Marine Flying Base, for outstanding bravery and skill in combat in the Solomon Islands in the South Pacific, last summer. The presentation was made at Cherry Point, North Carolina in the presence of the entire Air Wing.

The citation credited First Lt. Simpson with making a direct hit on a Japanese destroyer and sinking it, and performance of duty in combat in accordance with the highest traditions of the service. He was awarded the Air Medal while in the South Pacific.

First Lt. Simpson is a Virginian. He was a student at Shepard College, Shepardtown, West Virginia, when he joined the Marines in the Fall of 1941. He graduated as an officer at Pensacola, Florida earning his wings as a pilot in the summer of 1942.

He was at Guadalcanal six weeks and spent a year in the South Pacific. He returned to this country recently and was assigned to the Cherry Point Marine Air Base as an instructor in air combat. He is now assigned to VMSB343 at the Greenville, North Carolina Marine Air Base as an Instructor of Air Dive Bombing.

Note: This report was obtained from the Micro-film at the Shepard Memorial Library, Greenville, North Carolina.

MY FLIGHT IN THE ARMY A-25

by Will Kalmoe

In the summer of 1944 our squadron at Greenville, North Carolina received two Army A-25's for the pilots to check out in. These planes were similar to the SB2C's we received when we got to Ewa, Hawaii. I, Lt. Kalmoe, was up in one, and Lt. Alerik was up in the other. As I was returning from my familiarization flight I saw the other A-25 down on the field just off the runway cracked in two at the rear cockpit area. That wasn't a pretty sight with me about to make a landing. Thankfully, Lt. Alerik was not hurt and I landed safely in ONE piece.

SIGHTED SUB - SANK SAME

by George Bobb

From November 1, 1942 through February 28, 1943 (end of first tour) VMSB 131 aircrews and some of the ground personnel periodically rotated between Henderson Field, Guadalcanal and the rear base at Espiritu Santo. While at the rear base they maintained and sharpened their skills by flying simulated torpedo runs, night familiarization hops, gunnery practice and Anti-Sub Patrols.

On February 19, 1943, Captain William Dean and his aircrew, turret gunner SSgt. Harry Johnson and radio gunner SSgt. George Bobb departed Espiritu Santo in TBF BU NO 06084 on a 3.6 hour Anti-Sub Patrol. The first and second leg of the triangular search, flown at altitudes of 2000 to 5000 feet, proved to be routinely dull - but unknown to this alert crew, an opportunity to engage the enemy lay ahead.

Approximately twenty miles out from Espiritu Santo on the third or inbound leg of the patrol, Captain Dean reported to the crew; "We have a sub below at 10 o'clock". SSgt Bobb looked out of the port window and saw what appeared to be an overturned boat with waves lapping at the keel. Captain Dean, satisfied that this was a sub, opened the bomb bay, made a low pass over the intended target but for some reason, failed to drop the two depth charges. Pulling up, he circled around again and made a second pass and a perfect drop. SSgt Bobb saw the two depth charges straddle the sub amidships and detonate with a tremendous upheaval of the sea.

Captain Dean then instructed Bobb to radio the base, identify themselves and their location and report "Sighted Sub - Sank Same" a phrase originated by the Army Air Corps earlier in the war. SSgt. Bobb turned on the radio and waited for it to warm up while Captain Dean circled the doomed sub. Just as Bobb was about to transmit the message Captain Dean exclaimed, "WAIT! WAIT!" Captain Dean then made another low pass over the target and found a very large whale in several huge pieces floating in a sea of red.

Switching back to the intercom, SSgt Bobb transmitted the following message to Captain Dean - - "Sighted Whale - Sank Same".

The whale's remains floated around the area for a few days in full view of all flying in and out of Espiritu Santo. Captain Dean became famous and received many comments on his exploit.

See log book pages (2) back of "Anniversary Book. 2nd page of log,
19 Feb., 43   BOMBED WHALE

On the 24th of October 1942, Turret Gunner Robert Gough and Radio Gunner George Bobb left the Marine Air Base, Ewa, on the Island of Oahu, with Captain George Dooley in a TBF-1, BU No. 00559 and flew to Ford Island, Pearl Harbor where we landed and went aboard the USS Nassau. The Nassau, CVE-16, was an Escort Carrier, a class of carrier more commonly referred to as "Jeep Carriers" or "Baby Flat Tops". It was being used to ferry replacement aircraft and squadrons to the South Pacific. All aircraft were loaded at pierside.

We departed Ford Island with the hangar deck loaded to maximum capacity with aircraft. Two-thirds of the flight deck was filled with aircraft, wings folded, to make optimum use of available space. Five Army P-40's, which were not designed for carrier operation, did not have wing folding capabilities. Our TBF's were spotted forward on the flight deck. Two Grumman F4F Wildcats were positioned on the bow catapults for air defense. Some of the VMSB-131 pilots were put on "Standby" to man the fighters. If they were launched and survived an attack, they would have to make a water landing along side the carrier for recovery. As we moved out from the pier, the port catwalk, forward, struck a gun sponson on the USS Curtis, a seaplane tender. Only minor damage was incurred by both ships, so we continued our departure.

The Gunnery Officer aboard the Nassau was on the Lexington (CV-2) when she was hit by two torpedoes and three bombs in the

Battle for the Coral Sea, May 8, 1942. Burning uncontrollably and ripped apart by violent explosions, she was abandoned and sent to the bottom by several torpedoes from the destroyer Phelp (DD361). This experience made him a firm believer in gunnery practice. As soon as we cleared Pearl, he held a drill with the twin 40 Millimeter and 20 millimeter guns firing at balloons. If the balloons escaped this hailstorm, he would have the five inch mounts open up. This practice continued daily and some of us were assigned as backup crews for the 20 millimeter guns. I was one of the lucky ones as I had an opportunity to fire - never did hit a balloon.

All squadron personnel not assigned to gun position were assigned an area to which they had to report when "Battle Stations" sounded. One thing I learned quickly was not to get caught in a passageway or on a ladder between decks when the alarm sounded as the sailors, in their frenzy to get to their stations, would trample you to death.

We crossed the Equator on the 31st day of October 1942 and all "Pollywogs"-- personnel aboard ship crossing the Equator for the first time-- were initiated into the "Ancient Order of the Deep". All were given a sound paddling except Captain Jens Aggerbeck, who was given the "honor" of pinning a diaper on King Neptune's Royal Baby.

We stopped at Noumea, New Caladonia to deliver five F4F's to the Enterprise (CV-6) tied up there for repairs. She had a damaged elevator and bomb holes in the flight deck. Five Enterprise pilots came aboard the Nassau and were catapulted off in the Wildcats. We nearly lost one as his engine cut out just prior to the Cat Officer giving the launch signal. It turned out that the pilot was running on an auxiliary tank instead of the main one.

BATTLE STATIONS

By George Bobb

On the way into the harbor, we received a visual signal that we were nearing the "War Zone". We passed a freighter, outbound, riding high (empty) in the water with a huge hole clear through its hull, just above the water line. It dwarfed the seaman standing there watching us go by. This message was reinforced as we left the harbor when "Battle Stations" sounded, sending us scurrying to our assigned positions. From the flight deck, we watched a destroyer dropping depth charges as he chased a submarine over the horizon. Some thirty plus minutes later the "All Clear" sounded. The tense moment ended with the sub escaping.

We arrived at the launch point, some seventy or eighty miles from Espiritu Santo, the rear base for the Solomon Islands Operations, located in the New Herbridies. The five P-40's flew off first. Since there was only one third of the flight deck available to build up flying speed, a number of us had doubts that the P-40's could do it. With full flaps and screaming engines they cleared the deck and immediately disappeared from view, only to reappear several miles in front of the carrier, low on the water with props clawing the air to gain altitude.

Robert Gough and I left the Nassau with Captain Dooley at 0930 on the llth of November 1942 to TBF-l, BU, NO. 11559 and landed at Espiritu Santo at 1100 the same day. I do believe that we landed in a heavy downpour that continued through the afternoon and into the night. The ground crews worked all night long preparing six aircraft for a four and one half hour flight to Guadalcanal.

At 0530, the morning of the 12th, Gough and I left with Captain Dooley in TBF-l, BU, No. 00440. The six TBF's, led by Major Pat Moret, our commanding Officer flew wing on a DC-3 belonging to the South Pacific Combat Air Transport Command, more fondly known as "SCAT". The transport pilot's job was to escort us safely to Henderson Field, since he knew the Combat Operational Procedures for the area. We arrived over the channel off Henderson Field somewhere around l000 (my flight log indicates we landed on Henderson at l045) and as we approached the Island I saw a number of ships, which I identified as American Cruisers and Destroyers, moving about in the channel. A few minutes later, I wasn't so sure.

Looking out the right hand window (located in the door) I spotted a Cruiser ahead and to the right, flashing a recognition signal toward our flight. I was unable to respond because of my location and I had little concern about it because I knew the ships were friendly and the DC-3 crew would acknowledge the challenge. For some unknown reason (possibly landing preparation) the transport crew failed to respond and "All Hell" broke loose. We had flak exploding all around us with the resulting concussions rocking and rattling the plane. Gough exclaimed over the intercom, "They are firing at us!" and then over the radio I heard the transport pilot yelling to the base radio - "Cactus Control, Cactus Control, tell those SOB's they have friendly aircraft overhead". Within minutes the firing stopped - one of our planes had holes in a wing panel and in the resulting confusion we landed on the fighter strip instead of Henderson Field. We took off again and this time landed on Henderson, between falling artillery shells being lobbed onto the field by a Jap dubbed "Pistol Pete" located in the hills above the field.

We learned later that the same ships that fired at us (remember we were still in formation, taking no evasive action, only 800 feet in the air) were attacked by sixteen Japanese torpedo planes the day before and they shot more than half of them down. Upon hearing this a few of us decided we were living on borrowed time.

An hour or two after we landed, I was walking toward the communications tent a few steps behind Pat Moret when we heard a shrill whistling sound. Both Pat and I dropped flat on the ground, burying our faces in the dirt. But this time, the whistle had come from one of the radio receivers and not from one of "Pistol Pete's" incoming shells.

TOKYO EXPRESS DERAILED AGAIN

by George Bobb

Late Thursday afternoon, December 3, 1942, a Japanese Naval Force consisting of four cruisers and eight destroyers was spotted just South of New Georgia, 150 miles Northwest of Guadalcanal, heading for Henderson Field. There was grave concern that this latest element of the "Tokyo Express" would arrive off Henderson Field during the early hours of December 4th, and subject the Field to an intensive shelling that would destroy the all too few remaining aircraft dispersed around the field perimeter.

The ships were approximately one hour and thirty minutes away by air and there was less than two hours of daylight remaining. To accomplish the mission - sink as many ships as possible or inflict enough damage to cause them to turn back - it was imperative that the aircraft be launched immediately to place them over the target area before darkness settled in. A "Strike Force" consisting of eight dive bombers and torpedo planes had faced the murderous anti-aircraft fire thrown up by the Japanese battleship Hiei and accompanying cruisers and destroyers during the "Battle for Guadalcanal" November 12, 13, and 14th, and they knew they would experience more of the same. With memories of "Flak still fresh in their minds, and a warning that they could expect heavy air opposition from the Japanese fighters based on New Georgia, the crews, as they flew Northwest toward "Hell", experienced a feeling of gratefulness and love for the tough little Gumman Wild Cats and Bell P39's, in groups of two, criss-crossing the formation in a defensive maneuver known as "Thach Weave", a tactic developed by LCDR John S. "Jimmy" Thach, C.O. of VF-3, January 1941.

The weather was good, the sky was clear and the sun was low on the horizon. Around 1820, from an altitude of 11000 feet, the ships were sighted heading southeast in two columns. As the flight approached each ship in the left column initiated a turn to the left and began circling at high speed in a counterclockwise direction. Each ship in the right column initiated a right hand turn and began circling at high speed in a clockwise direction.

The dive bombers left the formation and headed for a position over the ships from which they could select their target and commence their dive. At this point, they were jumped by twelve or more Zeros on floats. As the TBF's opened their formation to start their descent, radio gunner Sgt George Bobb, in TBF-BU. No. 00404, reported to Capt. Hayter, "The F4F and P39 at 8 o'clock have dropped their external tanks and are heading for the Zeros." By this time the sky was full of black puffs of smoke along with red and orange fire balls from exploding anti-aircraft shells. The TBF's continued to twist and turn in their dive toward the sea and attack altitude. As they passed through 1500 feet, Bobb again reported to Hayter, "There are three parachutes high at 4 o'clock." Seeing the chutes in close proximity to each other led Bobb to believe that a TBF had been hit as this was the only aircraft type in the area carrying a crew of three.

The two large ships that had been leading each column were identified as light cruisers. Capt. Hayter, now low on the water, was still twisting, turning and "porpoising", boring a hole through a flak toward one of the cruisers. Bobb, riding in the tunnel with only a "loose gun position" safety belt to hold him in place, was bouncing from bulkhead to bulkhead as though he was on a "Bucking Bronco". Captain Hayter finally leveled off to make the drop and Bobb looked out of the side windows and saw five burning aircraft floating on the sea and water spouts caused by exploding shells, leaping at the plane. The torpedo ran true and in the waning daylight, was seen to explode against the side of the cruiser by Hayter's turret gunner Sgt. Ted Chikowski and Bobb. Another cruiser was reported hit by a torpedo dropped by either Lt. McShane or NAP Main and two more probable hits were scored for pilots Molvich, Dean, and Aggerbeck.

By the time the attack was over darkness enveloped the area, and as Hayter headed for home, only two other aircraft, a TBF and a F4F joined on him - the fate of the other twenty-four aircraft was unknown at this time. Bobb, reflecting back on what he had seen, the Zeros, the chutes, the five burning planes, and the heavy anti-aircraft fire, feared that our losses would be heavy.

Capt. Hayter landed at Henderson Field at 2000 and the crew was thankful to be on the ground again. Hayter, upon leaving the cockpit, headed straight for the bomb-bay where he retrieved the ring from the torpedo arming wire as a lasting memento. One by one, the remaining aircraft came straggling in. All aircraft returned except one TBF flown by Lt. Pelto. No one saw the plane go down and eventually Pelto, along with his turret gunner Sgt Gross and radio gunner Cpl Goodwin, were declared "Missing In Action".

The "Tokyo Express" was derailed again - 12 Zeros were shot down, five seen burning on the water by Bobb and two by Lt. Dalton. Four cruisers were damaged and left burning. Reports the following day said that three were still burning while one had gone down. The three parachutes were probably Japanese.

When Fleet Admiral Nimitz, at Pearl Harbor, received the report, he awarded all participants the Navy Commendation Medal.

Participating Aircrews - VMSB-131

PILOTS	TURRET GUNNERS	RADIO GUNNERS
Capt.Jens Aggerback	no record	no record
Capt.Bill Hayter	Sgt. Ted Chikowski	Sgt.George Bobb
Lt.Carrol Dalton	no record	Pvt.Oren Childres
Lt.Bernard McShane	no record	no record
Lt.Bill Dean	Sgt.Emmanual Ditiberio	Sgt.John Bruder
Capt.Arthur T.Molvik	Sgt.Robert T.Gough	Sgt.Gerald Champlin
MSgt.Bud Main	Sgt.Richard C.Ganther	no record
Lt.Bruce C.Pelto	PFC.Kenneth Gros	Cpl.Vernon Goodwin

Roster updated to correct spelling of some
names and to include full name and rank.
1-23-98 George Bobb

THE INVISIBLE ENEMY

by George Bobb

Shortly after noon, Wednesday, April 7, 1943 the Command Post at Henderson Field received a communiqué from a Coast Watcher on Bougainville. The Coast Watcher, who was monitoring activities on the Japanese airfield from an observation post in the mountainous jungle, reported eighty-five Japanese aircraft heading south. It was assumed by those in command that the aircraft were headed for Henderson Field and the shipping in Tulage Harbor.

At 1215 the transports and destroyers began moving at full speed toward the open sea, and the duty aircrews for all bomber type aircraft on Henderson manned their planes. These aircraft, SBD's, TBF's, B17's and B26's left the field and flew south of the island, "Out of Harms Way". They would be recalled after the enemy aircraft cleared the area.

The fighter planes, Army Air Corps P39's and P38's, Marine F4F's and F4U's scrambled and made initial contact with the approaching "Bandits", code word for enemy aircraft, some thirty miles North of Henderson, over Cape Esperance. TSSgt George Bobb, along with other "Standby" crewmen for 131, were standing just outside the Command Post, listening to the fighter pilot chatter coming in over the radio. Several memorable bits of conversation overheard were: "There must be a million of them."; "Someone get that S.O.B. off my tail."; and "They are not Bandits, they're P38's."

At 1220, the Signal Station at Koli Point flashed "Condition Red" which meant an air attack was imminent. Almost simultaneously the groaning engines could be heard as the combat drifted over the field, above the 6000 foot overcast. A four plane section of F4F's, led by Marine First Lt. James Swett of VMF-211, intercepted the Japanese aircraft over Tulage. Ignoring heavy anti-aircraft fire, Swett engaged and shot down seven Val Dive Bombers in fifteen minutes. For this action, he was awarded the Congressional Medal of Honor. Lt. Swett's F4F was extensively damaged by anti-aircraft fire and a burst of machine gun fire from the rear cockpit of a Val. The F4F, with a seized engine and trailing a dark plume of oil, was seen by those at the Command Post as it came through the overcast headed for the channel. Lt. Swett, who broke his nose in five places during the water landing, was picked up by a Navy Patrol Boat.

Suddenly a P39 Aerocobra punched through the overcast and made an emergency landing on Henderson Field in lieu of returning to the fighter strip. As the aircraft touched down, its landing gear collapsed, bringing it to a grinding halt in front of the control tower. SSgt George Bobb and others from 131 ran to the downed aircraft to assist the pilot. As they came along side, a young Army Air Corps Second Lt. stepped unharmed from the cockpit. While staring in amazement at his P39, which was a candidate for the boneyard, he stated that he and another P39 pilot flew through some clouds into a "hornets nest". As a result of the wild melee that followed, he lost track of his wing mate. Outnumbered and out-gunned by Zeros, he pushed the nose over and dove for the cloud cover below. During the short interval that it took to reach the clouds, the P39 was literally shot from around him, so he continued straight down through the clouds, landing at the first airstrip that came in view.

The ships at Tulage were not visible from the Command Post, but several Val's were seen diving toward the area. Word was received that two ships were hit, but escaped with minor damage. None of the attacking aircraft got through to Henderson. Some thirty-five Japanese aircraft were downed along with a few of our fighters.

The Japanese had staged an around the clock attack on Henderson Field and the surrounding area the night before. Wave after wave of enemy bombers came over the area dropping earth-jarring thousand pound bombs along with anti-personnel fragmentation bombs, also know as "Daisy Cutters". It was another one of many sleepless nights for all as 131 personnel were kept on the run between their tents and foxholes.

These two attacks and reports from reconnaissance aircraft of a vast increase in the number of enemy aircraft in the Bougainville area prompted operations to schedule a major early morning "Strike" against the airfield at Kahili on Bougainville. This decision proved to be a fatal one for the aircrews of 131 assigned to this mission.

Returning fighter pilots and a PBY-5A "Black Cat" on patrol up the Slot had reported rapidly deteriorating weather over a broad front in the vicinity of the Russell Islands. Conditions were ripe for the development of very severe weather and the telltale signs were already in place. Heavy convective currents produced by extremely high temperatures and a high moisture level were present as indicated by the towering cumulus and cumulonimbus thunder heads building up. Had the meteorologist and operations been aware of the violent air currents generated within these cells, the "Strike" would have been aborted. Unfortunately, this was not the case. The deadly destructive forces of the vertical updrafts and downdrafts caused by wind velocities that can reach 6000 feet per minute (FPM) were unknown as were the terms Wind Shear and Microburst. A Microburst, a cause of Wind Shear, is an intense highly localized vertical downburst of a very short duration with wind velocities that can exceed 5000 FPM. As the burst nears the earth's surface, associated gusts with wind speeds as high as 3000 FPM fan out horizontally in all directions, covering an area two and one-half miles in diameter.

Initially, an aircraft entering this area will experience strong headwinds causing an increase in indicated air speed and lift, the result of increase airflow across the airfoil. This increase in performance will cause the aircraft to fly at some level above the intended flight path. As the aircraft penetrates deeper into the area, the vertical component of the downburst takes over, causing a rapid decay in the indicated air speed and lift. The effect of the increased pressure on the top of the airfoil, combined with the low pressure area that develops below the airfoil, is negative lift. The aircraft rapidly descends from its intended flight path, literally flying into the ground, or as in the case of the aircraft of 131, into the water.

The planned "Strike", a coordinated Marine/Navy attack against Kahili called for 24 TBF's, divided into four divisions, to leave Henderson Field early Thursday morning April 8, 1943. The four divisions maintaining fifteen minute intervals, would fly up the "Slot" on the same heading through the area of bad weather, zero visibility, high turbulence and embedded thunderheads in various stages of development.

Each TBF carried a crew of three, a full load of 30 and 50 caliber ammunition, and four five-hundred pound general purpose (GP) bombs in the bomb bay. All internal tanks were topped off, providing enough fuel for the 5 1/2 hour round trip, and a twenty minute reserve, if all went as it should,

During the "pre-strike" briefing, the pilots were instructed to maintain "radio silence" and make a running rendezvous using only the night formation lights to establish and maintain contact. The climb to 12,000 feet, cruising altitude, was to be made using maximum range power settings and the use of oxygen was not contemplated.

The first division, consisting of six Navy aircraft, left Henderson Field at 0200. One aircraft with crew was lost due to the turbulence or to a navigational error enroute to the target. The other five aircraft reached the target area but failed to find Kahili because of the extensive cloud cover. They returned to Henderson Field early in the morning with bomb loads intact.

The second division, consisting of six Navy aircraft left Henderson Field at 0215 and failed in their attempt to rendezvous. Four aircraft were lost along with their crews and the other two returned safely to Henderson. It appears as though this division, like the third and fourth division, penetrated the storm during peak activity, encountering the severe turbulence of one or more embedded, expanding cells or thunderheads with their accompanying microburst. The missing aircraft, more than likely were involved in a collision caused by the turbulence or they flew into the sea as a result of an encounter with a down burst.

The third division, consisting of six Marine aircraft from VMSB-131, led by Captain Hayter, left Henderson Field at 0230 and joined up as planned. During the slow climb, through heavy rain squalls, they encountered severe turbulence. Occasionally the clouds would part revealing a star-lit-sky and towering Cumulonimbus thunderheads that seemed to have no tops.

Some forty minutes out, Captain Hayter signaled a right turn to return to Henderson Field. His left wingman, Captain Ritchey, could not hold position during the turn, so he flew clear of the formation.

The severe turbulence caused the aircraft flown by Captain Manthey, leader of the second section, flying on the right side of Hayter's section in the five o'clock position, to collide with the aircraft flown by Lt. Hatfield, Hayters right wingman. Both aircraft fell into the sea, killing Captain Manthey and his crewmen, turret gunner PFC Gannon and radio gunner SSgt Miller, along with Lt. Hatfield and his radio gunner PFC Hoss. Hatfield's turret gunner TSgt Lares survived the crash.

Captain Hayter and his crewmen, turret gunner PFC Winkle and radio gunner SSgt Zimlich, along with Lt. Nuzum and his crewmen, turret gunner Sgt Kweperer and radio gunner PFC Baum were also lost. It is quite probable that the aircraft flown by Lt. Nuzum, Captain Manthey's right wingman, collided with the one flown by Captain Hayter.

Captain Reese, Captain Manthey's left wingman, continued on and eventually flew into the sea, forced down by a microburst. Captain Reese and his turret gunner Sgt Bolen survived the unintended water landing but the radio gunner, SSgt Moyer was trapped in the tunnel and went down with the aircraft.

Meanwhile, Captain Ritchey set a return course for Henderson Field and climbed to 6000 feet in order to clear several island peaks in the area. His plan was to return to Henderson Field by dead reckoning navigation and circle until dawn. At about this point in time, "Radio silence" was broken. The fourth division consisting of four of the six Navy aircraft scheduled, had left Henderson Field at 0245 and also failed in their attempt to rendezvous. Three aircraft were lost along with the crew and the fourth returned to Henderson.

As Captain Ritchey was commencing his first turn around a point he estimated to be Henderson Field, a search light flared on far below. Captain Ritchey said "It was a simple matter to circle downward around the beam and find the mat." He and his crewmen, turret gunner Cpl. Merideth, and radio gunner Sgt Brandon, were de-briefed immediately after landing at about 0430.

The extent of losses at this time were not known, but by 0830 fear set in as thirteen aircraft with thirty-nine men were overdue. Plans were made immediately to launch an extensive air search. "Rosie the Riveter" would replace the aircraft, but the men were irreplaceable.

ARRIVING IN GREENVILLE, NORTH CAROLINA

by Ralph Heidenreich

December 1st 1943 - Greenville, North Carolina

VMSB-343 was moved from Atlantic Field, North Carolina to Greenville, North Carolina. We were to use the airstrip at Greenville for training and be housed at the NYA Center, which was not habitable until we cleaned it up.

The Squadron arrived at the airport with no quarters, so being Marines we paired up for pup-tent assignments. The lst Sgt. lined us up, sighted our lines, then we pitched tents. Everything had to be right for we were U.S. Marines on display at Greenville, North Carolina. After much confusion we completed our assignment. Tents were aligned, properly erected and anyone who observed knew we were trained to accomplish our mission. Lights out - Goodnight.

Guess what? Next morning when we crawled out of our pup-tents we found ourselves under two inches of snow. Welcome to the south in Greenville, North Carolina.

Thank goodness for our mess section, for they had breakfast prepared with plenty of good hot Joe.

MARINE KILLED IN CRASH HERE

Three Others Escape Injury In Plane Collision

In the first serious accident at the Marine Air Station here Sergeant Robert P. Templemeyer, 22, U. S. Marine Corps, met instant death yesterday morning when two planes taking off in operational flight collided on the runway of the field. Three other occupants of the two planes escaped injury. Both planes were badly damaged.

Sgt. Templemeyer's next of kin is listed by the Navy as his mother, Mrs Florence Templemeyer, of 6239 Plymouth Avenue, St. Louis, Mo. A short time ago Templemeyer's mother and fiancee visited him here and were guests in the home of Rev. and Mrs. Robert S. Boyd, while here.

The body was carried to the main base at Cherry Point yesterday to await instructions from the family. It will be accompanied by an honor guard when it is returned home.

Sgt. Templemeyer was a member of Marine Air Squadron 343 and this was its first training casualty since the organization was formed under commandership of Major W. E. Gregory. He entered the service in August 1943.

Body Of Marine Is Taken Home

The body of Sgt. Robert P. Templemeyer, who was killed at the Marine Air Station here in a plane collision last Sunday has been sent to his home in St. Louis, Mo., according to information released by the public relations department of the Marine command. The body was sent from Cherry Point late Tuesday and is due to arrive in St. Louis today. It was accompanied by Pfc Richard M. Shearer.

Sgt. Templemeyer was the victim of the only serious accident at the local airfield since it was developed and turned over to the Navy Department for use as a Marine air training station.

Marine Killed

A Pennsylvania youth, 18, enlisted in the United States Marines to help win the war against the Japs and Germans and while in training here was killed by a hit-and-run automobile driver on 10th Street Extension on the way to the Marine Air Station at the old NYA center last night shortly before midnight.

His name cannot be published until his family have been notified of his death. A Marine companion walking with him was painfully but not seriously injured.

State highway patrolmen, police and other officers and the Navy military police, working on a clue, expect to apprehend the hit-and-run driver.

Both Marines were knocked into a ditch near Jack Netherland's home. The injured man managed to get to the highway and hail a Marine military police car. The Marines were taken to Pitt General Hospital. One was dead with a fractured skull upon arrival; the other was given first aid treatment and sent to the Marine Air Station barracks at the NYA center.

Coroner Griffin H. Rouse and a jury viewed the body last night and recessed the inquest until further notice.

4/7/44

Officers Seeking Death Car Driver

By CHESTER WALSH

Pvt. Raymond Alvin Hahn, 18, member of U. S. Marine Bomber Squadron 343, stationed at the Greenville Air Training Station, who was killed by a hit-and-run driver on Tenth street extension Thursday night while on his way to the Marine barracks at the old NYA center, will be buried in his home town, Allentown, Pa. A Marine guard of honor accompanied the body home, Capt. Holmes Ninth Marine Air Wing public relations officer at Kinston, announced last night.

Pvt Hahn was a son of Mrs. Helen M. Hahn, 936 1-2 Tilgham street, Allentown.

"Hahn was a good soldier in every sense of the word, loyal to his command, ambitious and enterprising and had a personality that made him popular with the Marines and others, one of the officers of Major W. E. Gregory's squadron stated.

Hahn and a Marine companion, J. J. Jacobs Jr., were walking toward the Marine barracks when a hit-run driver struck Hahn, fracturing his skull and knocking him and Jacobs into a ditch. Jacobs, painfully hurt and dazed, made his way to the highway and hailed a Marine military police car.

An ambulance took the two Marines to Pitt General Hospital Hahn was dead upon arrival. Jacobs was given first aid at the hospital and sent to the Marine barracks.

When the two men were arrested they had replaced the broken windshield and headlight and touched up the car with new paint, officers stated.

Pvt Hahn was a son of Mrs Helen M Hahn, 936 1-2 Tilgham street, Allentown, Pa. A Marine guard of honor accompanied the body home Marine officers and enlisted men gave Hahn a good name as a soldier and a citizen. He was popular with the Marines and in Greenville.

Marine military police provided all of their facilities for local authorities in finding the driver of the death car

It is understood that the law does not provide for the holding of an inquest concerning a death when a confession of guilt is made to police Coroner Griffin H Rouse could not be contacted today

Spain and Riggs were ordered held under $1 000 bond each. They provided bonds and were released.

The next criminal term of Superior Court will be held here on April 17.

YOUTH HELD FOR SLAYING

William Earl Spain Driver Of Car That Killed Marine

By CHESTER WALSH

Working on a clue discovered by Police Traffic Officer M. E. Corbett, authorities Saturday afternoon arrested William Earl Spain, 18, of the Galloway's Crossroads community on a charge of being the driver of the car that struck and killed Marine Pfc. Raymond Alvin Hahn, 18, and injured another Marine, Cpl. J J Jacobs, Jr, while walking along Tenth street extension Thursday night to the Marine barracks at the old NYA center

The arrest was made at Spain's home

Marine Pays Tribute Servicemen's Home

The following letter from a Marine platoon sergeant is refreshing testimony of the warm and cordial relations between the service men and the people of Greenville, especially for the Servicemen's Home at the Vines House. It is also a fine tribute to Mrs. Mary Horne. "Mom." as she is affectionately known to thousands of the boys in service, hostess at the "fellowship spot." The letter:

"Feb. 20, 1944

"To The Salvation Army Board. "Dear Friends.

"I'm just one of the thousands of boys that have stayed at your "Service Men's Home" here in Greenville. This is one town I'll never forget, mostly because of the 'home' here.

"I would like to say that I've been in service clubs and homes from Maine to Miami but never have I felt more at home than here in Greenville. Each week-end. I look forward to coming up and spending the week-end with 'Mom.'

"'Mom' is a woman a Marine never forgets once he has met her —so full of life, so interested in 'her' boys and with a memory almost unbelievable. She can meet a fellow she's never heard of and even though it's six months later before she sees him again she'll call him by his name.

"Our 'Mom' is doing a wonderful job, friends. We just don't like to think that anything will ever happen to close this home and take 'Mom' away from us.

"Wherever you hear a service man mention Greenville you can bet your life if you stick around and listen to him talk he'll always ask you if you know 'Mom.'

"Yes, friends, 'Mom' is the one in a million. She cheers the lonely and makes life happier for the happy.

"We salute you Salvation Army workers and the wonderful job you're doing. Please for us keep up the good work.

Very Sincerely.
"Plt. Sgt. C. W. Calk.
"U. S. Marine Court."

2/24/44

Marine Officers To Entertain Thursday

Major W. E. Gregory and the officers of the 343rd Marine Scouting Bombing Squadron stationed here, will be hosts to the members of Greenville Elks Lodge No. 1645 and their wives and the members of the Greenville German Club at an informal reception and dance at the Country Club Thursday night at 9 o'clock. The event will be entirely informal.

3/21/44

USO NOTES AND NOTICES

By LUCY CHERRY CRISP

Special activities at the USO Club during the past two weeks have exhibited an interesting variety. First, there was the Monday night "ice-cream turning," which grew out of the statement of one of the marines concerning home-made ice cream."

"I've never seen any made in a freezer," he said. "And never eaten any, either."

Discussion followed and out of it came the "ice-cream turning." Old-fashioned freezers were found, somewhere. The custards were made, after the best "old southern" tradition. Ice and salt were on hand, though the role of salt in the proceeding remained obscure to some of the marines and navy boys who vigorously turned the handles of the ancient and somewhat creaky freezers. The results of the "turning" seemed to be completely satisfactory to everyone concerned, however, and between 80 and 100 servicemen and junior and senior hostesses enjoyed the novelty of eating—and making—home-made ice-cream.

Then there was the "Magnolia Garden" dance, with the club decorated in magnolias, cape jessamines and flower-decked pergolas, and the Cherry Point band, under Sgt. De Martino's able direction to make the music for us. Despite sweltering heat several hundred were on hand to enjoy dancing in the "Magnolia Garden."

After the War Bond Rally show on the college campus Thursday night, the club held open house for the players, soldiers and WACs from Seymour Johnson Field—with dancing and refreshments from 10 to 12 o'clock.

And now, tonight, at the municipal swimming pool, there is to be a swimming party from 9 to 11, with junior hostesses and men from the local field, invited.

Miss Flanagan Honored.

Miss Margaret Jones entertained at the Coca-Cola party on Wednesday afternoon at 4:30 in compliment to Miss Josephine Flanagan, bride-elect of this month.

The house was decorated throughout with a profusion of early spring flowers.

When the guests assembled Coca-Colas, sandwiches, cheese biscuits and bridal cakes were served by the hostess, assisted by her mother and Miss Beatrice Williams.

Miss Flanagan was presented crystal in her chosen pattern.

Miss Jones' guests included members of the bridal party, close friends of the bride-elect and the officers' wives of Squadron 343.

USO "House-warming"

A number of special events are scheduled at the USO Service Center next week to mark the official "House-warming" celebrating the completion of the club building renovation carried out by the USO. On Wednesday night there will be a formal dance for the men stationed at the local air base, with an orchestra from Cherry Point. Thursday night an informal open house is planned for the USO entertainment group appearing earlier in the evening at the college. Friday night from 7 to 11 o'clock, the club will hold open house for people of Greenville and the surrounding community who are interested in coming in to see the results of the USO .... work on the building. .... night there will be another formal dance, with orchestra from the local air base. Further announcements concerning the "house-warming" will be made during the week-end and early next week.

MAY 18, 44

Woman's Club Meets.

The Woman's Club held its monthly meeting at the club house Friday afternoon. Honoring war mothers was the special feature of this meeting. Patriotic emblems were given each war mother present. Mrs. Dink James presided over the business session which included reports from various department heads. Encouraging reports of Christmas activities were given. Knitters were urged to make gloves for use of the boys located at the Greenville airport. Following the business session, Mrs. James turned the meeting over to Mrs. J. Knott Proctor, chairman of War Service. Under activities in this committee, Mrs. Fred Haar reported entertaining officers' wives at a coffee hour at the club house. Mrs. John Warner reported on War Stamps and Bonds. Mrs. J. H. B. Moore introduced Mr. Herbert Waldrop, Pitt county chairman of war savings, who spoke on the coming Fourth War Loan drive. He made a strong plea for sacrifice during this "door-knocking" drive. At the conclusion of his talk, the club voted to assume the responsibility for selling $300,000 worth of bonds, equivalent to purchasing a bomber.

Miss Louise Kilgo, accompanied by Miss Ona Shindler, sang two appropriate war songs, "Say a Prayer for the Boys Over There." and "When the Lights Go On Again."

As a fitting close to the program, Mrs. Proctor introduced Capt. Russell Jansen of the local airfield, who spoke from experience on the relation of war bonds to the actual combat of war. He delighted his listeners with a few personal experiences on Guadalcanal, New Hebrides and other Pacific islands.

During the social hour, the hostesses served delicious tea and cakes from a tastefully decorated table featuring the patriotic motif. The hostesses were Mrs. R. C. Deal, Mrs. A. E. Gibson, Mrs. R. S. Boyd, Mrs. Guy C. Evans, Mrs. Charles Davis, Mrs. W. R. Jones, Mrs. J E. Dees, Mrs. B. F. Bullard, Miss Audrey Dempsey and Miss Lena Ellis.

JAN. 11, 1945   —Reported.

Entertain Servicemen's Wives.

The wives of enlisted men and non-commissioned officers who are stationed at the Greenville airport were guests of the End of the Century Club at the home of Mrs. L. R. Meadows on Fifth street Friday morning. An informal coffee hour was enjoyed between 11 and 12 o'clock. The guests were greeted at the front door by Mrs. Meadows and Mrs. Ficklen Arthur. Mrs. J. L. Fleming and Mrs. R. C. Stokes, assisted by Mrs. Withers Harvey, served sandwiches, cookies and salted nuts. Other members of the club enjoyed chatting with these newcomers and welcoming them to Greenville. These included Mrs. E. B. Ficklen, Mrs. F. C. Harding, Mrs. B. W. Moseley, Mrs. Ed Harvey, Mrs. A. D. Frank, Mrs. J. T. Little and Mrs. R. J. Slay.

This was the first opportunity that these wives had had to meet each other since coming to Greenville to make their home while their husbands are stationed here.

Among the guests were Mesdames Jarboe, Loomis, Migas, Hefty, Harris, Love, Snyder, Mead, Bowes, Pippitt and Pfc. Sandford. Mrs. Dink James, president of the Woman's Club, and Mrs. R. C. Rankin, who is chairman of the Woman's Club Hospitality Committee, were also guests.   FEB. 1944

Suppers And Dances For Marine Officers

Major W. E. Gregory, commandant of the Greenville Marine Auxiliary Air Base, and the officers and their wives, will be guests at numerous Christmas holiday social affairs during the coming week.

Manager L. R. Wheatly of the Olde Towne Inn, will be host to the officers and their wives at dinner tonight and tomorrow night at 9 o'clock.

The Elks Club will entertain the Marine officers and their wives at a barbecued chicken supper and dance at the club, Monday night.

The German Club will have them as guests at a reception and dance at the Country Club New Year's Eve.

Numerous other social affairs in honor of the Marine officers and their wives are being arranged for the holidays.   DEC. 13, 1944

Marine Commandant Guest Of Kiwanis

By CHESTER WALSH

Major W. E. Gregory, command and of the Greenville Marine Al Training Base and Lieut. R. I. Megowen, ground o icer, and Rev A Hartwell Campbell, pastor of Im manuel Baptist church, were specia guests of the Kiwanis club at it weekly supper meeting at the high ool last night. President-elect W J Bundy presided for President Jo Tait, who is ill. Otis Morton wa master of ceremonies. Mayor Bruc Sugg introduced the Marine offi cers

Major Gregory expressed pleasur at being stationed here and convey ed the appreciation of the squadro for the hospitality of the Greenvill people and the innumerable kind nesses extended the officers an men. Lieut. Megowen spoke f amiliar with P eloquently welcomed the Marine to Greenville. expressed the hop that they could be here a long time but realizes that in a short tim they will be on the way overseas t help the Allied Nations to complet the job of wiping out the German and Japs, he said.

Rev Mr Campbell made an im pressive after-dinner speech on th "Golden Rule in Business." Hi an dotes were witty, humorous an philosophic and he won applaus when he said "we don't need s much gold in this world, but mor of the 'golden rule'."

For a little fun and to rais money for underprivileged childre Otis Morton and Eli Bloom confis cated two of the members hat placed them in bags and had Mayo Sugg auction them off to the high est bidders. Phil Kramer, manage of an A. and P. store, bought th first one for $6. J. A. Collins, hea of J. A. Collins and Son's furnitur store, bought the other for $7. To day there are two Kiwanians minu their fedoras.

Ed (Little Lamb) Rawl led th singing of Kiwanis songs with Mr Ray Tyson as accompanist. Majo Gregory was much impressed whe he learned that Mrs. Tyson's so Lieut. Vernon Tyson, U. S. Arm Air Corps, had participated in t African and Sicilian campaigns an that Mrs. Tyson is a grandmothe "Wonderfully preserved woman." I said approvingly. DEC. 11, 1944

Haughton-Dudley.

Miss Margie Dudley, daughter of Mr. and Mrs. Lewis Patrick Dudley of Greenville became the bride of Lt. Gayle Haughton. III. on June 23 in Immanuel Baptist Church. Reverend A. Hartwell Campbell, pastor, officiated.

The bride, who was given in mar riage by her father, wore a wedding gown of lace and net, designed with a sweetheart neckline, fitted bodice and long full skirt and train. The sleeves were full at the top and came to a point over the hands. The bride's fingertip veil fell from a cor onet and was fastened with orange blossoms. She carried an arm bou quet of white gladioli.

Miss Florence Dudley, sister of th bride and maid of honor, wore a gown of blue marquisette, fash ioned on princess lines, and carried a nosegay of mixed summer flowers.

Lt. Wesley V. Carscaden of Seat tle, Washington, was best man. Ushers were Lt. William R. Laney of Tyler, Texas, and Lt. Byron W Franklin of San Antonio. Texas.

Mrs. Ola Tucker and Norman Wilkerson sang "The Sweetest Story Ever Told" and Mr Wilkerson sang "The Lord's Prayer."

Mrs. Haughton graduated from Greenville High School and East Carolina Teachers College.

Lt. Haughton is the son of Mr. and Mrs. Gayle Haughton, Jr., of Trona. Calif. He graduated from San Bernardino Union High School and attended the University of Southern California. He is stationed with the Marine Air Corps in Greenville.

Heidenreich-Jones

On Thursday evening, July 13 Miss Evelyn Louise Jones became the bride of Staff Sergeant Ralph Harry Heidenreich at the home of the bride on West Fourth street.

The vows were spoken before the Rev A. Hartwell Campbell pastor of the Immanuel Baptist Church with the immediate family and inti mate friends attending. The only at tendants were Staff Sgt and Mrs. James C. Love. The double ring ceremony was used

The bride is the daughter of Lieu tenant and Mrs. Lester Jones. She is a graduate of Greenville High School and East Carolina Teachers College. Sergeant Heidenreich is the son of Mr. and Mrs James F Heidenreich of Pittsburgh, Pa., and is serving in the United States Ma rine Corps.

On Friday evening Mrs. I. B. Tucker, Miss Jane Tucker and Miss Elizabeth Pollard entertained the couple and intimate friends at a cake cutting. The bride's table was centered with a tiered wedding cake topped with the traditional bride and groom After the bride and groom cut the first slice, the bride's mother continued to cut the cake.

arge Number Graduate At ECTC This Morning

9/5/44

Baltimore Editor Delivers Commencement Address; Richmond Pastor Baccalaureate Speaker

Dr. Gerald White Johnson, well-known editorial writer on the Baltimore Sun, biographer of President Roosevelt, and author of numerous other books, delivered the commencement address to 145 graduates in the Robert H. Wright building at East Carolina Teachers College this morning.

President H. J. McGinnis presided and welcomed the friends of the college. He introduced Dr Johnson as a native son of North Carolina who had made good in his chosen field of endeavor.

Dr. Johnson spoke on "Education for Life." He pointed out that the present war is the result of bad teaching of history, geography, and other sciences in the Axis countries. The truth was warped to fit the evil designs of Axis leaders. He urged the future teachers of the graduating class to teach truth, which leads the way to peace. They should educate, he said, for life, not death.

There is danger of education for death, he pointed out, even in this country because of racial, religious, and other prejudices which sometimes are present in teachers.

"Germany," he said, "looked upon itself and saw that its logic was sound, that its science was accurate, that its strength was great; therefore it looked upon itself as the Master Race, brushing aside as of no importance the warning of one of the greatest of its own leaders, the Iron Chancellor Bismarck: In politics the influence of imponderables is often greater than that of either military power or money. Not when Hitler started to scream, but

(Continued on Page Two)

(Continued on Page Two)

Engagement Announced.

Mr. and Mrs. John Flanagan announce the engagement of their daughter Josephine Skinner to tenant Victor Bernard Blanc ed States Marine Corps Reserve

Blanc is the son of Mr. and V. G. Blanc of Pasadena, Calif.

2/29/44

Blanc-Flanagan.

and Mrs. John Flanagan announce the marriage of their daughter Josephine Skinner to Victor Bernard Blanc nant, United States Marine Corps Reserve day, the seventeenth of March een hundred and forty-four at Paul's Episcopal Church Greenville, North Carolina

announcements sent in town.

wedding characterized by its city and dignity was solemn-in Saint Paul's Episcopal h Friday evening at six o'clock Miss Josephine Skinner Flan-and Lieutenant Victor Bernard were united in marriage. The ony was performed by Rev-Colgate Daughtery, rector of Paul's.

n-branched candelabra with g tapers against a back-d of greens with vases of flowers formed a lovely set-or the impressive ceremony. renade," by Schubert; "Ave " and "Venetian Love Song" among the selections rendered s. R. A. Tyson, organist, prior ceremony

before the entrance of the party, "Oh, Perfect Love" by y, was sung by Miss Louise

traditional Bridal Chorus Lohengrin was used as a pro-nal and Mendelssohn's Wed-March as a recessional.

ng as ushers were Lieutenant Butler of Columbus, Ohio. Lieutenant Richard Israel, of ington, D. C., both now sta-at the Greenville Marine Air

bride entered with her fath-hn Flanagan, and was met at tar by the groom and his best Lieutenant Allen S. Hart-of Los Angeles, Calif., also Greenville Air Base.

Heidenreich-Jones.

Lieutenant and Mrs. Lester Jones announce the engagement of their daughter Evelyn Louise to Ralph Harry Heidenreich Staff Sergeant, United States Marine Corps

Sgt. Heidenreich is stationed at the Greenville Marine Base. His me is in Pittsburgh, Pa. The wedding will take place in the near future.

BASKET BALL HERE TONIGHT

Phantoms To Play Marine Officers At High Gym.

Tonight at 8 o'clock in the Greenville High School gym the G. H. S. Phantoms will meet the Marine officers of the local airport in what should be a fast game.

This will be the first time the Phantom five has met the Marine quintet and very little is known about them. Last Friday night the Greenies won over the Elizabeth City Yellow Jackets but lost to a powerful Portsmouth, Va., team on the following evening and are expected to be out for vengeance tonight. The Phantoms are expected to use their powerful fast-break offensive against the Marine flyers.

The probable line-up for Greenville will be Posey and Futtrelle at forwards, Leggett, center, and Harrington and Fleming at guards. Probable starters for the Marine officers are Lts. Aitken, Holloway, avis, Peterson, and Edwards.

The admission will be 15 cents or students and 25 cents for adults.

JAN. 11, 1944

MARINES WIN OFF PHANTOMS

Flying Officers Take Basketball Game 41 to 33

By DAVID WHICHARD

The Green Phantoms' powerful fast-break offensive was stopped last night 41-33 by the Marine officers of the local airport in a fast, hard-fought basketball tilt. The Marines took an early lead which they held throughout the game except twice in the second quarter when the Greenies tied the score. At half-time the Phantoms trailed the Flyers by eight points 22-14.

During the second half the Phantom five tried all their tricks and fakes but were unable to overcome the eight-point lead which the Marine officers held at the half and when the game ended the Phantoms still trailed by eight points.

Lt. Aitken, lanky center of the Marine five, led the scoring of the game with 21 points to his credit. Lt. Studt was runner-up for the scoring of the Marines with nine points.

Flashy forward Jimmie Futrell and guard Billy Harrington led the play for the Phantoms. Futrell took the Greenies' scoring honors with 10 points followed closely by Harrington with seven markers.

The Phantoms travel to Kinston Friday night to meet the Kinston High School Red Devils. The Greenies have not met the Red Devils before this season and they will be out Friday partly make up for the losses they have suffered in the past two games.

JAN. 12, 44

Phantoms Lose To The Marines

Taking to the hardwood for the last scheduled game of the season the G. H. S. Phantoms suffered a 43-27 defeat last night by the Marine officers' five from the local airport. The game, from the opening minutes to the final whistle, was fast and rough as the Greenies attempted to stop the flyers' powerful offensive. The Marines took the lead in the first quarter and held it unmolested by the Phantoms scores, who could account for a little over one goal to the Marines two. The two teams were after the ball and each player did all in his power to keep his opponent from scoring as is indicated by the 16 personal fouls committed by Phantom players and 11 personal fouls committed by the Marines.

In the closing minutes of the third quarter and in the beginning of the final period the Greenies began to rally and closed the gap between their score and the officers lead but their attempt to gain the lead was futile as the Marines also began to rally and piled point after point on their already large margin.

Jimmie Futtrell and Amos Leggett led the Phantom scoring with nine points and seven points respectively while the Greenies' floor play and ball handling were sparked by Billy Harrington and Neil Posey.

High scorer for the Marines was Roe with 16 points followed by Holloway with seven markers and Aitken with six.

In the preliminary tilt the Pal Phantoms topped the Winterville high school team 24-17. Ed Williams, Henry Turner and Sherod White were the high scorers for the local junior team with six points each. The Winterville squad was led by Moye with five points and Ennis with four.

FEB. '44

DUSK PATROL - GREENVILLE, NORTH CAROLINA,

FEBRUARY 1944

by Ralph H. Heidenreich

I was at my desk, waiting for our dusk patrol to touch down, when Capt. Russell Janson, coming from the base control center, told me we had a plane down in a field next to Hwy 43 in the Bruce Area. Operations were secure except for those of us who were waiting for the return of our two planes. Capt. Janson instructed me to get foul weather gear out of the parachute hut and accompany him to the crash site. I drew flight jacket, pants, boots and helmet, fleece-lined, jumped into the jeep and off we went to the crash site. When we arrived we found our SBD-4 had crash landed in a corn field. Our pilot (?) was taken to the hospital for after-flight evaluation.

Capt. Janson instructed me to secure the area, which I did, so as not to let anyone infiltrate the area. Having this done, I sat on the ground in my flight uniform, then the farmers arrived. First thing, they brought a coal stove, set it up with a stove pipe up six feet in the air, and fired it up to keep me warm. Everyone of them thought I was the pilot, but Capt. Janson had taken the pilot for medical evaluation.

Next came the good North Carolina folks. They brought me collards, yams (two bushels), country hams, biscuits, coffee, chicken, blankets, and an oil lantern. I was relieved about two hours later, but when I left I filled the back seat of the jeep with the love, affection, and patriotism of the people of North Carolina.

AN INCIDENT AT GREENVILLE, SUMMER 1944

by Will Kalmoe

One nice summer day I, Lt. Kalmoe, was scheduled for a flight in a SBD. I started the engine, taxied to the appropriate runway, revved the engine to check the mags, and started down the runway. About the time of lift off, the engine started to miss. I couldn't abort because then I would end up in the river. I did get airborne and go over the river; then I was thinking of all those houses that I might crash into. But the plane kept flying and eventually I was over open land. I radioed the tower that the engine was missing and that I was returning to base. I reduced the throttle setting, as by then I had enough air speed. Then the engine sounded fine. To me it seemed that at full throttle the engine didn't get enough gas. I landed without incident and "downed" the plane on the check sheet.

A couple of days later the lead mechanic came to me and wanted to rev up the engine to see if it would miss or cut out again. So I started it and held the brakes as hard as I could. The mechanic held on outside the cockpit. I held it at full power for about two minutes before it started to miss. Then they fixed it.

MEMORIES

by Evelyn Jones Heidenreich

December 1943: The snowman paid a visit to North Carolina and everything is inundated! Nevertheless, Mrs. J. Keif Brown calls for a meeting of the U.S.O. Junior Hostesses at her home on this snowy night.

How we all got there escapes me, but nevertheless, my sister, Sarah, and I were in attendance. After the meeting we went to the Greenville U.S.O. to see what was happening on this cold and snow-covered night.

Sarah and I arrived with others from the meeting at the Greenville U.S.O. Club. To our surprise, there was a pretty good crowd assembled. All of us went into our usual mode, which was "make friends with the servicemen who are looking for a friend."

Spotting a U.S. Marine who had just arrived, and had seated himself in front of a gas heater going full blast, Sarah and I went over to talk and make friends. We had never seen such an obstinate individual!! Try as we might, we received only very curt answers to our questions or attempts to make friends.

Sarah Moore, another junior hostess, came over, apparently to "try her luck", at which point my sister Sarah and I gave up. However, sister Sarah whispered to me, "Look at his socks! It looks like the whole alphabet is on them." Of course, it was "H-E-I-D-E-N-R-E-I-C-H," which to "Jones" girls was a real oddity. We were so consumed with laughter we had to take our leave!!

Early February 1944:

I am talking to a good looking U.S. Marine at the Greenville U.S.O. In the course of our conversation we discover his birthday is the same as mine -- February 18th. His name was Eddie Galante.

Since all my girlfriends were coming to my house for a spaghetti dinner and to celebrate my birthday, I asked my new friend, Eddie, if he would like to attend. Being Italian, he accepted immediately.

My best friend, Elizabeth Pollard, lived next door. I told her about Eddie Galante and asked her if she would "take him under her wing", at my birthday party so I would be sure he was being taken care of. She agreed. She did, and of course, as you all know, continues to do so to this day, October 1996. Eddy and Libby are a happily married couple.

February 1944:

A big dance is being held at the old blind center, which has been taken over by VMSB 343. The Third Marine Airwing Band was coming to play! U.S.O. Junior Hostesses were invited. Wow!

I could not find a thing in my wardrobe that I wanted to wear. I said to my best friend, Lib Pollard, "Have you got anything you will let me borrow to wear to the dance?"
She told me I could wear anything I could find in her wardrobe. I looked and found just the thing.

That night all of us Junior Hostesses converged on VMSB 343. My main thought was to concentrate on dancing early on with Jimmy LaShan, who I had met and knew he was one fantastic dancer. All the junior Hostesses had the same thing in mind, for we all knew if you were lucky enough to snare a good dancer early on, you were set for the evening, because the others would know you could dance and would "break in" on you. My prayer was answered and there I was with that wonderful band playing, and dancing with Jimmy!! How fantastic. How could it get any better than this?

Now, so I was told, Ralph Heidenreich was on duty as the Sgt. of the Guard. When he was relieved of his duties, he decided to attend the dance, find Jimmy LaShan, his best friend, and break in on him, thereby making sure he did not find himself stuck with a little old southern girl who couldn't dance. You got it. When he came to the dance and looked for Jimmy, who do you think he got when he broke in -- me!!

What paces he put me through to the music of that wonderful band. It did not get any better than this. I was born with my toes twiddling. We began dating and, of course, I went through my 'dating' wardrobe and started over again. Ralph said to me "Why don't you wear the dress you wore the night of the dance?" I should have revealed my secret then and there. But, no. I borrowed Libby's dress again. Now you are probably way ahead of me. There came a night when Libby, Eddie, Ralph and I double dated. Out comes Libby in "my dress". Ralph was not pleased. He took me aside and said, "Have you gone crazy? Why are you letting Libby wear your dress knowing that it's my favorite?" There is a moral to this story.

What great times they were for such a short interval: Eddie and Ralph presenting Libby and me with corsage boxes filled with dead roses they had picked along the way to cover the real roses; Margaret, Libby and I waiting at the 400 Club in Margaret's car for Joe Ligman, Eddie Galante, and Ralph to jump the fence; all the good music and dancing; those were the days.

I must mention there came a time when my sister Sarah was to see that wonderful man I met at the U.S.O. She had heard all the accolades I had heaped on him. When Ralph walked in I said "There he is, Sarah, at the entrance."

She said, "I don't see him. There is only one man standing there."

I said, "Well, Sarah, that is him."

"What?!? You mean him? Don't you remember that cold night in December when we tried to make friends? I don't believe it. Remember the alphabet on the socks?"

How soon we forget!!

GREENVILLE NORTH CAROLINA APRIL 1944

by Ralph H. Heidenreich

Eddie Galante, Joe Ligman, and I found ourselves blessed with being associated with three southern belles. Margaret Savage, being an only child, was bestowed with a loving mother and father who at that time were considered wealthy. Mr. Savage, who owned Savage Stables on the corner of East Fifth Street and Cottanche Street, supplied Margaret with a Buick convertible town car. You can relate, I'm sure, these were big cars. Top down, seating six with a collapsible windshield and two spare wheels mounted on the side, and running boards. A sight to provoke the envy of anyone who observed this car.

Margaret was a beautiful woman who delighted in sun tanning. She gracefully wore dark brown on her body, which was accomplished after many hours of sun tanning.

Eddie, Joe and I would date these girls, Margaret, Libby, and Evelyn, pooling our nickels to see what we could do on our dates.

Gas being a priority at this time was something we had to be mindful of. Well, SSgt. Burkholder, who worked on the flight line had command of this situation. He would draw gas (flight fuel) at the flight line, having established a reservoir at our Marine barracks. The only two people who had wheels were, SSgt. Walter McCowie and Willie Clary. This was their pumping station.

Being friends of Burky, when we needed to get gas from Burky, we would drive to the 400 Club. The 400 Club was run by Mr. N. H. Barber. After the war he was a good friend of mine, for I worked for the postal service, and delivered his mail for a number of years. We would wait at the 400 Club to get a can of gas from Burky.

Margaret, Evelyn, and Libby would sit in the town car waiting for Joe, Ralph, and Eddie to report into the C/Q - (change of quarters) and then all three of us would go out the back gate at the 400 Club to meet our girlfriends.

Joe Ligman would, of course, drive Margaret's car to the pumping station where we enlisted men had our source of gasoline (Burkholder Supply, Inc.).

MY FIRST PLANE RIDE

Greenville, North Carolina Airfield, 1944

by Dick Haviland

I made the mistake of mentioning to Lt. Holloway that I had never flown in an airplane. A few days later we were out in the boondocks firing 50 caliber machine guns when a bomb cargo truck pulled up and I was told to report to the flight office. All the way back I'm wondering what I had done wrong. When we got there Lt. Holloway stood there with a parachute and a Mae West. He told me to put them on. I was hemming and hawing trying to talk my way out of going when he said he was ordering me to go.

We flew out over the Atlantic and made four simulated dive bombing attacks. The dives were started as 12,000 to 18,000 feet and pulled out just a few hundred feet over the water. It is a frightening experience to be in an airplane that is diving straight toward the ground. At the start he turned upside down and headed straight down. My stomach tried to come out of my mouth until he started to pull out then it went to the other end. I thought I was going to be crushed by the pressure pushing me down in the seat. I am told we pulled between 6 and 8 G's. However, by the last dive I was enjoying it. I will always believe that Lt. Holloway is one of the finest officers I know, but also is the greatest pilot in the world. So my first airplane ride was in a dive-bomber and, needless to say, it was a very big thrill.

A MARINE'S MOTHER

by Dick Haviland's mother (Leola)
while he was in VMSB 343

There's the Soldier and the Sailor
and the aviator keen;
As fine a group of fighting men
as one has ever seen.

But for me, I have a soft spot
for the boy in forest green.
The dashing, gallant leatherneck,
the United States Marine.

I will never be first lady
and grace a magazine.
I'll never be world famous
nor will I be a queen.

But I would never change my lot
for any that I've seen.
For you see, I am the mother
of a United States Marine.

I'd like to shield this boy of mine
from all that's wrong and mean.
I'd gladly sacrifice my life,
but he needs no go-between.

For God has given to my son
the gift of life supreme.
The "Red, White and Blue," blood
of the United States Marine.

A SALTY OLD TALE, 1944

by Frank P. Kittle

As everyone knows a kind of folk lore exists about "Salty" Fuller (Clifford Fuller) and the time he has spent in the Brig. All the while he was in Greenville he was in the Brig, which at the N.Y.A. camp was a tent. I was the Sgt. of the Guard on the day he was released and told he could finally have liberty in town. Salty took off for town and within a few hours, here come two Army Military Police with Salty, drunk as a skunk. He couldn't even walk. I threw him over my shoulder like a sack of potatoes and carried him to the barracks and threw him on the bunk. Later one of the guys came to me and said Salty had thrown up, straight in the air and it had come down right on his face. They complained he was stinking up the barracks. I told them that was not my responsibility. The next morning Salty woke up out in the yard. They had carried him and his mattress outside and left him there.

Story as told by Frank P. Kittle to Wally LeTendre

BASE FIRE DEPARTMENT, 1944

by Jim Love

R. D. Deines was appointed officer in Charge of the Base Fire Department at the Greenville Air Base. Jim Love was appointed NCO in charge under him. Jim had six men including Burkholder, L. B. Leonard, Dugan, and three others. The crew was assembled and they brought up a 4" pump from Cherry Point. It had two 4" outlets. Jim hooked it to the 8" outlet on the City Fire Hydrant, and L.B. Leonard was out on one hose and Burkholder was on the other. After priming the pump, Jim Love fired up the pump. The hose men were flailing around in the field throwing water all over everything in sight. All of a sudden the water petered out and was dripping on their shoes. They checked the pump and figured they had burned it out.

About two and one-half hours later the City Fire Marshall drove up and wanted to know if they had a problem. Jim said the pump burned out. The Marshall said we had emptied the entire fire-main system for the City of Greenville. He said, "Don't ever do that to us again."

Jim Love said, "YES SIR."

The group was later sent to a Southeastern Regional Training School to compete with others from the area. They had to climb inside a four story tower taking their hose to the top landing and shooting it out the window. Love calculated if he put his big man on the nozzle and spaced a man every twenty feet they could effectively negotiate the many landings. They blew the whistle and the 343 crew took off up the tower and actually set a record for the best time in the tournament. Jim Love still has the certificate they were awarded in the event.

AS I RECALL -- FIFTY YEARS AGO

by George Bobb

SUMMER 1944 - Greenville, NORTH CAROLINA

VMSB-343, a new Dive Bombing Squadron equipped with Douglas SBD-5's was in the middle of an intensive training program, in preparation for action against the Japanese in the Fall.

A heavy flight schedule was being maintained, Dive Bombing, Fixed and Free Gunner, Navigation, Radio and Radar Exercises and Section Tactics, both day and night.

The Squadron was operating from Greenville Airport, an auxiliary field for the Marine Corps Air Station, Cherry Point, North Carolina. Squadron personnel quarters and mess facilities were located in an old barracks a few miles from the field. Food for the noon meal was prepared at the barracks in large aluminum vats and trucked to a garage mess tent at the field.

LEMONADE AND THE ALUMINUM VAT

One day after completion of the morning Flight Schedule we went to lunch at 1200 and enjoyed a hearty meal topped off with several glasses of lemonade.

A nine plane Dive Bombing Mission was scheduled for 1300 and all pilots and gunners arrived at the flight line on time. All aircraft cleared the field and formed up and headed for the target area.

Some ten minutes into the flight, one pilot after another called the Flight Leader, declared an emergency and requested to return to base. It wasn't long before half the planes had turned back, so the mission was aborted and all aircraft returned to Greenville --- just in time ---as most of the pilots and gunners were suffering from stomach cramps and diarrhea.

The Squadron Medical Officer determined the cause to be the lemonade which was made and served from the aluminum vat - a very toxic combination.

COAST GUARD "BEWARE"

The Marine Corps maintained and operated a Target Boat in the Pamlico/Neuse River area. The boat had an armored clad top and was available to the squadron for Dive Bombing Practice.

Regulations required that the lead plane establish radio contact with the boat crew upon arrival in the area and to make additional contact announcing the "Start" and the "Completion" of each dive bombing run.

One afternoon (1300) a flight of nine planes led by Capt. Russ Janson departed Greenville for the Target Boat. Each aircraft carried six miniature cast iron bombs containing a shot gun type shell, but larger, that produced a lot of smoke so the aircraft crew could see the impact area.

I was flying with Russ and as we arrived over and circled the target area, at 1000 feet, I tried repeatedly to establish contact with a boat visible below. After several failed attempts, Russ, by radio, called the flight and stated that we were going down to identify the craft below. At the same time, he instructed all other planes to hold their position.

Well! We peeled off, dove down toward the bogey craft, and as we leveled off and passed the starboard side a couple of hundred feet off the water, I looked back and up.

Yes! You guessed it. The other eight planes followed us down and each released a bomb. I looked again at the boat and counted eight splashes high-lighted by puffs of smoke.

I called Russ, told him what had taken place and he ordered all planes to join up and return to base. Later we found out that the bogey craft was a thirty or forty foot private yacht taken over by the Coast Guard for the duration of WWII.

NOTE: That was one time that the pilots were thankful for a miss --- never did find out what Russ had to say to them.

BRIDESMAID WANTED

Charlie Depke had spent several years in Quantico and had a girl friend, Marie, in Washington, DC. Toward the end of Summer, 1944, rumors had it that we would be shipping out soon, so Charlie and Marie decided to marry.

The wedding was to take place on a Saturday afternoon (1400) in a church in Greenville with a reception to follow at the Old Town Tavern Inn. Charlie had asked me to be the Best Man and I was delighted.

Saturday morning, the day of the wedding, around 1100, Charlie, myself and several others are in the tavern going over the plans of the day. Charlie was a little upset because Marie did not have a Bridesmaid.

I was sitting facing the open door of the tavern when I saw a cute little WM go by. I turned to Charlie and said, "Sit tight, I'll be back in a minute with a 'Bridesmaid'," and then I headed for the door.

I caught up with the young lady Marine and introduced myself. I then explained our problem and asked her, "If you have the time, would you like to be the Bridesmaid and attend the reception?"

She responded with an enthusiastic "Yes", and we both returned to the tavern. Charlie was surprised and pleased. At the church, Marie was also surprised and very happy. The wedding went off without any further hitches and a good time was had by all at the reception.

THE COWBOY AND THE MULE

by L.D. "Buck" Buckner

During our tour at Greenville, NC, a lot of the local people would invite Marines out to Sunday dinner or other special occasions.

A family named Turnage was just one of those families, and they were having a family reunion. This family also had a family member who was a General in the Marine Corps. Well, they invited me, D.D. McKelvy, and Red Larson. They had a barbecue in the yard of a large frame house on a farm just out of Farmville, North Carolina.

Well, there were several large mules in a lot not too far from the house. McKelvy asked one of the family members if he could ride on one of the mules. They told him they didn't think so because the mules had never been ridden. Being from Texas, Mack just had to try one. Well, he picked out a large gray mule that seemed gentle enough. He grabbed hold of the mule's mane and swung up on his back. He hardly was seated when the mule bucked and Mack's seat never touched the mule again. Needless to say, a great time was had by all.

THE APPROPRIATION

by L.D. 'Buck' Buckner

While VMSB-343 was at Greenville, North Carolina, I had my brother bring my old 1934 straight eight Pontiac auto over from my home in Clarksville, Tennessee. During this time gasoline was rationed at three gallons per week per auto, and you can imagine how far that went in an engine about six feet long.

If someone came around and said lets go somewhere this weekend, I would tell them they would have to get the gasoline. Well, Burky Burkholder wanted to go some place one weekend and said he would get the gas. A couple days later I went out and got my car and the gas fumes were really strong. Then I noticed something covered up in the back seat. I uncovered it, and there was a ten gallon milk can filled with aviation gasoline.

Needless to say, Burky had guard duty the night before and had drained a small amount of fuel out of several different airplanes. I am sure he was just making sure there was no water in the tanks of the planes.

The next night he and I drove out to Clark's Drive Inn. Clark's Drive Inn is the same place Ralph Heidenreich threatened to burn down one night when Mr. Clark wouldn't sell him any beer after hours. Needless to say, he got his beer. We borrowed a funnel from Mr. Clark and poured the gas into the old Pontiac. Best I remember the milk can was thrown over an embankment there by the Gar River. All you milk can collectors can search for it there.

THE BUGLER

by Harry W. Gibbs

I am a little late in writing to you and Wally but nevertheless here is a true story concerning myself, and Fred Reynolds who died last year.

Fred and I were leaving the barracks to go into Greenville on leave when we passed the flag pole. The bugler had laid the bugle down to go back to the barracks for something or the other. I picked up the bugle and blew assembly and all the guys came out of the barracks, pulling their pants up, half dressed, shaving cream all over their faces, and wondering what to do. I laid the bugle down and Fred and I went on our way - past the Administration Building - got into the taxi which was waiting, and innocently went on our way into Greenville.

Just another great and glorious evening spent in Greenville, North Carolina.

STRIKE THREE - YOU'RE OUT

by Richard "Dick" Haviland
Rocky Mount, North Carolina - 1944

Our squadron baseball team had just won our game against Rocky Mount and was celebrating the win in one of the hotel rooms where we were staying. Len Haney and I were being introduced to the fun of drinking by some of the old salts. Len seemed to be learning much faster than I was, so they asked me to take him to our room and put him to bed.

On the way we took a wrong turn and ended up in the hotel lobby. We sure raised a few eyebrows because we were only dressed in our skivvies.

I finally got Len to the room and myself back to the party. I don't know how he did it, but he beat me back. So we both slept on the floor in that room.

The next day we were in trouble with the hotel people, but Lt. Holloway gave them a big sob story about how we would soon be overseas and some of us might not get back, so they forgave us.

If the C.O. had found out it would have ended the baseball team.

ALL'S WELL THAT ENDS WELL.

GOING TO CHURCH IN GREENVILLE - 1944

by Walter "Joe" LeTendre

I joined the Marines, as most of us did, to defend our country against the tyrannical governments of Germany and Japan. In joining I felt I was putting my life on the line, but I was prepared to do that. I also had a deep faith in my God, and if it was my destiny to lose my life in the line of duty, I wanted to be walking hand in hand with the Lord.

In looking for a church to attend in Greenville we found a wonderful missionary church, St. Gabriel's, that was run by the Passionist Missionaries. The missionary priest was Fr. Maurice Tew, C.P. Most of the parishioners were black folks and there were always a lot of children attending. On the average, probably twelve to fifteen Marines from our squadron would attend Mass each Sunday morning. Since it was a very poor parish the collections normally did not gather much money, but the Marines, seeing the church's plight, were always very generous and the average Marine gave a dollar each Sunday.

God held my hand throughout the war and fifty-five years later he continues to walk with me.

And now that the remaining members of VMSB-343 continue to hold yearly reunions with one another for the past twelve years, it is very interesting to see that, almost to a man, every single one is a religious person: Catholic, Lutheran, Presbyterian, Greek Orthodox, Southern Baptist, Jewish, and Methodist. All practicing their faiths and showing their love for one another.   Thank you God.

SUNDAYS WALKING DOWN EVANS STREET IN GREENVILLE, NORTH CAROLINA DURING JANUARY TO JULY 1944

by Ralph Heidenreich

Sundays in Greenville, North Carolina during WWII was something to remember.

As you walked down or up Evans Street, which was the main street in Greenville, local folks, after leaving church services, would cruise main street, as it was called, looking for Marines to invite to Sunday dinner. It made no difference how many were in the party, a window of the car was rolled down, a voice asking, "Do you Marines want to come home with us for dinner?" I, as many others did, accepted their offer and were the recipients of Southern Hospitality from the residents of Greenville, North Carolina.

Not only that - we had to send members from the duty sections to attend constant invitations to church affairs or whatever as these folks extended their love and support to our men and women serving in the military in defense of our country. Muster (roll call) would be sounded, invitations read, who would go from the liberty section. No one would answer for they had other dates or plans for that night. The only alternative the Sgt/Major had was to draw from the duty section, so as not to offend the kind offers from the populace of Greenville, North Carolina.   Semper Fi.

CURFEW ON BEER

One night in January, 1944, after a hard days work at the Greenville Marine Air Strip, a crowd of us VMSB-343 Marines went out on the town of Greenville - drinking all the beer we could find. You remember, of course our only means of transportation was Pat & Charlie for we walked almost everywhere we went.

About 11:30 PM, we were across the river at the foot of the river bridge (the one Lt. Frank Lange flew under) at a drive-in called "Clark's". We, all eight of us, went in and demanded beer. Mr. Clark, who was practically blind, said he would not sell us any because of the eleven o'clock curfew. We argued and pleaded, but to no avail. We then asked for a gallon of gas. Mr. Clark asked what to put it in for he saw no car. We said - put it in a gallon jug, which he did. He then asked what we needed the gas for, because we had no car. One of us said, "We'll use the gas to burn your damn place down if you don't sell us some beer." Reluctantly, he sold us beer, and we were on our way, leaving the gallon of gas setting on the counter.

Just another typical liberty night in the lives of VMSB-343 Marines.

P.S. This is a true happening.

LOOSING A BUDDY

by Bernie Gallagher

This is the letter I promised you concerning Templemeyer's death.

As I recall, it was a typical gorgeous day in Greenville, North Carolina, cloudless, sunny, and a perfect day for flying.

It was to be a regular training flight for the squadron, and up and down the flight line several engines of the blue and white Douglas Dauntless' were already warming up. The checkout sheet attached to a clipboard was lying on the ground slightly behind the right wing. I picked it up and climbed up the walkway of the wing to the pilot. Handing the sheet to him, I realized I didn't recognize him as one of the regular pilots. As he signed it and handed it back to me, I was about to ask him if anyone would be going with him, and if not, could I go along. Normally it wasn't my habit to ask for a ride, but this did not cross my mind that morning. At that moment I looked up and saw my plane captain, Templemeyer, crossing the apron carrying a parachute.

After the pilot signed the sheet and I was sure he was ready for flight, I went back to Templemeyer to see if I could aid him in any way. He had climbed into the gunner's cockpit and was adjusting his shoulder strap for the seat belt, and without looking at me asked if the pilot had signed the sheet, and I said, "Yes". Getting down off the plane I went around to the front and, after warming up the plane, the pilot signaled "thumbs up and out" and I removed the chocks. He seemed to be in a hurry and cut into the line of airplanes taxiing by. I watched him taxi down the apron. After passing the hangar on his right, he disappeared from my sight.

Somehow I had a peculiar feeling of apprehension, but when I saw Tom Gibbons - seeing his plane safely on its way - I dismissed the feeling and we both walked across the apron toward the "snack shack" where we'd meet the rest of the line crews, such as McAloose, McGlinchy, Duggan, Gordon, Fickling, Harvey, Leonard, and the rest.

Suddenly there was an uproar from the direction of the flying field, beyond the hangar - and then the loud siren of the ambulance. Inwardly I felt that there was an accident of some sort and Templemeyer was involved. It was a rare feeling of dread which I never felt before and haven't felt since. I'm not sure I shared my thoughts with Tom Gibbons, but I'm positive I had them.

It wasn't too long before we learned that of all four involved, only Templemeyer was killed instantly.

The pilot he was with had taken a short cut over the old approach which led to the runway and got into flight position to be first to take off. He probably thought the other pilots would see him and have to wait. He hadn't figured - if a plane is behind him ready to take off, the nose would block off any view of the runway ahead until he had achieved enough flying speed that the tail lifts up and the nose goes down. That apparently was what happened. As the plane behind was racing down the runway, the pilot finally saw the other plane, but it was too late to stop. With what speed he had achieved, the pilot managed to lift his wing enough to clear the top of the tail and body sections, but not the gunners canopy. The pilot's life was saved by the bullet proof steel behind his seat. I don't don't recall seeing him around the squadron again.

THE 400 CLUB - 1944

by Walter G. Letendre

While we were in training in Greenville, North Carolina our planes were at the Greenville air station and our barracks were at the old N.Y.A. (National Youth Administration) buildings located on 14th Street.

At the far end of the property where the N.Y.A. camp was located was a little unpainted, clap-board shack that couldn't have been much more than 10 x 15 feet in size. It had shuttered windows, a screen door that would slam by the pull of the long spring attached to it, and the walls were adorned by signs saying "Double Cola", "Orange Crush", "Prince Albert", and "Camel Cigarettes". The store was owned by Mr. and Mrs. Barber, and was facetiously nicknamed the "400 Club" by the Marines comparing it to the famous club of that name in New York City.

When we returned from our duties at the airfield, and we had some free time we would walk over to the 400 Club for a double cola, cigarettes, or a can of tobacco. The couple that owned the store were incredibly friendly "down home" folks. We would often gather in small groups, sitting on little chairs and benches shooting the breeze about world events, things that happened while working on the planes, and our girlfriends. We all have a lot of wonderful memories of the time we spent at that wonderful little store in the beautiful city of Greenville, North Carolina.

After the war, in 1951, I drove back to Greenville with my new bride, Kitty, and looked for, and found the 400 Club. I also found two buddies, Ralph Heidenreich and Billy Wells working at the Post Office. We're still close friends.

THE 400 CLUB

by Ralph Heidenreich

How many of VMSB-343 members remember the "400 Club"? This was a little shack on 14th Street behind our N.Y.A. center/NORTH CAROLINA Department of Rehabilitation for the Blind Center which was our enlisted barracks while in Greenville, North Carolina.

This was at the back of our encampment, the front being on Elm Street. On the Northwest corner we had our Brig tent and fuel supply dump which S/Sgt. "Burkie" Burkholder would store gas for the few civilian cars which were owned by some of our squadron members. I can remember only two - S/Sgt. Walter McCowie and PFC. Willie Clary. There may have been more.

We cut the fence wire and could go to the "400 Club" for a soft drink anytime. I can remember Major Gregory during inspection saying, don't repair it, they will only cut another hole. This way we know where the outlet is.

Eddie Galante, Joe Ligman, Jimmy LaShan, and Ralph Heidenreich used this hole in the fence regularly. We would be dropped off at the main gate, check in with the CQ (Charge of Quarters) then go out the hole in the fence. Many times we would check with Burkie Burkholder to get some aviation gasoline. (Of course, you can remember gasoline was rationed at that time.)

During working hours, base personnel at the NYA center knew they could get a soft drink, snacks, or tobacco at the "400 Club".

After I was discharged from the Marine Corps in March 1946, I made friends with N. H. Barber and his wife, and daughter, Thelma, and son, Joe, who owned the property until they sold same to East Carolina University. This same property is called Dormitory Hill of ECU.

"SHAKEY" 1944

by Walter G. LeTendre

The first time I ever met "Shakey" was when I joined the squadron in the Spring of 1944 in Greenville, North Carolina. His real name was Frank G. Bluemlein, and he was from Brooklyn, New York. He was a sort of a nervous and fidgety guy, and hence the nickname "Shakey". He had a great sense of humor and a million jokes and, best of all, he could really play the chromatic harmonica. It seemed that most of the guys in our squadron that were from New York City or Brooklyn were extremely outgoing, if not pushy, but not "Shakey". He was more on the quiet and reserved side, but just ask him to play a song on his harmonica and he was more than ready to play.

"Shakey's" real gift was as an artist and spray painter. He designed the squadron insignia for Gregory's Gorillas, the gorilla holding a bomb. He spray painted all the planes with their characteristic sky blue top and white bottom, which made them harder to spot against the blue of the ocean or the white of the sky. Whenever a plane was damaged -- and we suffered considerable damage on Midway from Goonie Birds flying into the planes, and sheet metal had to be replaced -- Bluemlein would repaint them. He cut all the stencils for marking and identifying everything we owned and kept us looking ship-shape at all times.

After the war, Frank Bluemlein went to work for Tiffany Jewelers in New York City as an engraver, and worked there until he retired in February 1990.

PAYDAYS AT GREENVILLE NORTH CAROLINA

by Ralph Heidenreich

When I went into the Marine Corps in early 1942, the base pay was $21.00 per month. You must understand this included housing, meals, and uniforms. Needless to say the military at that time was saturated with folks that could not support themselves on the outside. The 1st Sgt. was the one who could drink more liquor or beer than anyone in the command, plus be able to punch out anyone who challenged his right to give orders. As things changed with WWII, the base pay was raised to $38.00 per month. Later another pay raise, and basic pay of a private spiraled to $54.00 per month free and clear. Housing, uniforms, and meals were an added bonus. To make a statement, the Marine Corps has changed.

Master Sergeant Stanley I. (Horse Cock) Harris was a senior HCO in the service. You may have many interpretations about the nickname "Horse Cock" but, in truth, this was associated with the Sunday meal at all Marine Stations. The Mess section would prepare breakfast and the noon meal for the troops, so Sunday evenings after lunch they would prepare a cold meal for whatever troops would eat at the mess hall. Horse Cock was balogna, you know the big 6" round, sliced into 1/4" thick slices. Well Stanley "Horse Cock" Harris loved this, I don't know why, for he was a gambler from the Philadelphia, Pennsylvannia, New Jersey area. (Only a ferry trip from Phil to New Jersey to gamble.)

When we were paid, it made no difference what day of the week it was, Stanley "Horse Cock" Harris would stay at the NYA Center, our base barracks, playing poker or shooting craps until he either was broke, played even, or wiped out the other players. This went on for days with the game being postponed during working hours -- 0700 till 1630 when we secured.

Meanwhile his wife, Emily, living at the Perkins house next to the Pitt Theater would call base inquiring about Stanley's existence. Most calls were directed to me because Stanley, M/Sgt. Jim Bowles and T/Sgt. Jim Love were good friends of mine. All of them except me lived at the Perkins House. Emily would ask, "Ralph, is Stanley all right?"

I would answer, "Emily, he's fine - just playing poker."

She in turn would say, "Okay, just tell him I love him and he should come home soon."

I might add that after the war, Evelyn and myself decided to make Greenville, North Carolina our home. Mrs. Perkins, her son, Dave, and her daughter, Helen, became very good friends.

The Perkins home has since been demolished and now is only a parking lot in downtown Greenville.

Semper   Fi

MESS DUTY AT GREENVILLE NORTH CAROLINA

by Jay Higgins

I was stationed in Greenville. I served on Mess duty for thirty days. My job was in the spud locker. Peeling potatoes was my primary job -- along with the onions. If I remember correctly, Norman Brown was also in the spud locker.

After doing our job for several weeks, wearing gas masks for the onions, we thought up a great idea. We talked to Pappy Kilgore to see if we could cut up a large supply of potatoes in advance, store them in our portable containers and fill them with water so they wouldn't spoil. All this hinged on whether or not we could get a Pass.

We must have caught Pappy after he had a few shots and he told us to go ahead and do it -- if we got the Pass we wanted.

We did some promoting, got a seventy-one hour Pass for the weekend. We peeled potatoes day and night and stored them in the walk-in cooler. We were ready to go. We caught rides to Cherry Point and Rocky Mount, then took a train to Washington, D.C. We spent one day and two nights -- had a great time, from what I remember! We caught a train back to Rocky Mt., and hitch hiked back to the spud locker.

MY ONLY ACCIDENT

by Jay Higgins

One night in Greenville, North Carolina, it snowed. I was driving the liberty truck, made one trip into town and returned to the base to see if I had another group going in. I went to the mess hall to get a cup of coffee to warm up. While there, Pappy Kilgore decided he needed a ride to pick up a bottle. As we started back to town, ice was on the streets, and a car stopped in front of us. I hit the brakes and slid fifty or sixty feet into the rear of this stopped vehicle. Did I mention that I had never driven on ice before?

I got out and spoke to the man who was driving. As I did this, I saw Pappy get out the other door and disappear. After checking the damage -- about $100.00 in those days, the man said not to worry about it -- it wasn't that bad. I told him I had to make out an accident report. He assured me he would not report the accident, but gave me all the information that I requested. I turned in the information to Sgt. Berstein in transportation. He took my report and held it, and said he would only use it if the man complained. On my return trip to the base, I picked up Pappy with his brown bag. So I guess, in spite of the accident, the liberty run turned out okay after all.

ALL FOR THE GREATER HONOR AND GLORY
OF THE CORPS

by Bernie Gallagher

Returning from a leave, I was in Washington, D.C. and had to wait till 11:00 PM for a train to take me to Rocky Mount, North Carolina. I had my ticket and had eaten my supper earlier so I had time to relax and have a beer. I found a spacious restaurant with perhaps a dozen tables and a long counter. I preferred the bar stool at the far end so as to enjoy myself and reminisce about my visit home. I remember it must have been winter, because it was cold outside and I had my overcoat on over my greens.

A commotion several tables away caused me to turn to watch a young sailor as he went from table to table annoying both sailors and soldiers alike. Obviously, he had been drinking the hard stuff, and was very obnoxious to the extent that another sailor came over to me and said he wished this guy would pick on him, cause he'd like to knock him on his fanny. I agreed with him, this sailor was looking for trouble, but since I had a train to catch I told the sailor he wasn't bothering me. I turned and went back to my reminiscing and, as fate decreed, in short order I was unluckily approached by the "obnoxious one". After a few choice remarks such as "I wore out more sea bags than you." "You look like you're just out of boot camp." In truth I had already been assigned to the squadron and had a stripe. He was loud and boisterous so that every one was watching us. In his boasting way he claimed he was a corpsman and served with the Marines.

Finally I had had enough so I asked him "So you're a corpsman?" He answered in the affirmative, so I said, "How about giving me a short arm inspection?" With that he lunged at me and pinned me to the bar. We exchanged punches and fought for a while, banging into tables and back up against the bar stools and bar. Finally someone separated us and his buddies subdued him.

Someone suggested to me "You'd better leave, Marine." I appreciated that since I'd had a few beers and wasn't exactly ready for such violent exercise, so I left.

Walking up the sidewalk past the plate glass windows of the restaurant, I thought I had conducted myself pretty well except for the gurgling in my stomach. I thought it was all behind me until I heard a voice call out, "Hey, Marine, do you still want that inspection?" What could I do but get ready to continue round two. He again lunged at me and drove me into a parked car, while I tried to get a clean shot at his chin. When he drove me into the plate glass window, I was really scared but it held both our weights so the fight continued. Twice some guys tried to stop us, which I was grateful for, but the consensus of opinion was, "It's too good a fight.", so they wanted us to continue, even though there was one opposing vote. After a while, someone shouted, "There are MP's coming!" which finally broke up the fight and dispersed the crowd. A cab with about four soldiers pulled up at the curb and they ushered me inside and whisked me away to avoid the MP's. They already had my overcoat, my green jacket and belt. They were enthusiastic and patted me on the back and told me it was a great fight. I don't remember being hit, a fact I guess most fighters wouldn't admit.Fortunately, I wasn't the worse for wear. I had no marks on me and only a dislocated right thumb to show for it, which I have to this day. The soldiers were great and they took me to the First Aid Station and wished me all kinds of luck. I, of course, caught my train back to camp.

Looking back a half century later, I marvel at the way our country conducted a war on two oceans. This is particularly true when I realize how poorly prepared we were on December 7, 1941. Except for the needless slaughter of young American boys, both the dead and the injured, I appreciated this time in my life. It was a time when we Americans united and sacrificed to do all in our power to win on both fronts. With a war effort this country will never see again, we supplied thousands of planes, ships, tanks, vehicles of all sizes, through Lend Lease to all of our Allies at the same time that we built our own military force. I was, and am, proud to have been a part of it.

OUT OF THE BLUE

by Frank Pryg

Marine Air Field: Greenville, North Carolina 1944:

The drill for our squadron of SB2C's was to put as many aircraft in the air as possible in the shortest time. Normally, we took off staggered two at a time. This time, two were half way down the runway when our tower operator went berserk. "Get off the runway now. I mean now!" he yelled. "Something is coming in." Our two planes became airborne just as, out of the blue, a P47 Thunderbolt landed on our runway. Fishtailing its rudder to slow down, it lost control, started to slide sideways for a hundred feet or so, finally slid off, blew a tire, and came to an abrupt stop. We all rushed out with the crash crew. The pilot climbed out with oxygen mask half on, half off. We were all very young, but this pilot looked sixteen. "Did I hurt my plane?" he asked.

Our O.D. answered, "To hell with the plane are you all right?"

"Yes, sir," he saluted. "I lost my engine at thirty thousand feet. My squadron leader radioed there was an air field somewhere below." The young pilot explained that he had managed to pump his landing gear down and proceeded to land at a very fast rate of speed. Needless to say he had very little braking. The Lieutenant, who was from a fighter squadron out of Goldsboro, North Carolina, took a physical. Almost immediately the Lieutenant and our engineering officer took off in our S.N.J. It was a practice insisted on after a crash, so the pilot will not suffer any mental anguish.

The next day a big Army truck and a couple of jeeps with a big tech crew arrived at Greenville. They repaired the P47 and on the 3rd day the very young Lieutenant flew back to his home base. He was one lucky guy!

THE SWIMMING HOLE

by Charlie Franzo

While stationed in Greenville at the N.Y.A. barracks we found an abandoned swimming pool in a yard where the house had been removed. The pool was full of dirt up to the top. Looking for a place to have a little fun, we got permission from someone to remove the dirt, clean it up, and fill it with water.

One night about eight or nine guys, myself included, decided to try it out. I didn't swim because I don't know how. The other guys decided since it was dark they would go skinny dipping. Unfortunately, no one owned any trunks. They all got in the pool figuring no one would see them.

As the fates would have it, they heard a bunch of women approaching with one of them saying, "Let's go in too." Butt naked, the guys got out of the pool and beat a hasty run to hide in the bushes where they crouched down to hide. It seemed forever, but finally the ladies left so they could sneak back to the base. To their surprise, the next day all of them broke out from waist to ankles with Poison Ivy.

Lesson for the day: they should have stayed in the pool; or maybe, it's sometimes better not to know how to swim.

STANDING TALL - 1944

by Charles "Chuck" Luedtke

While stationed at Greenville, North Carolina Air Station, our squadron VMSB-343 would stand split duty sections, with one section on liberty on Saturday and the other on Sunday.

On Sunday morning the Saturday liberty group came back to the NCO Base. Sgt. Mead called the group to attention to call them to duty. Joe Swenarski standing in the back rank unbuttoned his fly, pulled out his tool, and started to urinate on Lloyd Jefford's leg. Chuck Luedtke said, "You can't do that".

Swenarski answered questioningly, "I can't?" Put his tool back in his pants, buttoned up, and proceeded to pass out, falling flat on his back. It's a fact!

DIVE BOMBERS IN GREENVILLE, NORTH CAROLINA
1944

by Frank Lange

While on assignment in Greenville, North Carolina our orders called for us to participate in:
practice gunnery exercises,
practice bombing exercises,
practice group activities,
Our complement of pilots was thirty.

During our Gunnery exercises we would fly out over the Atlantic Ocean and engage in target practice, firing at targets towed by Navy tow-planes. This involved both the pilot and his gunner, coming at the target from different angles. We also fired on fixed targets on Raccoon Island.

During our bombing exercises we again flew out over the Atlantic Ocean and practiced dive bombing runs on target ships that had been immobilized in Pamlico Sound, off Cape Hatteras. Our bombs were ten pound training bombs with a charge in their heads and were about fifteen to sixteen inches long. The target ship was used by Army, Navy, and Marine Corps pilots.

Water evasive tactics.
Our group activities practices involved flying in wing formations. The various formations were:

3 plane formations,
6 plane formations,
9 plane formations,
12 plane formations,

15 plane formations,
18 plane formations.

These groups would engage in practice recognizance, practice strafing runs, practice dive bombing runs and cross-country flights. We also practiced water evasive tactics where we flew just above the water, twisting and turning as we flew. An unexpected side benefit was that we would fly over the East Carolina Dormitories where the co-eds would be sun-bathing on the roofs. That only lasted until the commanding officer got wind of it, and forbade us from flying over the dorms. So much for fun.

One unfortunate guy who never adhered to that last order forbidding flights over the dorms was a maverick, Frank Lange. He paid for it.

IT'S ALL RELATIVE

by Walter G. LeTendre

Have you ever wondered how we made it during our early years? After I got out of highschool I worked at the first A & P supermarket that opened on Milwaukee's South Side. There was no such thing as a forty hour work week. I routinely worked sixty hours a week. When I left the A & P, Feb. 1, '43 to join the Marines my hourly rate was 18 ¾ cents. I had just gotten a ¾ cent raise. Since we got paid every two weeks I had $22.50 coming, which my mother wired to me in boot camp.

Once I'm in the Marines my Private's pay was $21.00 a month. (Of course, they fed and clothed me.) But everything was cheaper then. Following are some ads from the Greenville newspaper the Daily Reflector, showing prices in 1944.

SHOES

Every hour that man is ringing our back door bell and delivering New Spring Shoes

$3.95

to

$6.50

You will want to own at least one two-piece dress, and we have such a wide selection of these in all materials —

$5.95

To

$19.95

SUMMER COMFORT

New styles in cool, comfortable, summer cotton

DRESSES

$1.69 – $1.98

$2.98

2-Pc. Cottons

$5.95 – $7.95

Better DRESSES

Spun Rayons, Linens, Chambray and other materials.

$5.95 – $7.95

HOSIERY VALUES!

Cannon
51 Guage $1.20
48 Guage $1.15
45 Guage $1.08

Hudson
45 Guage   96c

Sheer! Flattering!
Long Wearing!

5/44

Dining Room Suites

These Beautiful 9-piece Dining Room Suites Consist of Buffet, China, Table with extension leaf, 5 Side Chair And One Arm Chair.

You Will Like The Beautiful Finish And Style of These Attractive Suites. The Low Price of –

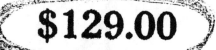

$129.00

Is A Special Value For You. See These At Once.

You Will Be Pleased With Our Easy Terms And Low Prices.

Taft Furniture Company

"Fine Furniture At Reasonable Prices."

GUARD DUTY IN CHERRY POINT

by Dick Haviland

Len Haney was on guard duty at the brig. Len was not the kind of guy who wanted to wear his "45". Len asked the Sergeant of the day what these guys in the brig were in here for. The Sergeant answered, "Murder, beating up their wives, assaulting a civilian."

Len, on hearing the charges, wheeled around, went back and strapped on his "45", and said, "Now I'm ready for guard duty."

A SALTY TALE

by Len Haney

Salty Fuller was in the brig all the time. He'd get out on Tuesday and the next thing you'd know he'd be back again, usually for insubordination to an officer. The Ordinance Group was the base MP's, so when Salty went in the brig he'd be on Piss & Punk for ten days or whatever. But we'd hollow out a loaf of bread and get Lou Mascolo, our base cook, to give us some goodies and we'd fill the loaf of bread that we'd hollowed out with Mascolo's goodies. Salty would be on P & P for ten days and end up gaining weight. No one could figure that out, but the MP's guarding him knew the story.

Salty was in the brig more than he was out. . . I think he loved the treatment we gave him.

RECONNOITER, JANUARY 1944

by Walter Viator

Youngsters that we were, sometime in the winter of '44, 343 was sent to Quantico, Virginia on a cross country and mission of inter-type tactics. On one of the flights we were at ten or twelve thousand feet and Capt. Simpson called Lt. Smith and said "Smith, take your wingman, go down and reconnoiter.

Smith came back, "Captain, what's reconnoiter?"

"Smith, go down and just look around."

"Oh!"

FAMILIARIZATION FLIGHTS SB2-C AIRCRAFT
GREENVILLE, NORTH CAROLINA March 1944

by Ralph Heidenreich

Captain Russell Janson our operations officer ordered all pilots to familiarize themselves to our new aircraft. After much instruction each pilot would fly solo in the new plane with a take-off, circle the field (360 degrees), touch down, take off and then land. This was done according to assignment, one after another being eager to fly our new plane. In the operations center things were hectic because all the pilots (officers) were on my ass asking, "When will I fly?"

Capt. Janson took care of this and he gave me the scheduling. Major Harold G. Schlendering, our executive officer, Captain Hap Simpson, and Capt. Russell Janson were all veterans of the battle of Guadalcanal, Marshall Islands, and the South Pacific area of operations. These three officers, particularly Janson and Simpson instructed and trained our pilots to achieve high proficiency in their assignment as dive bomber pilots. They know how important familiarization with one's aircraft must be.

After flight after flight, 1st Lt. George Alarik took control of an SB2-C, took off, began to circle the field, when he ran into mechanical problems. Trying to complete his 360 degree turn he lost power, then at 180 degrees, brought the plane into the field at "full alert". After losing air speed and altitude, he hit the grass between the runways, cartwheeled, leveled flat, and tore the engine from the front of the plane. Both wings severed and pushed through the front of the plane.

Immediately, Air Rescue, fire control, medical assistance, were at the scene. Dr. Bryon Hawks, our Medical Officer, took George Alarik to the Medical tent to examine him (S.O.P. after a crash of any kind the people involved must be examined). What had happened was Lt. Alarik ran out of fuel, had to switch tanks, but being unfamiliar with the aircraft, actually shut it off. Dr. Hawks, after the examination, observed Lt. Alarik's wings were missing. They are worn on the left chest above the pocket. They then went to the crash site to look for the wings. Upon arrival, Lt. Alarik, who was assumed to be all right, looked at the plane, debris, and all, then fondly and thankfully fainted.

LEAVING GREENVILLE July 15th, 1944

by Ralph Heidenreich

After being alerted to send all our pilots, gunners, and support elements to Norfolk, Virginia to receive new SB2C's, and to board an aircraft carrier for deployment to the European theater of operations in support of the Normandy invasion, our orders were revealed. Fact being, this was to be an all Army effort. They did not want Marines in support, so we were assigned another mission. Our pilots and support elements returned to Greenville, two weeks later we left for the West Coast.

Saturday, July 15, 1944 we boarded railroad coaches off 14th Street in Greenville, North Carolina to go to who knew where. We traveled on a coal fired train through South Carolina, Georgia, Florida, Alabama, Mississippi, Louisiana, Texas, New Mexico, Arizona, and finally to San Diego, California. The trip took approximately two weeks with many stops. I can remember on one of our stops, everyone disembarking in formation and going to a restaurant where we were fed a wholesome meal. It was in Montgomery, Alabama.

Master Sgt. John Dolgate, our flight line chief, was NCO in charge of the railroad car to which I was assigned. Johnny, a career Marine, had found his love and married before we left Greenville. Having had his love experience, just as we departed, he found out he was going to be a father. Johnny never recovered from his loneliness. At Midway he was relieved of duty, reassigned to the States, and ended up in a hospital. Throughout the trip to the West Coast, I was instructed by Johnny to be NCO in charge. I can remember forming the squadron in Alabama to march downtown for dinner at the above mentioned restaurant.

The most memorable thing I remember was our stop at Waco,

Texas. We had a S/Sgt. BoBo Beauford who came from there. You know how Texans are; the great wide state, we do everything big. As we stopped for water (keeping in mind we were on a coal fired locomotive) Mexican children came running to the train saying, "Daddy". As Marines will be, we all were delighted in assigning these children to BoBo who, as you know, was from Waco, Texas. We had many laughs about Bo and all his children.

After another week, without showers, proper facilities, etc., we arrived at San Diego, California - our departure point to the South Pacific.

P.S. Can you imagine how much in need of a shower, shave, and proper body maintenance we all were?

DEPARTURE PARTIES AT GREENVILLE,
NORTH CAROLINA

by Ralph Heidenreich

We arrived at Greenville, North Carolina from Atlantic field on December 1st, 1943. Our Squadron VMSB-343 was commissioned August 1, 1943 and stationed from Cherry Point, Havelock, North Carolina to Atlantic Field in Atlantic, a fishing village on the outer coast of North Carolina.

With the expansion of the 3rd Marine Air Wing headquartered at Cherry Point, we did not have enough air space to train all the squadrons. The Defense Department acquired all the area airfields in local counties and cities to occupy for training, thus taking the burden off air space from Cherry Point to these outlying airfields. We had auxiliary fields at Atlantic, Bogue, New Bern, Kinston, Greenville, Edenton, and Elizabeth City, North Carolina.

We moved from Atlantic field to Greenville, North Carolina around December 1, 1943. Guess what greeted us? SNOW! In the sunny South! We pitched pup-tents at the air field for our barracks were on the other side of town and were not ready for habitation. Our advance party would correct this as we occupied the old NYA center, which had been occupied by the North Carolina Department of the Blind. Can you imagine the task the forward party had?

After occupying the NYA center we fell on downtown Greenville to find a refuge from Military Chow. We were easily led to the Olde Towne Inn on East 5th Street, downtown, close to East Carolina Teachers College. ECTC was a coeducational facility to educate teachers, but the war took all the men to service, except the 4F's, so the students were all women, one of which later became my wife. It did not take long for VMSB-343 to learn where to go downtown and where to eat--The Olde Towne Inn. We instantly became favorites. When orders came down in July 1944, the management of the Olde Towne Inn gave going away parties to our squadron. We, of course, at that time were a part of the Navy. As SOP (Standard Operation Procedure) we were organized into a port (on the left of ship) and starboard (on the right of ship) liberty sections, liberty being off duty.

The management gave us going away parties for two nights so they could reach all the squadron Marines. What a gracious gesture on their part. Some of us attended both parties.

Let me say in regard to us being part of the Navy during WWII, it is fact. All the ship guards on Navy vessels were Marines. They were called sea-going Marines. Captains of all these vessels demanded much from the ships' guard. I can also remember that Marine Guards would be on duty at all Naval Base entrances. Also all of our medical personnel--officers, and enlisted were Navy personnel. They of course, took care of all medical needs.

What two great parties we had, thanks to Greenville, North Carolina citizens. They loved the U.S. Marines and could not do enough to support the war effort and to support the troops. Semper Fi.

JIMMY AND CHERRY GET MARRIED
June 2, 1944

by Jimmy LaShan

I was nineteen and madly in love with my girl, Cherry. It was now or never! Faced with the likelihood I would be going overseas soon, I proposed to Cherry. We decided to elope to South Carolina. There was no waiting time in South Carolina for getting a marriage license.

After the USO dance was over, I took Cherry home. She packed a small suitcase with her nighty and underwear and sneaked it to me through a window. I headed back to the USO.

We planned to meet at 12:00 noon on Saturday at Cherry's parents' main gate and catch a bus for South Carolina. Well, back to the USO; I was headed for my cot when the bag fell open spilling Cherry's panties and all that in the middle of the floor causing a Hu-La-Ba-Lu and a lot of crazy remarks.

We did meet the next day as planned and "tied the knot" about 9:00 PM on June 3, 1944 in Dillon, South Carolina.
Major Gregory had lent me $50.00 - it paid for a gold wedding band, bus fair, hotel and food. Needless to say I paid him back.

A NEW BRIDE LEFT ON HER OWN
July 1944

by Cherry LaShan

It was July 1944. Jimmy and I had been married one month. VMSB 343 had received "shipping-out" orders. They came to the train station by truck convoy, marched to the train and began to board. Jimmy and I held hands and embraced for a little while and then said our "goodbyes". When the train pulled out there were a lot of sad wives left behind.

Afterwards, Babs from Bayonne, who was also a new bride, and I stopped at a nearby store and bought some milk. We didn't feel like eating. We talked and cried all night - packed and got ready to catch a train to New York City around noon the next day.

About 6:00 in the morning, I discovered I had lost my wallet. I had left it at the store. It was gone and I had no money and no ticket.

We walked down to the Greek restaurant and pretty soon everyone in there knew what had happened. The proprietor gave us breakfast, then a Lieutenant from VMSB 343 offered his help. He had a car (a rarity in those days) and drove me to the Red Cross Office to ask for help. The answer was "Sorry, it will take several days to even consider it". Next, we went to the Salvation Army Headquarters - they lent me $30.00. Then two of the USO ladies gave me another $20.00. That gave me enough to buy my ticket.

We made it to the train station in time and were on our way to New York. My first trip to a big city. A young couple on the train took me under their wing. We arrived at Grand Central Station and there was nobody to meet me. The young couple took me by cab to the address where Jimmy's mother lived - eventually we found each other.

When I look back on this day and realize how much help I received from strangers, I think God was watching over me. And I also do try to offer help whenever I see someone in need.

BEST REMEMBERED MEMORIES OF VMSB-343

by Jack Milarch

Seventeen years old, anxious for new experiences of grown-up proportions, eager to sample life's limits and intrigued by anything different from farm chores and school discipline, I joined the Marine Corps and started a three-year adventure consisting of many memories, both good and bad.

Those three years afforded me growth and maturity, as well as an awakened social consciousness, built on education and discipline that would serve me well through life.

The adventure of travel and enlightened awakenings as to architecture, climates, speech, geophysical and gastronomical differences were constant topics to write home about.

The education I received for skills I (and others) would use was beyond my comprehension only a short time before. My horizons for life were expanded beyond my wildest dreams.

Now I find it difficult to sort out the most special memories of my experiences -- those very special times -- but I think my memories of Greenville, North Carolina probably head the list. I've never forgotten how people of all ages, economic and social differences, accepted us and made our tour of duty there pleasant and downright enjoyable.

The most specific were two gentlemen, Mr. Tournage and Mr. Hearne, as I knew them. For example: my mother and sister wrote that they were coming to Greenville for my nineteenth birthday. It was exciting for me but also a little worrisome as to know how I would accommodate them. I had decided to reserve a room at the Proctor Hotel; however, my opportunity to spend time with them would be limited to evenings when I had liberty and one weekend. I related my plight to Messrs. Tournage and Hearne who both assured me that they would make my mother's and sister's stay enjoyable.

On their own they rented a beautiful room in a lovely old home in town. They purchased flowers to await them when they arrived. They picked them up at the bus station and took them to lunch, showed them their accommodations and drove them around the countryside to acquaint them with the area. They entertained them when I couldn't be there.

That experience was never forgotten by my mother and sister and they talked about it long after the war was over. My mother also felt better about me being away from home and that I had such fine friends.

And, as I have related, I have never forgotten it either.

SECTION IV

SHIPPING OUT

EXPLOITS BY BILL

by William G. Barry

I went through boot camp in January 1943 when I was thirty years old. From there to Tent City at New River. Officer Candidate School at Quantico, then Reserve Officer Class, and Commissioned June 16, 1943.

I wanted to get home in Boston for Christmas 1943 and selected Intelligence School at Quonset Point, Rhode Island and that was why I was an Intelligence Officer in VMSB 343.

I joined VMSB-343 in Spring 1943 and was berthed in BOQ which was a squad tent. Because I was a line officer, the Major wanted me to run the camp as Camp Commander. This was not to my liking as a different officer would be officer of the day and advise me what to do. At my suggestion, a squadron order was cut to read that Lt. Barry, Camp Commander, would be under order of Major Gregory, Squadron Commander only.

I took out punishment marches of about ten miles with rifle and pack several nights a week. I carried rifle and pack and enjoyed running up and down the column. Made sure we were able to each have a beer on the way back on me.

Our men were paying too much for beer downtown. A search by me revealed that an ex-Marine was in charge of Budweiser Beer in Goldsboro, North Carolina. I took a truck with a detail of four men to Goldsboro. I went to see the man and was informed that all of their beer went to the Army. After a lengthy discussion between an ex-Marine and myself, we were allotted thirty-three cases a day on credit.

Under my direction we opened a slop shute in camp with my barracks detail and myself as bar tenders selling Budweiser at fifteen cents per bottle. We would close up at 2300, clean up, and have a few beers.

One evening about 2320, we had a bang on the door, and I opened it. In rushed the OT, a short pilot captain whose name I do not recall. We had some unfriendly words and he was going to run us all in for being open after hours. I informed him that I was the Camp Commander and instructed him to leave. Finally I picked him up and he left the premises. (The camp security detail was under my command).

The next day I was brought up under charges before our Executive Officer, Capt. Janson. After listening to all of the many charges, I asked to have squadron order # _____ read to the Executive Officer. They were forced to drop all charges. After this the pilots were not friendly to me. They wanted to buy beer from me for the officers' mess, and I refused.

When we arrived at Ewa I went to Honolulu with a rotor for a jeep in my pocket. I selected a good Army jeep and put the rotor in the distributor, drove it back to base, had it painted gray and with Navy numbers. I used it regularly for Honolulu trips with my buddy, Ben Shriver (Material Officer).

We would run the blackout with Army MP's chasing. I would turn the lights off and slide into Cane Field. After they roared by, and turned back, we would speed back to safety of the base. Army MP's would be held back.

The squadron shipped to Midway Island. The Colonel of the 6th Defense Battalion wanted a flight jacket from Major Gregory who could not produce one. I was not entitled to another one. I had traded a new automobile tire in Cherry Point for my spare jacket. First I asked the Material Officer for a chit for a new jacket. This could not be done.

I was due to make First Lieutenant. The Major called me in. "I want your jacket. If I get it I will approve your promotion. If not - NO."

"You win. Here is my jacket," I said, handing him my only flight jacket.

That night I worked on W. O. Burke, ADJ. I bet him ten dollars that he could not use the Major's jeep and drive through the front and out the rear of the Major's Quonset hut. W. O. Burke accepted the bet. The Major's Quonset hut was wrecked.

One time when we were flying from Ewa to Midway in a C-46 or C-47, I was Troop Commander with thirty troops aboard. We approached Midway and the field was closed down. We didn't have enough fuel to return to Ewa. We approached French Frigate Shoals, an atoll two-thirds of the way back to Ewa with a runway of about 3,400 feet. Never had a plane our size land there before, and there were cross winds. Our plane had an interior gas tank which was leaking. The pilots and I had a conference. They were for ditching. I wanted to attempt a landing. We landed, dragging everything, and ended up on a sea wall.

On Midway, when our food did not arrive monthly, we'd go out to Pearl & Hermes Reef to go fishing. We usually got a lot of tuna. This enhanced our food supply until our regular shipment came in.

2

4a

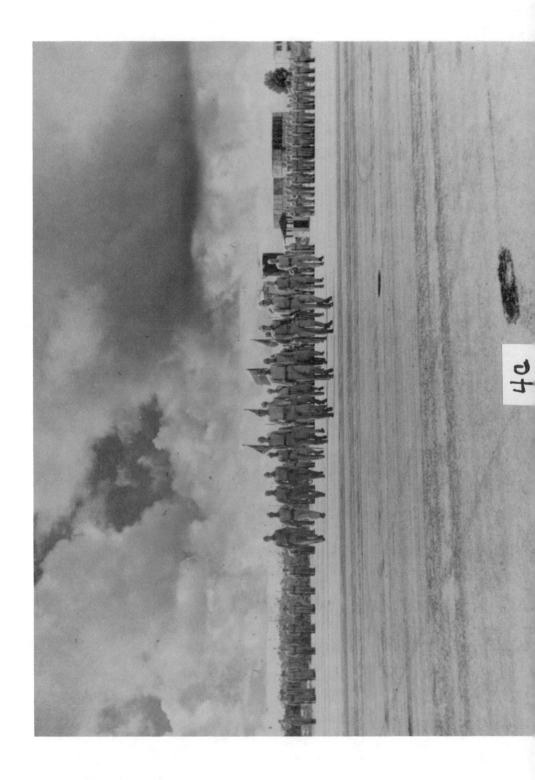

4a

5b

6

11

11a

12a

12b

13

14

15a

15b

15c

16a

16d

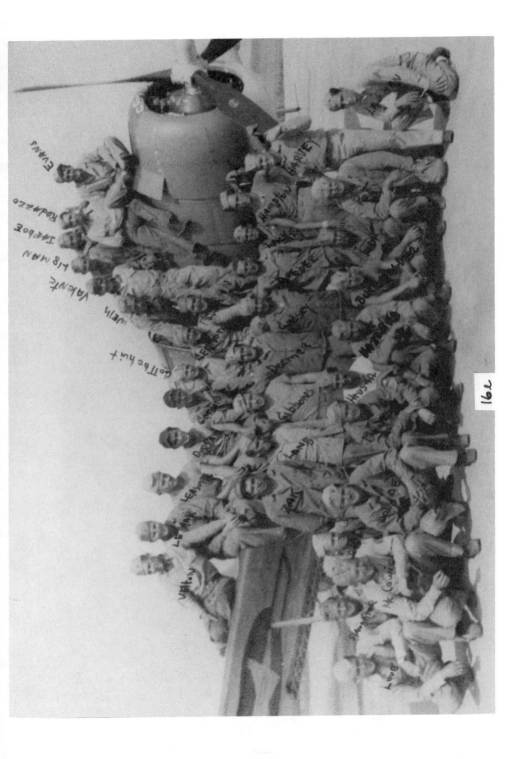

162

191

16g

17

18

19

20

21

22a

22b

GREENVILLE   23   1944

27

28a

29

30

31

32

34

DR
HANKS

BILL
DRUM

SAM
MATTOLA

33

These two Marines are telling it to each other in no uncertain terms. Cpl. Gail M. Gillbreath, USMCR, Long Beach, Cal., is shown being told with a left hook to the jaw from Pfc. Steve Graytak, USMCR, Bridgeport, Conn. This was one of the bouts recently conducted as a part of the Navy Welfare Department program at Midway Island. A capacity crowd, including all hands from the Commodore of the base to the most recently arrived boot, was present to witness the fights.

35

37

38

36

Update on Betty Hutton

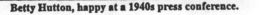

Betty Hutton, happy at a 1940s press conference.

The August 1993 *Midway Mirror* carried an article on Betty Hutton visiting Midway during the war years. We thought the following thumbnail sketch would be of further interest to the readers.

Actress Betty Hutton — the original "incendiary blonde" of the 1940s and '50s — fell on hard times.

Despite her effervescent exterior, Hutton (real name: Betty June Thornburg) was haunted by a troubled childhood. Her father committed suicide, and her mother was an alcoholic who died in a fire. Hutton married four times, became a drug addict, had trouble with alcohol and attempted suicide. She fell from public view after her last film, *Spring Reunion,* in 1957 and eventually was rescued by a Catholic priest, who put her to work as a housekeeper and cook in his Rhode Island rectory. When other celebrities learned of her problems, a benefit was organized in 1974. Unfortunately, she wasn't cured, and later required hospitalization. In 1980, Hutton made a Broadway comeback as Miss Hannigan in the musical *Annie.* Today, at the age of 72, she is battling Epstein-Barr virus.

Article submitted by Jimmy Cotta — San Francisco.

U. S. ARMY HOSPITAL SHIP
"ACADIA" ARRIVES
AT CHARLESTON, S. C.

42a

426

44

45a

45b

46

47

48

49

50

51

52

53

54

55

56

57

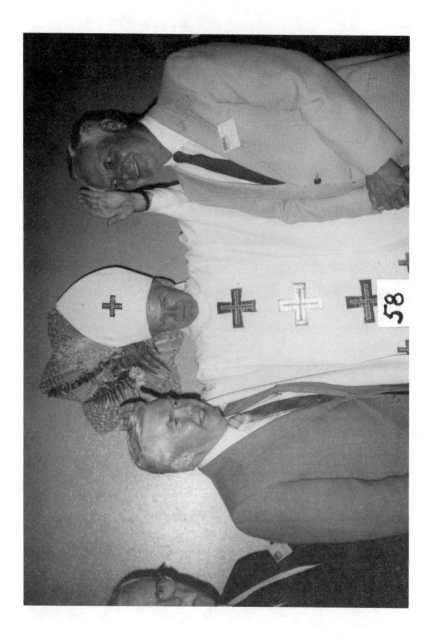

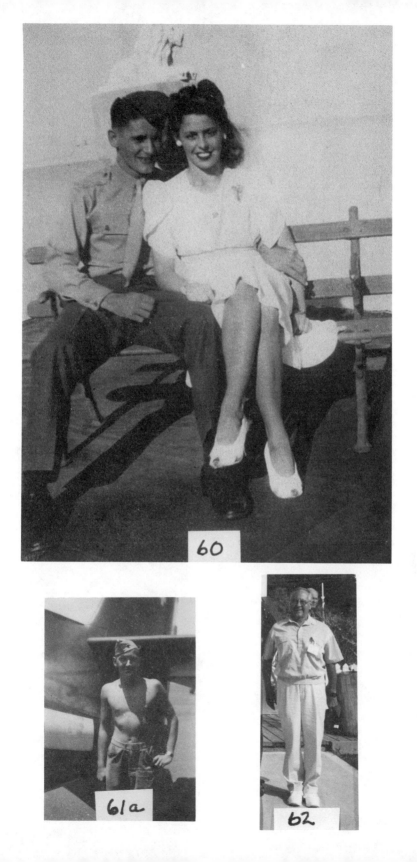

60

61a

62

TROOP TRAIN TO SHUMAKER, CALIFORNIA

by Clark Herrman, Control Tower Operator

We were all in dungarees, and when we stopped in Cincinnati, we all got off (thirty of us) and were walking around. We ran into four little old ladies, who asked, "Are you servicemen?"

One of our men could speak German, and had the accent to go with it. He answered, "No we're all prisoners of war from a submarine going to a concentration camp."

With that the ladies all ran off saying, "My God, they're letting them run around loose!"

SHORE LEAVE

by Charlie Franzo

August 1944

While we were stationed at Camp Miramar, California (San Diego), prior to shipping out, we were on liberty in San Diego. We went to Carley's Bar in Dago, to have a few beers. A sailor approached me looking for a fight. He asked me if I was a Dago. I answered, "I'm from New York."

He repeated again, "Are you a Dago?"

I answered again, "I'm from New York."

By now he was very irritated, and raising his voice, he asked "Are you an Italian?"

I said, "Yes!"

So he said, "Oh, then you're a Dago."

I answered, "For years, back East, I was called a 'Wop' and a 'Grease Ball'."

He laughed and said, "Come on, I'll buy you a beer."

TRAVEL ITINERARY

by "Burkie" Burkholder

Troop train from Greenville, North Carolina to Miramar, CA. 1944.

Boarded USS Altamaha (CVE18) at San Diego, California to Ewa, Hawaii.

Pilots ferried SB2C to Midway.

Flight crews flew in Curtis Commando's.

Emergency stop made at French Frigate Reef due to rain storm.

Returned to Ewa via USS Colusa, ll August 1945.

Returned to US from Hawaii on USS Saratoga.

Arrived at Treasure Island, California.

GUARDIAN ANGEL

by Bernard M. Gallagher

Being the youngest in a family of eight children, I never expected preferential treatment, especially when it concerned Guardian Angels. I suppose I could have managed with a mediocre one and then lived life very cautiously. But as it happened, I am blessed with a super Guardian Angel who takes excellent care of me

For instance, early in life, before I went to school, my brother Chink (for Charles) and I were coming back from grocery shopping and were almost home. We were going up close to the high curb, facing uphill, and he was pulling the wooden wagon with me holding on to the groceries. Suddenly a car, out of control and speeding, swerved from the curb and made a sudden turn and headed right for me and the wagon. Chink saw the car but couldn't help so he jumped back. The car trapped the wagon bed up against the curb, and I was catapulted up over the sidewalk and landed on our neighbor's lawn. Amazingly, the wagon was demolished, but I didn't receive a scratch -- thanks be to God and my Guardian Angel.

The summer before eighth grade, some buddies and I raided Fuller's Orchard early in the summer, and I returned home with a shirt full of not-so-ripe apples. Green apples are difficult to digest, and I ended up pretty sick and miserable. After no relief for a week, my sister, Henrietta, walked with me to the doctor's office. He examined me and took her aside and said, "Take this young man to the hospital immediately".

She said, "Okay, first thing in the morning!"

"Never mind then, take him to the undertaker!"

My sister was very quiet on the way home. Finally, that night I was rushed to the hospital and was operated on, thanks to her and my Guardian Angel.

During the summer, after graduation, I was working at Bethlehem Steel, and a good friend, Laurie Knight, saw me at the pool and asked if I'd like to join the Marine Corps with him. I said "Good". So we both went down to the Recruiting Office and passed all tests.

When I asked my Dad to sign for me he said, "Why don't you wait till it's closer to the draft?"

I said, "Okay," and then notified my friend who joined anyway. Later in the summer I joined with another friend, and when we went to Tent City at Camp Lejuine to shoot the range, I got in touch with Laurie who was in the Fleet Marines. He was in great shape and was really 'Gung Ho' and ready for combat. I am sorry to relate that Laurie was killed in Saipan by a sniper's bullet. Except for my father's advice, I probably would have been with him in Saipan. I thank my Dad and my Guardian Angel.

Working on the line at Greenville, North Carolina I was attending to the pilot who was warming up the Douglas Dauntless Plane -- I was second in command. He was in a hurry to get into the air since there was some kind of bet among the pilots as to who would be first in the air. It seemed like no one would be in the Gunner's seat and I was on the verge of asking if I could get a chute and go along for the ride, when I saw Bob Templemeyer coming across the black top with a chute over his shoulders. Thanks to my Guardian Angel, and I guess Bob, I was saved again. Sgt. Robert Templemeyer was killed in a collision of two ground planes on April 16, 1944 in Greenville, North Carolina in a training accident, in the plane I was going to fly in.

SHIPPING OUT

San Diego, California - August 31, 1944

by Ralph Heidenreich

VMSB-343 departed the continental limits of the United States to parts unknown. We were aboard the USS Altamaha, a light aircraft carrier, in a convoy. Ships were exercising evacuation and deployment to confuse the enemy. We stood on the flight deck, watching the landscape of the USA floating out of sight. None of us knew if we would ever see the mainland again. We were in convoy – orders unrevealed to all of us, for we were only fighting men going to our call of duty. We swerved and turned day after day until we reached our assigned destination, Oahu, Hawaii.

Upon arrival we were confined to ship for twenty-four hours. This, however, did not apply to the ship crew. Immediately they established the port and starboard duty sections for four-hour liberty. We stood on board watching the sting rays (two feet in width) eating and washing against the carrier. Then we saw the port liberty section going ashore. White Navy suits, black shoes, looking military, going ashore for liberty. Then as we watched, here comes the port section reporting back for duty after three and three-quarters hours of liberty; monkeys hanging off their shoulders, uniforms dirty and torn, hats missing, obviously drunk - a complete embodiment of what an American GI can do to himself in four hours of liberty, after being confined to duty.

After being lifted from our quarantine, we were assigned to barracks on the main island at Ewa, Oahu. We worked, did our duty, not knowing what was coming next. One day as we went to noon chow and were standing in line to enter the mess hall, we observed planes overhead. Barber's Point was the field where all planes landed. U.S. Forces, taking advantage of the expense of loading and unloading military aircraft from carriers, made a training exercise of unloading a squadron of SBD's from a carrier, with F6F's fighter support. The aggressors were Army P-38's as the attacking force.

This, unknown to us as we stood in the chow line would be a show we would never forget. In disbelief we watched a P-38 fly into one section of SBD's hitting two planes, which immediately exploded. The P-38's, which were silver, sat in the sun's rays for cover and attacked the flight. Unfortunately, the pilot misfigured the speed of the flight and crashed into the number one and two planes of one section.

Next thing, we saw the sky lit up with flames and explosions and there were parts of the aircrafts flying everywhere. When the parts landed on the ground they were all around us. One motor crashed into the mess hall entrance. We saw a seat with a parachute coming down. All rushed to the scene to help. There lay a torso of a Warrant Officer - legs and arms gone - strapped into his flight chair. What a sight. None of us will ever forget that day. Plane parts and remains of American boys lying all around us. We didn't have any appetite for chow that day.

REMINISCING - USS ALTAMAHA CVE18
August 31, 1944

by Al Vazac

Our departure from San Diego, bound for USMC Air Station at Ewa, Oahu took place on board a small carrier, USS Altamaha, with our planes on deck, and accompanied by escort vessels. Most of us tended to sleep on the decks under the wings, enjoying the beautiful nights under the stars.

Marines, being by nature curious, we were wondering especially about the ship's name, Altamaha, so we prevailed upon our hosts (the swabbies) to share their knowledge about that unusual name. They responded that the name was Indian for "Leaky Canoe", which got lots of laughs.

Actually we later discovered, it was named for the river of that name in the state of Georgia!

Altamaha She lived up to her name

By GRANT FARRIMOND
Progress Staff Writer

Sailor John Kennedy was through with the war. It was 1946. With his brand new wife, Nelliejeannee, he was traveling through Georgia after a brief stop in Jacksonville, Fla.

It was a time for the two to get reacquainted. All the fighting was done .

Kennedy had served in the second world war aboard three ships: the U.S.S. Lexington, one of the biggest war vessels at that time; the U.S.S. Langley, one of the fastest ships in the American fleet; and of course that other ship.

The one that was too small. The one that creaked and groaned at night. The one Kennedy just knew he would wind up going down with — hopefully not to Davey Jones — but down and wet none the less.

Then the sign caught his eye. A green marker flashing the name of a local stream.

The Altamaha River.

"Well doesn't that beat all," he said to himself. "I knew that ship was named after a river."

Kennedy's other ship duty was aboard the U.S.S. Altamaha, a "baby Flattop," a small class of carrier designed to carry 28 replacement planes behind the main fleet.

The couple had been driving for a while now. They stopped to rest.

He struck up conversation with some locals.

The main topic — that winding Georgia river bearing the name of his ship.

"I was on an aircraft carrier, Altamaha in the war," Kennedy said, beginning the conversation.

"That so?" one Georgia native said. "Do you have any idea what that word means in Indian?"

Mr. Kennedy became interested instantly.

"I'd sure like to know," he said.

The chatty stranger continued.

"Well, the word Altamaha means leaky canoe in Indian."

Kennedy fell to the floor laughing hysterically. Mrs. Kennedy had to help her husband off the floor. She's the only one of the two who could speak now. Tears were streaming down his face.

"At the time they were on rough water and there was this plate that would go twang, twang, twang and he had always just waited for it to break right in half," Mrs. Kennedy said. "You can obviously see why he is on the ground right now."

NAVY VETERAN JOHN KENNEDY

A ship of war is more than just fused metal to the sailors who spent time aboard. Each man has a story. Like precious cargos being hauled through tranquil seas, these stories are sometimes told.

For the men of the U.S.S. Altamaha, one theme runs through each and every remembered tale — character.

The Altamaha had a personality all its own.

The Altamaha wasn't very fast; it only averaged 18 knots and that's when the captain chose to shut down the laundry facility to create more steam. It's speed dropped down to around 13 to 14 knots when clothes were tumbling.

The ship was caught in a violent typhoon 220 miles off the coast of Luzon the Philippines in December of 1944 that capsized three destroyers and killed 778 men in the U.S. Third Fleet. It didn't sink.

The Altamaha missed mines, dodged torpedoes and faced down German attacks in the Indian Ocean. It floated many missions unescorted in the far reaches of the Pacific Ocean under moonlit skies. The Japanese never found her.

Bob Hope, Frances Langford and Jerry Colona staged a show aboard the Altamaha near Guadacanal. Many sailors said they just know some high ranking officer on the ship had a Hollywood connection — Bob Hope didn't entertain on just any ship you know.

British pilots practiced landing planes on the Altamaha off the coast of San Diego, it was occa-

ALTAMAHA SAILORS RECOVER TYPHOON DAMAGED PLANES

Please see NAVY page 2A

... Navy

(Continued From Page 1A)

sionally used for pilot training.

The Altamaha was the first aircraft carrier to experiment with rocket-assisted takeoffs, the first to land and refuel blimps and it spent time pioneering the art of hunting and sinking enemy submarines.

This canoe may have leaked, but its character never let it sink.

Two-hundred sailors who spent time on the U.S.S. Altamaha and their wives 'll be meeting this week for their ninth reunion. They will reunite in Tulsa, but come to Claremore for a tour of the museums Wednesday.

There are many stories to tell and retell. The favorite topic of conversation is their leaky canoe.

Kennedy remembers that day in Georgia when he found out what the word Altamaha meant. To him the name just fits.

"I thought it would break in half at any time," he said. "Boy, you were out there in the middle of nowhere by yourself and you would hear that twang, twang. It was just hilarious when I found out what word was. War is not all hell, I guess.

"But I'll tell you, there were a lot of guys on board that would have said 'Yeah, that's right' if they would have known what the name meant at the time."

Kennedy said there were many times when he wondered when the craft would sink. Yet, the old girl

never did.

Born in the Seattle shipyards, the Altamaha was rushed into service less than a year after the December 7, 1941 Japanese attack at Pearl Harbor, It's main assignment was to lag behind the main fleet and replenish larger carriers with planes.

Joe Vandevier, father of Claremore resident Kay Henry, was aboard the Altamaha when it was overloaded with 65 planes that were to be transported to other carriers. The rendezvous point was east of Luzon, a northern Philippine Island.

December 18, 1944. Vandevier remembers.

"Refueling at sea is usually a routine operation, but not this time," he said. "The helmsman of the tanker and I were both fighting the rudder; we couldn't hold a true course. The vessels would drift apart and then merge dangerously close. It seemed the seas were angry, the waters became too turbulent for refueling."

The Altamaha, and the rest of the Third Fleet, were in the path of a typhoon.

Soon, the ship was in 25 foot swells with winds ripping over the ship at 120 knots. Vandevier watched as plane's propellers rotated by themselves. Waves were breaking over the bow like a rushing waterfall.

The carrier was made to with-

stand only 27 and a half degree rolls when the water crashed over the deck. Vandevier said he experienced 30 degree rolls soon after the typhoon hit. The pilot house inclinometer, used to measure the ship's tilt, read 45 degrees three times during the storm's fury.

On the hangar deck, a huge crane used to lift aircraft broke loose, ramming planes and jeeps alike. Gas tanks ruptured spilling fuel onto the deck. Vandevier said he thought the crane would ram right into the side of the ship, dooming the crew.

"The captain tried reversing the engines to get out of the trough, but that proved useless," Vandevier said. "However, it did pull tons of sea water over the fantail into the elevator well creating needed ballast."

Luck was with the men of the Altamaha.

"I don't know if you can call it fate or the hand of God," Vandevier said. "Perhaps all three were at work in the Altamaha's survival. I prefer to think it was God's miracle."

Another enormous wave thundered over the ship's deck. The 45 degree turn almost capsized the vessel. It hesitated for what seemed like forever before going upright again.

Other, larger ships weren't as lucky.

"All during the afternoon I could hear the ship's radio reporting 'Man overboard, man overboard' from the ship's fleet," Vandevier said. "I remember the report of a ship disappearing from radio contact."

During the storm, the Altamaha lost 43 of her brand new fighters. But, she survived to deliver another day.

Of the three ships Mr. Kennedy served on during the war, he will remember the Altamaha the most. He wears the tattered navy blue hat with gold trim adorned with the name of his ship.

He speaks of it with pride.

He served on a battleship that measured 10 times the size of the Altamaha. He also finished his tour of duty of a ship that could outrun any Japanese destroyer in the Pacific.

But, his favorite memories don't involve the U.S.S. Lexington or U.S.S. Langley. His hat says Altamaha.

For many sailors the Altamaha may have leaked.

HOW TO GET A GOOD MEAL

by Vic Kalfus

While stationed on Oahu many of the Marines would go to the Sea Bee's chow hall to eat because their food was better than the Marine chow.

The Sea Bee's finely had to put up a large sign saying "Marines, We love you like a Brother - But we can't afford to feed you."

This comes to us from good friend, FRANKIE WALAS, (C 13th F '40-'43), of 6410 Waikiki, Bradenton, FL. Eat your hearts out:

"Do You Remember When"
Sampling Of Items From The 1941 Menu
Of
BLACK CAT CAFE
Honolulu, Hawaii

Breakfast Dishes

Hot Cakes	$ .10
Waffle	.15
Oatmeal	.15
Corn Flakes	.15
Ham, Bacon or Sausage & eggs, Buttered Toast and Hash Browns	.35
Poached eggs on toast	.30
Egg & tomato scramble	.30
Oyster omelette	.45
Hard boiled egg, pickled egg, or raw egg	.05

24-Hour Specials

Breaded Veal Cutlet	.35
Roast Turkey with dressing	.50
½ Fried Chicken with bacon	.60
Roast Pork & applesauce	.40
Swiss Steak & brown gravy	.25
Corned Beef & cabbage	.30
Spaghetti & meatballs	.25
Hot Pork or beef sandwich	.25

Steaks, Chops and other meats

Porterhouse & mushrooms	1.00
T-Bone	.60
Rib steak	.40
Hamburger .30,with onions	.35
Liver & onions .30,with bacon.	.35

Fish & Sea Foods

½ doz. Fresh Frozen Oysters, fried, stewed or raw	.35
Fried Shrimps on toast	.35
Fried Ulua, tartar sauce	.30

Salads

Fruit salad with whipped cream	.25
Crab	.50
Shrimp	.35
Potato	.15
Alligator Pear (Avocado)	.10

Cold Meats with Potato Salad

Boiled Ham	$ .35
Assorted cold cuts	.35
Pig's foot	.20
Sardines	.25

Soups

Chicken	.20
Corn Chowder	.20
Vegetable	.20
Turtle	.20

Sandwiches
(Any sandwich under .20 - on toast .05 extra) Potato salad with any sandwich .10

Black Cat Special	.20
Bacon & Egg	.20
Cold ham	.10
Bacon & tomato	.20
Hamburger	.15
Hamburger & cheese	.20
Peanut butter	.10
Club House	.50
Denver	.25
Barbecued Beef	.15
Hot dog	.10

Desserts

Strawberry shortcake with whipped cream	.20
Pies (per cut)	.10
Pie a la mode	.15
Brown bobbies	2 for .05
Ice Cream	.10
Banana Split	.25

Drinks

Buttermilk	.10
Milk (second glass .05)	.10
Postum	.10
Ovaltine	.10
Milk Shakes	.15
Malted Milks	.20
Coca Cola & other sodas	.10
with meals	.05

AFTERNOON SHOWER

by Al Vazac

While awaiting our orders at USMC Air Station at Ewa, Oahu, it was normal procedure for our engineering section to march to the mess hall for lunch in a military fashion. The buildings at the airfield where we performed our maintenance work had low pitched roofs with long overhanging eaves, approximately six feet to eight feet overhanging on all four sides, in keeping with the style in Hawaii. They were safe to walk on, as "Crazy Jack" Sauffer, metalsmith was doing. He carried what later proved to be a pail of water, which he intended for some unsuspecting member of his fighter squadron walking past on the ground. Fortunately for the targeted victim, he eluded his stalker.

While Jack cautiously peered over the edge of the roof, he misjudged and sent the contents of the bucket down over the freshly pressed uniforms of four officers who kept right on with their conversation, well aware that it had to be the work of none other than "Crazy Jack".

What became of the culprit after that incident we never knew, but our platoon, on the way to chow, went into hysterics that day!

FROM EWA TO MIDWAY

by Charlie Franzo

While transferring from Ewa, Oahu, Hawaii to Midway in a C-47(?), with forty other buddies, about two hours out of Hawaii our left engine began to fail. Master Sgt. Reeves, who stuttered when excited, went up to the pilot and said "D-D-Don't y-you t-think wa-we sh-should turn b-back?"

The pilot said, "As M/Sgt. it's my plane and I'll make the decision".

Reeves turns to go back when Al Crocetti asks, "What did the pilot say?" When Reeves told him, Crocetti ran to the center of the plane, dropped to his knees, made the sign of the cross repeatedly, and said, "Lord, I don't want to die by drowning. I don't want to die, please God, I don't care if I get shot, but I don't want to die out here in the middle of the ocean. Please God, no one will find me!"

About then the pilot, laughing, turned the plane around and flew back to Hawaii. M/Sgt. Reeves said, "Thank you."

SQUADRON FLIGHT FROM EWA, HAWAII TO MIDWAY ISLAND

by Ralph H. Heidenreich

After receiving twenty-four new SB2C-3's, Curtiss Hell Divers, our pilots began familiarization flights. During October, 1944, orders were received for the 1100-mile flight to Midway Island. Here were our pilots with new planes and only familiarization flights being advised and they must fly this 1100-mile flight over open water to an atoll, a tiny dot of land in the Pacific Ocean. One can only imagine the anticipation, as well as the apprehension the pilots and gunners were experiencing! Flight plans were delivered to Control and off they went, all twenty-four SB2C-3's to Midway. The flight was uneventful, except for pilots constantly checking their fuel gauge for reassurance. I believe all planes had wing tanks attached for an added supply, but I am not sure of this. All sections made the trip with excellent air navigation. One plane did experience a problem and Lt. Frank Lange had to land at French Frigate Shoals, a landing strip between Pearl Harbor and Midway which was operational only if the tide did not overwash the runways. Lt. Lange can write why he was forced to land. Perhaps he will relate this in another story.

As stated previously, all our SB2C's made the 1100-mile trip to Midway, completely over water, without mishap. Keep in mind that at this time we were in radar and guidance infancy. Flight crews had to rely completely on plotting courses and flying by compass. What an accomplishment our pilots made!

The entire support element flew to Midway aboard C-46's and R5C's, Navy aircraft, along with all of our support equipment. What was left behind was transported by ship.

A great arrival at Midway was celebrated by all of us. We lost no aircraft or personnel! We were ready to continue our war efforts in support of our country, the United States of America!!!

FROM EWA TO MIDWAY

by Winton Studt

This is my best recollection of an incident which occurred during the flight of twenty-four SB2C's from Ewa, Hawaii to Midway Island.

The SB2C's did not have the range to make the 1100 nautical mile trip from Ewa to Midway. An intermediate refueling stop was required.

The first leg of the flight was about 480 nautical miles from Ewa to French Frigate Shoals. French Frigate was a tiny strip just barely above sea level. The landing strip was short and narrow and it could well have been constructed by dredging rather than naturally occurring. There were very few buildings on the strip and I think personnel stationed there lived on small vessels tied up along side.

We did not do our own navigating, probably with good reason. It would have been interesting to know how we would have done using our little plotting boards. Instead we followed a C-47 lead plane.

We refueled and on the second day took off on the remaining leg to Midway. The planes joined up in some sort of formation with the C-47 as the lead plane.

The sky was overcast and the plan was for us to follow the C-47 up through the clouds. For some reason the C-47 either reduced air speed too much or turned back into part of the formation. A number of SB2C's stalled out and there was lots of scurrying around for a time.

At any rate about half the planes were no longer in formation. Someone called the flight off for the day and we returned to French Frigate.

The next day we continued the flight to Midway without further incident as I recall. Someone else may have more details on this trip.

SECTION V

MIDWAY

SECURITY AT MIDWAY ISLANDS

by Ralph H. Heidenreich

Midway Islands was something none of us expected. Two small Atolls in the middle of the Pacific Ocean. When one looked right, left, forward or back all you could see was ocean. What little land there was, was surrounded by a white coral reef, sort of making a small sound between the ocean and the land. There were two islands, Sand Island, being the largest, and Eastern Island where we were first stationed, the smallest.

After about six months, we were transferred to Sand Island, and no one knew why. In later years, we learned the move was a conservation one because we were killing too many "Gooney Birds" with our flights taking off and landing. Many times we had to clear the runways of birds so the planes would not be in jeopardy.

Our islands were protected by the 6th Marine Defense Battalion, ground troops who had been stationed there during the Battle of Midway.*** They had dug-in gun emplacements at all strategic points of the island, their anti-aircraft guns, range cards for field of fire, plus covers to protect the weaponry from elements of weather. These foot Marines worked at night; we worked during daylight hours except for our "Dawn and Dusk Patrol". Both units had a NCO (non-commissioned officer) club. Theirs was open during the day after they secured - ours at night after we secured. To this day I still do not know why I was the NCO in charge of our club. Being good Marines though, we exchanged club cards, thus giving us access to beer and "torpedo juice" twenty-four hours a day.

I became friends with Gunnery Sgt. Turner of the 6th Defense Battalion. One night he invited five or six of us to a party in one of their outpost buildings on the very end of Eastern Island. We partied, had fun, got a little drunk and careless. The entire island was on total blackout from dusk to dawn for Japanese submarines would surface occasionally and fire on us. On party night, one of our blackout shades was not fully down!! The inside lights could be seen for miles!! Naturally, the 6th Defense duty officer making his rounds spotted us, and he surprised us. We were arrested, and put on report. We six Marines were turned over to our duty officer and instructed to report at 0600 hours for Adjutant Officer call. Our Adjutant was Warrant Officer Jim Burke. (He was a friend of mine. We first met at Eagle Mountain Lake, Texas where I was in Glider Pilots training early in 1943. Jim was a corporal in supply. Later he replaced Lieutenant Witt as our Adjutant before we left Greenville). All six of us went before Gunner Burke for office hours. He read us the riot act and restricted us to our barracks for thirty days. Now where in hell could one go on Midway Island? This was a break for us but he warned if the skipper, Major Gregory, got hold of this he was sure all of us would be court-martialed!!

Upon leaving Jim Burke's office he called me aside and said, "Sergeant, if you have another party and do not invite me, you are in deep S--- trouble!!

***The Battle of Midway was early in 1942. The Japanese wanted to occupy Midway in order to have a submarine base and airfields that would enable them to attack the United States mainland. Admiral "Bull" Hawlsey, Commander-in-Chief of all Pacific forces had thought differently. Warned through military intelligence he sent our aircraft carriers, battleships, and destroyer escort ships to engage the enemy, hoping that their destination was Midway Island. He was right. We engaged them there and defeated them with great loss to their Navy, sinking their mainstay of aircraft carriers and battleships. This was the United States' greatest sea victory, one which turned the war in our favor after the devastating loss of ships and aircraft in the sneak attack on Pearl Harbor. We had avenged our dead and salvaged our honor.

VOLUME 7
NUMBER 1

Reflections of the Past and Present

FEBRUARY 1994

1994 SIXTH DEFENSE BATTALION, USMC AND DEFENDERS OF MIDWAY ISLANDS REUNION ASSOC.

History of Midway Islands

An interesting account of the history of Midway was found in a booklet authored by a Fred C. Hadden of the Hawaiian Planters Association and was listed as a second printing, dated 1941. The account is in chronological order of geology and modern history (up to 1941) of the region. The establishment of an airport at Midway by the Pan American Airlines Company in 1935 has resulted in making this American possession popular with large numbers of people who have since stopped over there en route to or from the Far East.

Midway — The Middle

If one will look at a map, he will find that Midway is in the middle of the North Pacific Ocean, located at the northwest end of the Hawaiian Island chain at 28° N latitude and 177° W longitude, approximately 1150 nautical miles northwest of Honolulu, Hawaii. The atoll consists of two islands. Sand Island is about 1.8 miles long by 1.2 miles wide covering 1,200 acres. One mile to the east is 334 acre Eastern Island. Surrounding these tiny islands is a coral reef.

Not only is this atoll located almost in the exact center of the North Pacific Ocean, but it is also halfway around the world from Greenwich, at which point our time begins.

The reef and the two islands are called Midway Islands, or simply Midway. Actually, there is a third tiny piece of land rising from the ocean between Sand and Eastern and has been named Spit Island.

Midway was first discovered July 5, 1859 by N.C. Brooks, skipper of the Hawaiian bark *Gambia*. He promptly named the atoll the Middlebrook Islands. It is recorded that a Captain William Reynolds of the *U.S.S. Lackawanna* took formal possession of the islands for the United States on August 28, 1867. He named the outer harbor after the Secretary of the Navy — Welles Harbor, and the roadstead after the Secretary of state, Seward Roads.

Continued on Page 11

History of Midway

Continued from Page 1

Distances

Distances from Midway to other parts of the world are approximately as follows:

Midway to:

Johnston Island	S.E.	1,000 miles
Honolulu	S.E.	1,300 miles
Wake	S.W.	1,200 miles
Kamchatka	N.W.	2,000 miles
Canton Island	S.	2,200 miles
Aleutian Islands	N.	1,600 miles
San Francisco	E.N.E.	3,200 miles
New Guinea	W.S.W.	3,400 miles
Alaska	N.N.E.	2,000 miles
Shanghai	W.	3,600 miles
Samoa	S.	2,800 miles
Australia	S.W.	3,800 miles
Japan	N.W.	2,600 miles

Sand Island, the larger of the two islands in the south side of the lagoon, was colonized in 1902 by the Commercial Pacific Cable Company. At that time, there was no vegetation on Sand Island — it was nothing but a blinding glare of white, shifting sand, inhabited only by several million sea birds. However, the other island in the lagoon, now called Eastern Island, was even at that time fairly well covered by Scaevola, wild grasses, and Boerhavia. The roots of Boerhavia furnished castaways on Midway their only vegetable food, and it very possibly prevented death from scurvy.

Many passengers passing through Midway ask: "How old is Midway?" Geologically speaking, the atoll is probably very old, possibly 100,000 years or more — perhaps millions of years old. There is no way at present to determine how old it is. However, the atoll is a coral and sand platform resting upon what must be a very old volcanic mountain top, with the living and dead coral exposed in a ring at the outer edge of the reef in a somewhat circular barrier, which breaks the force of the giant waves from the open sea. Waves inside the lagoon are rarely more than two or three feet high. However, great waves from 20 to 30 feet high often break on the outer reef during winter months in stormy weather. As they break on the reef the spray sometimes flies upwards for from 50 to 100 feet.

The reef was very likely formed as follows: a million years ago, or more, lava began to erupt from a weak place in the earth's crust on the bottom of the ocean. As more and more lava poured out, it built up a great volcanic cone that may have emerged from the sea to a height of several hundred or even several thousand feet above sea level. From sea level to the bottom of the ocean at this point is about 12,000 feet or well over 2 miles. The small part of this volcanic mountain which was exposed above the sea was worn down by the action of waves, or perhaps by the great ice cap that may have moved this far south during the ice age (possibly 1,000,000 years ago). The land was worn down to, or even a little below, sea level at that time. Eventually, the ice cap melted, slowly raising the sea level as the ice disappeared. Then both coral building animals and plants began to grow on the submerged mountain top, until the lava was buried under hundreds of feet or coral rock. We do not know how far down we would have to drill before the laval rock would be reached. At first, the coral probably formed more or less uniformly on the flat-topped lava rock. Later, it grew more rapidly on the outer edges of the reef, and thus built up a ring of coral. Then the sea subsided a little so that this outer ring of coral was exposed above the surface of the sea, as it is now, leaving an irregular shallow lagoon inside the reef. The deepest water inside the lagoon is only 60 feet, and the average depth is about 8 feet.

Then, the action of waves and wind built up the small island of broken coral, shells and sand, which is now called Eastern Island. Later on, under somewhat different conditions, another island was formed of sand only. This is now called Sand Island and has been colonized by the Cable Company and by Pan American Airways.

Eastern Island, being the older island, has had vegetation on it for hundreds of years. Because the island is constructed of coarse pieces of broken-up coral, shells, gravel, and coarse sand, it is very porous, and the water there is quite brackish, containing much salt from mixture with sea water. However, donkeys that were turned loose on Eastern Island managed to survive by going down to the edge of the beach, where they pawed holes in the sand and drank the water which trickled out into these holes. This is a mixture of rainwater and a little sea water; brackish, but just barely sweet enough to support life.

In 1902, when the Cable Company first started operations at Midway, Sand Island was a level waste of wind-blown, glaring sand, with only a very few bunches of grass, one or two small Scaevola bushes, and a few Boerhavia vines growing in widely scattered locations. There was one large sand dune about 30 feet high where the Cable Company light is now situated, and the rest of the island was only a few feet above sea level. The Cable Company planted San Francisco grass. *Ammophilia arenaria,* and hundreds of ironwood trees around their compound. After a few years, the trees were large enough to protect the rest of the north end of the Island from the terrific wind storms which come intermittently throughout the winter months. This allowed the San Francisco grass, Scaevola, and Boerhavia to spread rapidly, so that 20 years later, sand dunes 10 feet high had formed around the island. Every place a Scaevola bush had got a good start, it formed a sand dune as the sand accumulated in and around it. As the sand filled in, the bush kept growing, and more sand was collected among the branches, so that now some of the dunes are 30 to 35 feet high, with just the tops of the bushes appearing above the sand.

Because sand is finer on Sand Island, it holds rain water better than Eastern Island, and consequently, the ground water on Sand Island is only slightly brackish. This almost-fresh water is held up in the island by pressure from the sea water, which is denser or heavier. It has only a slightly salty taste, but does have a rotten egg odor — due to the hydrogen sulfide which comes from the millions of eggs that broke or rotted on the island, and also from bird guano, and the remains of the millions of birds that have died there. Many thousands of birds die every year, either from disease or from starvation. Flies breed in these dead birds, and at various times of the year, they are very bothersome. Small white crabs that live in holes in the sand all over the island, also eat the dead birds.

Shipwrecks at Midway

For some strange reason, Midway has acted as a magnet, attracting ships to it and then wrecking them. More ships have been wrecked on Midway than on any other leeward island of the Hawaiian group.

Continued on Page 12

History of Midway Islands
Continued from Page 11

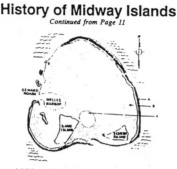

Fig 1. Map of Midway Islands prior to improvements. A: Coral reef, mostly submerged; B: Shallow water in lagoon; C: Deep water in lagoon.

The *General Siegel* with Captain Jacobsen in charge, was wrecked at Midway during a storm on November 16, 1886. Immediately, many weird things began to happen. First, one of the sailors, named Latkin, had his hand blown off while fishing with dynamite, and a few days later died complaining of great pain in his stomach. Another sailor, named Brown, accused the captain of poisoning Larkin. Then Brown and Captain Jacobsen went over to Eastern Island, but the captain returned to sand Island alone, stating that Brown has accidentally killed himself.

Jorgensen, another sailor, then went with the captain and a German boy to Eastern Island, and the captain showed them where he had buried Brown. The captain stood by indifferently while they dug up Brown's body — and found a bullet hole in the back of his head!

Several days later, the captain and Jorgensen went again to Eastern Island, and Jorgensen returned alone to Sand Island, saying the captain had disappeared! The captain was never seen again.

Jorgensen's shipmates outfitted a boat which had drifted from the wreck of the *Dunnottar Castle* on Kure or Ocean Island, 60 miles northwest of Midway, and sailed for the Marshall islands, leaving Jorgensen marooned and alone on Midway. They had accused him of killing the captain and were afraid to take him with them. He remained alone on Midway for nearly a year, until the *Wandering Minstrel* arrived.

On February 8, 1888, the *Wandering Minstrel,* commanded by Captain F.D. Walker, was wrecked in Welles Harbor — all hands, including Captain Walker's wife and three sons got to shore safely in small boats.

On October 13, 1888 (Saturday), John Cameron, Adolph Jorgensen, and a Chinese boy named Moses, left Midway in a small boat. On November 25, 1888, after a voyage of 43 days, they landed at Mille Island, 1540 miles from Midway.

According to Mr. Munro, there were no gooneys, boobies, or bosun birds on Sand Island at the time (1891), and only one or two small colonies of sooty terns were nesting at the other end of the island. Apparently, all of the gooneys, bosun birds, and moaning birds had been eaten by the castaways!

The sloop *Helene* was wrecked on Sand Island during a northwest storm (date unknown); she brought to Midway the crew of the bark *Kellogg,* which had been wrecked on Dowsett Reef.

Saved By a Toe

About two o'clock one morning in December, 1903, the schooner *Julia Whalem* struck the north rim of the reef "bow on." The lifeboat was lowered and the crew scrambled into it. They discovered they had no oars, so they climbed back aboard the schooner to look for some, but none could be found. The only thing they could find to use as oars were brooms, and these were used to row around the reef into Welles Harbor, and to shore at the Cable Company dock. Not only were there no oars, but the boat started to fill with water and sink. They then discovered that there was no plug for the drain hole in the bottom of the boat. Happily, they found that one of the "kanaka" sailors had a toe big enough to satisfactorily plug the hole and this saved the day. The ship broke up and sank two hours after striking the reef.

The Anchor on the Southeast Reef

On Christmas Eve, 1906, the bark *Carlton* went aground, "bow on" on the southeast reef. Apparently, they threw the anchor overboard in order to hold the ship on the reef and keep it from sliding off backwards and sinking into deep water. The anchor is still there, and shows plainly in calm weather. The captain and crew took to the boats, and rowed around the reef and into Welles Harbor to the Cable Company dock. Three trips were made, each time salvaging as much cargo as they could. A few days later, a southwest storm came up and on New Year's Day, the ship broke in two and was demolished.

According to A.R. Tinker, a Cable Company employee, at that time, there were no ironwood trees on the island, and very little plant life of any kind, so the wreck could be plainly seen from the second floor of their quarters at the Cable Company. The ironwood trees were planted in 1907. In 1940, 33 years later, the trees were from 60 to 70 feet high.

The Commercial Pacific Cable Company

In order to maintain and operate a submarine cable across the Pacific it was necessary to establish a relay station at Midway.

In 1902, the Cable Company landed on Midway and started the constrtction of their compound at Sand island. All of the material and equipment had to be brought ashore in whaleboats and lighters. It was a long haul from Seward Roads or Welles Harbor in to shore, or in through the treacherous S-shaped, small-boat channel in the south rim of the atoll. In those days, everything had to be moved by man power — it was really tough.

However, they did build substantial steel and concrete buildings, water towers, windmills, a very large concrete cistern for fresh water storage, a steam ice plant, a dock, and everything needed for operating the cable and for the comfort of the men stationed there.

Four times a year, for 15 years, 150 tons of soil were brought to Midway, after that 2-1/2 tons were brought in on each supply ship. It is estimated that over 9000 tons of soil were imported for use in the three-acre vegetable garden, and to scatter around on the sand for lawns to keep the sand from blowing out from under and around the buildings.

San Francisco grass and hundreds of ironwood trees were planted for protection from the winter storms. They now have a little paradise of their own, with ducks, chickens, turkeys, pigs and cows. The vegetable garden supplies them with fresh vegetables after the supply brought in once every three months

Continued on Page 13

History of Midway Islands
Continued from Page 12

runs out. Most of the men stay for a year or two — some stay longer.

Only the chief and his assistant could have their wives on Midway. Often for many months at a time, there was only one woman on the islands; at other times, there were no women there. The inhabitants led a calm and peaceful life, disturbed only by a flurry when the supply ship arrived.

Pan American Airways
In 1935, the first expedition of the P.A.A. arrived at Midway and began to "dig in." They, too, had all the difficulties of unloading equipment and building materials from the ship on to lighters which had to be towed to shore, and then unloaded and the materials reloaded onto sleds which were hauled up to position by a Diesel caterpillar. The "cat" has moved many thousands of tons of cargo — all the building materials, and thousands of drums of gasoline, each weighing about 450 pounds. It is still running.

The P.A.A. set up quarters for the men, a fine hotel for passengers, a power plant consisting of three large Diesel motors and generators, two windmills with tower tanks, and 20 1000-gallon steel tanks for the storage of rain water caught on the roofs of the buildings.

Thus, a modern little town was set up within seven or eight months' time, with electricity, running hot and cold water (sun heater), modern plumbing and nearly all of the comforts of home.

Instead of waiting three months to hear from home, the Cable Company personnel received mail once a week, and how they complained if the plane was delayed a few days by weather. It is amazing how much cargo besides mail and passengers is brought to the island on the planes.

On nearly every ship, hundreds of pounds of fresh milk and cream, eggs, vegetables, fruit and local express are unloaded at Midway and Wake, and even Guam. Once a week, the plane also brings a new "movie" for our entertainment. Two dozen potted palms, each weighing 20 to 30 pounds, were brought here by air.

Grass and ornamental plants supplied by the Hawaiian Sugar Planters' Association have been planted around the hotel, as well as trees for protection from strong winter wings. Ironwood trees planted four years ago are now from 25 to 30 feet high.

Only the "old timers" who saw the place as it was at first can now appreciate all of the work that has been done here.

Chronological Account of the History of Midway Island

July 5, 1859 (Discovery Day). As previously stated, the Midway Islands were discovered by Captain N.C. Brooks of the Hawaiian bark *Gambia*. Captain Brooks took possession in the name of the United States of North America under the Guano Islands Act passed by Congress in 1856. He named his discovery the Middlebrook Islands.

August 28, 1867 (Annexation Day). Captain William Reynolds, USN, in command of the U.S. Steamship *Lackawana*, took formal possession of Brook Island and reefs (Midway Islands) for the United States. This was the first island annexed to the United States beyond its shores. Captain Rey-

nolds named the outer harbor after the incumbent Secretary of the Navy — Welles Harbor, and the roadstead after the Secretary of State, Seward Roads.

November 16, 1886. The schooner *General Siegel* was shipwrecked at Midway during a storm.

February 3, 1888. The British bark *Wandering Minstrel* was shipwrecked in Welles Harbor during a storm. Mrs. Walker, wife of F.D. Walker, master of the *Wandering Minstrel*, was the first woman to land on Midway. Shipwrecked with her husband and sons, all were rescued by the schooner *Norma* of Honolulu, Charles Johnson, master, on March 26, 1889.

January 20, 1903 (Naval Administration Day). Due to recurring complaints of Japanese squatters and poachers being found on Midway Island, President Theodore Roosevelt issued the following Executive Order: "Such public lands as may exist on the Midway Islands, Hawaiian group, between the parallels of 28°05' and 28°25" north latitude and between the meridians of 177°10' and 177°30' west longitude, are hereby placed under the jurisdiction and control of the Navy Department."

April 29, 1903. Commercial Pacific Cable Company's first contingent arrived on Midway Islands.

June 3, 1903. Lt. Cdr. Hugh Rodman, USN, commanding the *USS Iriquois*, ejected Japanese poachers and squatters and appointed Mr. B.W. Colley of the Cable Company as Naval custodian of the islands, emphasizing especially that he should prevent "the wanton destruction of birds that breed at Midway, and not let them be disturbed or killed except for purposes of food supply." Mr. Colley was also appointed justice of the peace.

July 4, 1903. First "round the world" cable message was sent by President Theodore Roosevelt. Midway was a relay station.

May 1904. U.S. Marine Corps garrison of 20 Marines was established on Midway Island.

May 13, 1906. Dr. Miller, USN, died at 5:20 a.m. on Midway and was buried there. This was the first Naval death recorded on Midway.

1908. Marine Detachment was ordered away from Midway Islands.

1921. U.S. Navy commenced using Midway Islands as a rendezvous for Naval vessels on the East-West Pacific runs. Washington Naval Treaty (1921 - 22) forbade fortifying Midway through commercial enterprises were authorized.

1923. Cable Company blasted an entrance for the cable between Sand and Eastern islands in the south reef.

1924. Midway Islands were investigated by Commander Rodgers of the *USS Pelican* as a seaplane base. Later in the same year, Midway Islands were used as a rendezvous by the *USS Seagull* and eight submarines.

1934. Japan denounced the Washington Treaty (1922). Naval armament race was on.

April 12, 1935 (PAA Day). Pan American Airways ship *North Haven* arrived at Midway to set up a PAA airbase. Weekly (seaplane) clipper service followed soon after.

May 1935. Fleet maneuvers conducted off Midway. Advance base was established and amphibious operations were carried out.

May 19, 1938. *USS Oglala* and *USS Beaver* arrived at Midway with men and materials of the Hawaiian Dredging Co. to dredge a channel for seagoing ships.

Continued on Page 14

History of Midway Islands

Continued from Page 13

March 4, 1940. *USS Swan,* a mine sweeper type aircraft tender, entered Midway lagoon by the new channel in the south reef.

March 27, 1940. *USS Sirius* arrived with men and materials for the construction of a Naval Air Station. Arrival of Lieutenant D.B. Ventries, USN, Naval representative in charge of the project, automatically relieved Cable Company superintendent of Naval custody of Midway Islands.

June 1940. Marine Garrison returned to Midway Islands. By February of 1941, the garrison, under command of Lt. Col. Pepper, was 850 strong.

July 18, 1940. Arrival of part of U.S. fleet for a surprise visit brought attention to the splendid results of the Cable Company's planting program over about 1/6 of Sand Island. Under the Pacific Naval Air Base program, Midway began to fulfill its destiny as a strategic base in the Pacific.

August 1, 1941. U.S. Naval Air Station Midway Islands, commissioned under the command of Commander Cyril T. Simard, U.S. Navy.

August 11, 1941. Advance parts of 6th Def. Bn. arrived at Midway to start the relief of the 3rd Def. Bn.

September 11, 1941. Main body of 6th Def. Bn., 750 strong, arrive on the *USS Wharton* to relieve the 3rd Def. Bn.

November 9, 1941. Pan American Clipper arrived en route to Washington with Japanese Ambassador Kurusu and his secretary, Yuki. Departed November 12 for the Peace Conference.

December 7, 1941 (0630). Received notice of commencement of Japanese-U.S. hostilities.

December 7, 1941 (2135) WAR WITH JAPAN. Midway Islands was bombarded by a Japanese raiding force of two destroyers. Return fire from defense batteries struck the Japanese ships and forced retirement under a smoke screen. Some damage to facilities on Midway Island was sustained and the following were killed by the Japanese bombardment: 1st Lt. George H. Cannon, USMC; Ens. Donald J. Kraker, USNR; Pfc. Elmer R. Morrell, USMC; and F 2/C Ralph E. Tuttle, USN. Seaplane hanger and the hospital were hit and burned (the latter, completely). Reinforcements for Midway were rushed from Hawaii.

June 3, 4, 5, 1942. A major invasion effort was set up by Japan to take Midway. This huge task force was met by carrier- and Midway-based aircraft far at sea. On June 4, Midway's Marine fighters intercepted the Japanese bombers and inflicted heavy damage, cutting down much of the Japanese bombing attack, but in their turn, they took heavy losses from the supporting Japanese Zero fighters. The scale of victory was on the Marine side by count of kills. The Japanese bombing attack severely damaged almost all of the above-ground facilities at Midway. While the Marine fighters defended Midway and Midway Army's B-26 and B-17 bombers, the Midway Navy's TBFs, and the Midway Marines' SBDs dive-bombing produced hits on an enemy carrier, but lost half their force to enemy fighters. All losses were more than made up for by the U.S. Navy carrier squadrons. Boring in from all directions, the carrier planes smashed Japan's mighty Naval Air Force. Sinking most of the Japanese carriers, the U.S. carrier aircraft seized complete control in the air. The Japanese Navy never fully recovered from this terrible air loss.

With control of the air completely lost, the Japanese invasion force turned away in defeat and raced for home. The value of Midway as a strategic base was brought to world notice.

By post-war analysis of Japanese war records and interrogations of High Command officers of the Japanese Navy, the Battle of Midway was determined to be the turning point of the war — in favor of the United States.

America's faith in U.S. Naval aviation, Navy and Marine, the finest in the world, was vindicated.

After the battle was over, Mr. Stroupe, the Cable Company's superintendent, offered the Cable Company buildings for use as a hospital to replace the one bombed out by the Japanese. His offer was accepted.

Upon the recommendation of the commanding officer of the Naval Air station, Sand Island was developed as an air field.

July 15, 1942 (Submarine Day). U.S. Submarine Base at Midway Islands was established under command of Commander W.V. O'Regan, USN.

July 29, 1942. Naval Operating Base, Midway Islands, was established border of the secretary of the navy. The commanding office of NAS was ordered to additional duty as commander, Naval Operating Base, which embraced all attached activities on Midway Islands.

August 18, 1942. Captain H.M. Martin, USN, relieved Commander Simard as commanding officer of the Naval Air Station, Midway Islands.

January 1, 1943. Sand Island landing field, composing three landing strips, was completed and ready for use.

August 9, 1943. Commodore G.E. Short, USN, relieved Captain H.M. Martin, USN, as commander of Naval Operating Base, Midway Islands. The war progressed westward and Midway fell into a sad state of disrepair. Maintenance of the equipment took second place to construction of new facilities.

August 1944. Extensions to Sand Island's landing strips were completed, and large land-plane activity shifted from Eastern to Sand Island.

September 16, 1944. Commodore Gail Morgan, USN, relieved Commodore G.E. Short, USN, as commander, Naval Operating Base, Midway Islands. Regulations for the administration of the Naval Operating Base were drawn up. A sand stabilization program was set up. Planting of shrubs, grass and trees commenced.

October, 1944. Naval Air Transport Service was set up on Sand Island.

1945. During this period, air activity on Eastern Island began to slow up and a gradual shift to Sand Island took place. During the period subsequent to July 29, 1942, the submarine base came to its peak of utility. War patrols out of Midway began to take tolls on Japanese shipping, and the Navy's roll up to westward of the Japanese Sea Empire was speeded to its victorious end.

Motor torpedo squadrons performed faithfully in anti-submarine patrols and participated in the Battle of Midway. They returned to Pearl Harbor in May of 1945.

August 14, 1945. Japan surrenders. Soon after came the fulfillment of the Navy's promise to a loyal nation — speedy demobilization.

October 1, 1993. It has been officially announced that except for wildlife operations, Midway will be completely closed down as soon as closure activities are completed.

Next issue will deal with wildlife and seabirds on Midway.

THE HISTORY OF MIDWAY ISLAND

5 July 1859 (Discovery Day)	The Midway Islands were discovered by Captain N. C. Brooks of the Hawaiian bark GAMBIA. Captain Brooks took possession in the name of the United States of North America under the Guano Islands Act passed by Congress in 1856. He named his discovery the Middlebrook Islands.
28 Aug. 1867 ·(Annexation Day)	Captain William Reynolds, USN, in command of the U.S. Steam-ship, LACKAWANA, took formal, possession of Brook Island and reefs (Midway Islands) for the United States. This was the first island annexed to the United States beyond its shores. Captain Reynolds named the outer harbor after the incumbent Secretary of the Navy— Welles Harbor, and the roadstead after the Secretary of State, Seward Roads.
16 Nov. 1886	The schooner GENERAL SIEGEL was shipwrecked at Midway during a storm.
3 Feb 1888	The British bark WANDERING MINSTREL was shipwrecked in Welles Harbor during a storm.
	Mrs. Walker, wife of F.D.-Walker, Master of the WANDERING MINSTREL was the first woman to land on Midway. Shipwrecked with her husband and sons, all were rescued by the Schooner NORMA of Honolulu, Charles Johnson, Master, on 26 March 1889.
20 Jan. 1903 (Naval Admini- istration Day)	Due to recurring complaints of Japanese squatters and poach-ers being found on Midway Island, President Theodore Roose-velt issued the following Executive Order: "Such public lands as may exist on the Midway Islands, Hawaiian group, between the parallels of 28°05' and 28°25" North latitude and between the meridians of 177° 10' and 177° 30' West longitude, are hereby placed under the jurisdiction and control of the Navy Department."
29 April 1903	Commercial Pacific Cable Company's first contingent arrived on Midway Island.
3 June 1903	Lt Cdr. Hugh Rodman, USN, commanding the USS IRIQUOIS, ejected Japanese poachers and squatters and appointed Mr. B.W. Colley of the Cable Company as Naval Custodian of the Islands empha-sizing especially that he should prevent "the wanton destruc-tion of birds that breeds at Midway, and not let them be dis-turbed or killed except for purposes of food supply." Mr. Colley was also appointed Justice of the Peace.
4 July 1903	First "round the world" cable message was sent by President Theodore Roosevelt. Midway was a relay station.
May 1904	U.S. Marine Corps garrison of 20 Marines was established on Midway Island.

13 May 1906 — Dr. Miller, USN, died at 5:20 a.m. on Midway and was buried there. This was the first Naval death recorded on Midway:

1908 — Marine Detachment was ordered away from Midway Islands.

1921 — U.S. Navy commenced using Midway Islands as a rendezvous for naval vessels on the East-West Pacific runs. Washington Naval Treaty (1921-22) forbade fortifying Midway through commercial enterprises were authorized.

1923 — Cable Company blasted an entrance for the cable between Sand and Eastern Islands in the south reef.

1924 — Midway Islands were investigated by Commander Rodgers of the USS PELICAN as a seaplane base. Later in the same year Midway Islands were used as a rendezvous by the USS SEAGULL and eight submarines.

1934 — Japan denounced the Washington Treaty (1922). Naval armament race was on.

12 April 1935 (PAA Day) — Pan American Airways ship NORTH HAVEN arrived at Midway to set up a PAA airbase. Weekly (seaplane) clipper service followed soon after.

May 1935 — Fleet maneuvers conducted off Midway. Advance base was established and amphibious operations were carried out.

19 May 1938 — USS OGLALA and USS BEAVER arrived at Midway with men and materials of the Hawaiian Dredging Co. to dredge a channel for seagoing ships.

4 March 1940 — USS SWAN, a mine sweeper type aircraft tender, entered Midway lagoon by the new channel in the south reef.

27 March 1940 — USS SIRIUS arrived with men and materials for the construction of a Naval Air Station. Arrival of Lieutenant D.B. Ventries, USN, Naval representative in charge of the project, automatically relieved Cable Company superintendent of Naval custody of Midway Islands.

June 1940 — Marine Garrison returned to Midway Islands. By February of 1941 the garrison, under command of Lt. Col. Pepper, was 850 strong.

18 July 1940 — Arrival of part of U.S. Fleet for a surprise visit brought attention to the splendid results of the Cable Company's planting program over about 1/6 of Sand Island. Under the Pacific Naval Air Base program Midway began to fulfill its destiny as a strategic base in the Pacific.

1 August 1941 — U. S. Naval Air Station Midway Islands, commissioned under the command of Commander Cyril T. Simard, U.S. Navy.

9 November 1941   Pan American Clipper arrived enroute to Washington with Japanese
                     Ambassador Kurusu and his secretary, Yuki. Departed 12 November
                     for the Peace Conference

(0630)
7 December 1941   Received notice of commencement of Japanese-U.S. hostilities.

7 December 1941   Midway Island was bombarded by a Japanese raiding force of
    (2135)   (estimated) two cruisers and two destroyers. Return fire from
WAR WITH JAPAN   defense batteries struck the Japanese ships and forced retire-
                     ment under a smoke screen. Some damage to facilities on Midway
                     Island was sustained and the following were killed by the
                     Japanese bombardment:

                              1st Lt. George H. Cannon, USMC
                              Ens. Donald J. Kraker, USNR
                              Pfc. Elmer R. Morrell, USMC
                              F 2/C Ralph E. Tuttle, USN

                     Seaplane hanger and the hospital were hit and burned (the latter,
                     completely). Reinforcements for Midway were rushed from Hawaii.

3,4,5 June 1942   A major invasion effort was set up by Japan to take Midway. This
                     huge task force was met by carrier and Midway based aircraft far
                     at sea. On 4 June, Midway's Marine fighters intercepted the
                     Japanese bombers and inflicted heavy damage cutting down much of
                     the Japanese bombing attack, but in their turn they took heavy
                     losses from the supporting Japanese Zero fighters. The scale of
                     victory was on the Marine side by count of kills. The Japanese
                     bombing attack severely damaged almost all the above-ground
                     facilities at Midway. While the Marine fighters defended Midway
                     and Midway Army's B-26 and B-17 bombers, the Midway Navy's TBF's,
                     and the Midway Marines SBD's dive bombing produced hits on an
                     enemy carrier but lost half their force to enemy fighters. All
                     losses were more than made up for by the U.S Navy carrier
                     squadrons. Boring in from all directions the carrier planes
                     smashed Japan's mighty Naval Air Force. Sinking most of the
                     Japanese carriers the U.S. carrier aircraft seized complete con-
                     trol in the air. The Japanese Navy never fully recovered from
                     this terrible air loss. With control of the air completely lost,
                     the Japanese invasion force turned away in defeat and raced for
                     home. The value of Midway as a strategic base was brought to
                     world notice.

                     By post war analysis of Japanese war records and interrogations
                     of High Command officers of the Japanese Navy, the Battle of
                     Midway was determined to be the turning point of the war- in
                     favor of the United States.

                     America's faith in U. S. Naval aviation, Navy and Marine, the
                     finest in the world, was vindicated.

3,4,5 June 1942   After the battle was over, Mr. Stroupe, the Cable Company's super-
                    intendent, offered the Cable Company buildings for use as a hos-
                    pital to replace the one bombed out by the Japanese. His offer
                    was accepted.

                    Upon the recommendation of the Commanding Officer of the Naval
                    Air Station, Sand Island was developed as an air field.

15 July 1942   U. S. Submarine Base at Midway Islands was established under
(Submarine Day)   command of Commander W. V. O'Regan, USN.

29 July 1942   Naval Operating Base, Midway Islands, was established by order
                    of the Secretary of the Navy. The Commanding Officer of N.A.S.
                    was ordered to additional duty as Commander, Naval Operating
                    Base which embraces all attached activities on Midway Islands.

18 August 1942   Captain H. M. Martin, USN, relieved Commander Simard as Command-
                    ing Officer of the Naval Air Station, Midway Islands.

1 January 1943   Sand Island landing field, composing three landing strips, was
                    completed and ready for use.

9 August 1943   Commodore G. E. Short, USN, relieved Captain H. M. Martin, USN,
                    as Commander of Naval Operating Base, Midway Island.

                    The war progressed westward and Midway fell into a sad state of
                    disrepair. Maintenance of the equipment took second place to
                    construction of new facilities.

August 1944   Extensions to Sand Islands landing strips were completed, and
                    large landplane activity shifted from Eastern to Sand Island.

16 Sept. 1944   Commodore Gail Morgan, USN, relieved Commodore G. E. Short,
                    USN, as Commander Naval Operating Base, Midway Islands. Regu-
                    lations for the administration of the Naval Operating Base
                    were drawn up. A sand stabilization program was set up. Plant-
                    ing of shrubs, grass and trees commenced.

October 1944   Naval Air Transport Service was set up on Sand Island.

1945   During this period air activity on Eastern Island began to
                    slow up and a gradual shift to Sand Island took place. During
                    the period subsequent to 29 July 1942 the Submarine Base came
                    to its peak of utility. War patrols out of Midway began to
                    take tolls on Japanese shipping and the Navy's roll up to
                    westward of the Japanese Sea Empire was speeded to its
                    victorious end.

                    Motor torpedo squadrons performed faithfully in anti-submarine
                    patrols and participated in the Battle of Midway. They re-
                    turned to Pearl Harbor in May of 1945.

14 August 1945   Japan surrenders. Soon after came the fulfillment of the
                    Navy's promise to a loyal nation- speedy demobilization.

MIDWAY AT MIDWAY

by Ralph H. Heidenreich

Being stationed at Eastern Island, we had our entire squadron entrenched in assigned revetments, Quonset huts, etc. A small building was designated as the Officer's Club and another one as the Senior NCO Club. I had no association with the workings of the Officer's Club, but I was the NCO in charge of the NCO Club.

After months of operation, we found ourselves a little more than solvent, so with the funds the Board decided to invest in beer when it was available. When a new shipment of Narraganset Beer became available at Sand Island, off I went on a barge, bought four hundred cases for the NCO Club, and returned to Eastern Island. In Marine fashion, only then did I learn we were moving over to Sand Island in April!!

With the South Pacific war now in our favor, Japan retreating, and our forces penetrating the entire Pacific, things became somewhat less formal. I remember being called for a conference with Major Gregory. "Sergeant, what kind of money do you have in the NCO account?" I told him the amount. He then advised me we had to spend it all or turn it over to the government, which was regulations. With our funds, plus three hundred fifty cases of beer (fifty cases having been already consumed by the NCO's), he decided we would have an outing for the entire unit.

A softball game was planned with officers playing the enlisted men. It was decided that the officers would also cook hot dogs and hamburgers to go along with the NCO beer. At the conclusion of our Midway Show, sports event, and games of chance, I recall our Marines going to their bivouac areas with cases of beer on their shoulders. No one got into trouble. Everyone had had a great time.

After our funds were expended I used to watch Pfc. Russell Zurface make trips to the stacked cases of beer. I often wondered how many trips he made!!! For the next two months Russell was observed walking to the motor section every morning with a ten quart bucket filled with ice and beer. Lord knew where he got the ice! After all he was a Marine, and as everyone knows, Marines appropriate when the need arises!!!

Midway at Midway was successful for both officers and enlisted personnel. We had had a great time!! Still, we never jeopardized respect for each other as to our job assignments. Nor did we forget our major concern, defeating Japan!!!

MIDWAY STILL AMERICA'S FIRST LINE OF DEFENSE IN THE PACIFIC

Letter to the Folks at Home
written by Walter LeTendre

Midway, October 11, 1944

About two and a half years ago Midway Island and the surrounding waters was the scene of one of history's crucial battles.

Our Pacific front has moved westward since that time - in the Southwest Pacific, the Solomons, the Central Pacific, and through the Aleutians. But, in this area the front is just where it was two years ago - at Midway. Between here and Japan itself there is nothing but 2,600 miles of ocean.

American Marine and Navy forces stationed here have been on the alert all that time ready to throw them back again should they try to retake it.

Sidelights on the activities here:

The editor of the local daily paper, "The Midway Mirror," calls it "the most westerly daily newspaper printed in the world." He points out too, that if we were sixty miles farther west we'd be over the date line, and be the most easterly paper. That gives you some idea of where we are - west of everything and east of nowhere.

The closest land areas are the Aleutians, 1,600 miles to the north; Wake, 1,200 miles to the southwest; Johnston, 1,000 miles to the southeast; and Hawaii, approximately 1,000 miles eastward.

"The Midway Mirror" is published almost entirely by machinery improvised from war materials. The typographic casting box for instance was made from plates taken off a gasoline tank bombed by the Japs.

There is also a radio station here, a two-watter with a range of five or six miles. From six to ten every night the men can tune in and get re-broadcasts from the States, recordings and local news, and variety programs. Most radios can't get other stations.

The waters around Midway offer some of the richest fishing found anywhere. Recent catches have included a 222-pound tuna, a 93-pound striped marlin, a 100-pound blue marlin, and a 1,200-pound shark. Twenty-seven men are assigned to the permanent fishing detail, to augment the food supply for the local mess halls. Just the other day, a small boat brought in 447 pounds of tuna. Many men are learning to spear fish for the first time. Wearing flippers on their feet, and goggles over their eyes, and armed with a spear, they dive under the reefs and come up with aluus, moi, langostas, and other strange Pacific species.

Marine flyers on Midway are frequently bothered by birds that fly into their props and wings. There are more than a million birds here and the total droppings is so great that it affects the drinking water - giving a slightly brackish taste. When one leaves the island he notices that an unpleasant bird odor, given off by the thousands of broken eggs lying on Midway, clings to his clothes for several days.

Favorite birds are the Goonies. They bow and "talk" to the Marines and even put on dances for them. Most of the Goonies leave Midway in the early summer and don't return until around November. No one as far as is known here, has ever figured out where they go during this time.

Flies on Midway get so stuffed from feeding on the broken bird eggs that they become dopey. When they light on your arm they prefer death under the hand rather than to be frightened away.

Midway is one big blinding white beach. A newcomer must be careful or he will get a bad burn in an hour or two. Most men wear sun glasses while the sun is up to protect their eyes.

One of the tough problems here is to prevent the sand from blowing away from the pill-boxes. Fifteen horticultural experts are experimenting with plants in an effort to produce one that will grow fast and keep sand from drifting. Thousands of tons of dirt have been imported from Hawaii for the islands vegetable gardens and grass plots.

Hay has to be imported, too, for the three cows; one cow, one bull, and one calf on Midway. The cows provide fresh milk for the hospital patients.

Prized souvenirs among Marines here are colored fishing balls which the Japs use on their nets in place of corks. The balls float in from Japanese waters.

Where In the World Is Midway Island?

Excerpted from a recent travelog

Upon looking at a map, you will notice that Midway is in the middle of the North Pacific Ocean, and is also halfway around the world from Greenwich, England. Midway is about 300 miles north, and 900 miles west of Honolulu, T.H. It is not in the tropics, nor is it a "South Seas Island." However, it does have semi-tropical climate due to the effect of the warm water Japanese current which flows north of the island.

Midway is 3200 miles west of San Francisco, 3600 miles east of Shanghai, and 3800 miles north of Australia. Although discovered in 1859 by Captain N.C. Brooks, no permanent settlement was established until 1902, when Commercial Pacific Cable Company occupied Sand Island, the larger of the two, enclosed by a circular reef. Eastern Island, the smallest, was well grown with the morning glory, scaevola, and grasses, while Sand Island was a barren waste of ground coral.

The climate is considered to be ideal by the natives. To give you a better picture of our climate, a few statistics are as follows:

The rainy season is between mid-November and the end of March.

Average rainfall for the rainy season is 4 inches per month.

Average rainfall during the dry season is .40 inches per month.

Average winter temperature is 67 degrees F.

Low winter temperature is 52 degrees.

Average summer temperature is 78 degrees.

High summer temperature is 85 degrees.

During the months of July, August, and September, the relative humidity is extremely high, but fresh winds blow steadily during most of the year and keep the island quite comfortable.

Perhaps one of Midway's most outstanding features is its bird life, and one species, the "Gooney Bird" has become the island's symbol. The Gooney Bird is a species of the Albatross, commonly referred to as the Gooney Bird, because of its odd actions.

Many other seabirds make their home here, and the following is an estimate of their numbers:

Sooty Tern	600,000
Fairy Tern	3,000
Hawaiian Tern	2.000
Grayback Tern	500

Bonin Petrel (Small Morning Bird)	50,000
Wedge-Tailed Shearwater (Morning Bird)_	500,000
Bosun Bird	3,000
Frigate Bird	100
Red Footed Booby	100
Blue Faced Booby	500
Brown Booby	100
Laysan Albatross (White Gooney)	50,000
Black Footed Albatross (Black Gooney)	50,000
Wild Canary	100

The White Gooney is the king of Midway – a picture of the utmost grace and beauty while in the air, and a completely irrepressible clown on the ground. This beautiful bird, about the size of a goose, has a snow-white neck, breast, and underside, with beautiful gray shading around the eyes, a back and wings of brown and black, bright shiny black eyes, and a long powerful curved yellow beak.

The famous "Gooney" dance seems to be a courtship affair for mated birds before their eggs are laid in November, but later in the season only non-nesting ones perform. Being very polite, the birds start their dance by bowing to each other several times, then they liven to the tempo by fencing with their beaks. This is followed by two solo movements – one consists of a rapid snapping of the beak (reminiscent of a trip hammer) and the other of shaking their heads violently from side to side all the time emitting a high shrill whistle. The next motion is to lift and partially extend one wing and at the same time scratch themselves under the armpit, with the tip of their beak. Then they stretch skyward on their tip-toes and emit a loud cheer, known as the 'sky-call'. The action is fast and is repeated many times with each gesture being accompanied by a characteristic sound that persons familiar with the birds can visualize the action by just listening to the calls.

In any case, the dance of the Gooney or any other of his acts are always good for a long healthy laugh.

TOO SMART (OR DUMB) FOR OUR OWN GOOD
1944-1945

by John "Sandy" Sandefur

These couple of memories may help you with your history of events of VMSB 343. I still get a smile out of the situation when I relate it in the right groups. Their first event took place in the ordnance shack at Ewa Air Station.

M/Sgt. Joe Scott had need of several men to move 20 MM's to another room so that they could be handled in a better fashion. There were about ten of us sitting around and Sgt. Scott had most of the others paired up to move the 20's. It took two men to carry them. Stinson was sitting with me when Sgt. Scott came over and said "Stinson, you and Milarch help too."

I didn't move so of course Stinson couldn't to anything. In a short time Sgt. Scott came over and again told Cpl. Stinson and Milarch to help move the guns. I didn't move. This really made Sgt. Scott angry. He came over to Stinson and me and told us to follow him.

We went to the Sgt. Majors office where Cpl. Stinson and PFC Milarch were placed on report for disobeying a direct order. The Sgt. Major asked Cpl. Stinson his side of the story. Stinson said, "I couldn't carry the gun by myself". I was waiting for help.

The Sgt. Major turned to me and asked, "What have you got to say for yourself?" I pointed out that I was Sandefur not Milarch and that I had not been given a direct order. The severe look that the Sgt. had been displaying turned to great anger. Such arrogance could not be tolerated, so after a very strong tongue-lashing we were given extra duty.

We did the extra duty because we got off so easy and had got one up on Sgt. Scott. There must be a good moral here some place, but I'll leave it up to the readers to find it.

ANOTHER STORY

Jack Milarch and I were very good friends. Neither of us ever played Black Jack or Poker but we spent a lot of time watching. We became convinced that the best way to win was to be the dealer in Black Jack.

...We were on Sand Island as the squadron was breaking up and we had a lot of free time on our hands. Both Jack and I had saved a good sized nest egg and we agreed we should enlarge it by playing Black Jack. Jack was to be the dealer and I was to be his banker. Jack soon won the deal and we were ready to count the dollars that rolled in. However, in a short time both of our nest eggs had left our possession. I have never gambled at cards since. Jack and I still laugh about that experience.

WELCOME TO MIDWAY

by Walter LeTendre

When I first arrived on Midway in the Fall of 1944, I was assigned to a revetment that protected one of our dive bombers from a possible strafing attack by Japanese planes. All of our planes were protected in this way. A revetment is a horseshoe shaped mound of coral, open on one side and about eighteen feet high. The planes would be backed into the revetments when they were not in use. Built into one wall of the revetments were small tarpaper shacks with a couple of bunk beds. I had one of the bunks in one of those shacks. We had three major problems in those shacks that would really freak you out.

NUMBER 1: RATS. These huge roof rats, sixteen inches long would nest in the space between the shack wall and the coral revetment. They were constantly roaming in our shack looking for food, while we were throwing our boots at them. It finally got so bad they assigned Glenn Kelley to Doc Hawks to put out poison bait, and they wiped them out.

NUMBER 2: COCKROACHES. Our revetment shacks were constructed of 1"x 6" planks that were covered on the inside with tar- paper. Huge two-inch round, black oriental cockroaches lived in the tarpaper spaces. In order to get rid of them we sprinkled gas on the tarpaper and set it on fire. Once we felt the cockroaches were dead we had the fire truck hose it down.

NUMBER 3: SAND SPIDERS. Sand spiders look like a tarantula and they can jump three feet, and scare you to death. On one occasion I opened my foot locker and a sand spider jumped out at me and I set a new track record getting out of the way. Those pests we never did get rid of.

REMEMBER LANDING ON MIDWAY ISLAND???

by Steve Greytak

My good buddy Sgt. Frank Petrella, who I went to radio school with (Texas A & M), was in the Dive Bomber Squadron that we relieved. I believe the outfit was the Checkerboard Squadron, VMSB-312. After stowing our gear, I went looking for Petrella. I located him on the other side of the runway. Since he was leaving the next morning, we decided to have a few drinks together. He took me to the small NCO club they had and we started drinking. When the club closed, we went back to his barracks, or tent, I don't remember which it was. We continued drinking until the early hours of the morning. After saying our goodbyes, I left, thinking that I knew the direction to our barracks. Since being under the influence, I got turned around and ended up on the southern tip of the island. I had no idea where I was or where the barracks was. I wandered around until all of a sudden I heard "HALT, who goes there?" It sounded like it came from the sky. Actually it came from the guard on top of a revetment. At that moment I also heard a round being put in the chamber of a rifle.

I answered, "Steve Greytak".

They asked, "What's the password?"

I started to say, "I don't know", when I heard another round being put in the chamber of a rifle. Then I had to talk fast, because I thought I was going to be shot. I hollered, "Hold on. I just got here today with the Dive Bomber Squadron and I've been drinking with my buddy and lost my way to the barracks. Nobody gave me the password."

Now I could make out the shapes of the two guards on top of the revetment. They told me to stay where I was. One of the guards held his rifle on me while the other came down to where I was standing. He had a flashlight and flashed it on my face. I explained again what happened and that I was looking for my barracks. He got me going in the right direction. The first barracks I came to I went in and found an empty sack and went to sleep. In the morning I found our outfit which was close by.

A MIDWAY ISLAND HORROR STORY

by Reinholdt "R.D." Deines

The squadron historian, Mr. Wally LeTendre has requested that this story (nightmare) be told.

Before describing this in detail, I want to reiterate - it is a small world. In 1948, a man moved here from Hutchinson, Kansas, which is about 180 miles east of me. As we became acquainted he told me that he was a Naval Aviator and had been stationed on Midway about the same time that VMSB 343 was there. He was with the Navy patrol squadron that flew those Lockheed Venturas, based on the other side of the island. He alluded to those "hot" Marine pilots based on both islands and said, "One day we were watching a bunch of SB2C's land, when all of a sudden this crazy guy decided to do a slow roll, or something - we really couldn't decide what he was trying to do". That crazy was me! Sure thing! With gear and flaps down and about forty feet off the deck, that's what all hot Marine pilots do!

Anyway, on with the story. As best I can remember, this took place in early Spring of 1945 on East Island or "Sing Sing". We were completing a twelve plane flight and landing on the shortest runway, something like about 3,100 feet long and in a direction of 130 degrees.

The procedure was that the first to land, go all the way to the end and wait until the last plane landed and then turn around and taxi to their respective revetments.

In all of Naval Aviation it is an absolute must, that if you take a "wave off" or go around for another attempt at landing that you make a slight turn to the LEFT. The reason being that on an aircraft carrier the conning tower is on the ship's right or starboard side.

On this day and flight, I was to the rear in landing sequence, maybe in the last three or four. Routine procedure was the plane in front land on the left and the next one on the right and we usually hit the deck at about ten second intervals. The plane in front of me landing left side and I was approaching to land on the right, gear and flaps down, a few knots above stalling speed, and maybe about forty feet off - high. All seemed to be okay when suddenly the pilot in the plane in front of me applied full power, took a wave off going to the right instead of left, and gave me the full blast of the powerful prop wash turbulence. All hell broke loose in a split second.

My plane rolled to the right, slightly past vertical bank and turned me toward the control tower, which was not very far from the runway. Using all my strength trying to roll the airplane back to the left was not enough. As I was muttering every expletive and adjective I could think of at the pilot in that plane, in utter panic I rammed the throttle full open. It seemed an eternity before there was any response from the engine, but finally it took, and thank God it did, as I just knew this was it. The torque from my propeller under full power was the only thing that saved us. It helped roll us back to level attitude. In this case, us refers to my rear seat gunner, Leo Riersgord, and self. I have no idea how close we came to the control tower, as I was far too busy and terrified to notice. Later I heard rumors that the tower personnel were abandoning their station for fear that I was going to crash into them.

In all of my fifty-six years of flying, I have had some close calls and a few good scares, but this incident was probably the most terrifying I have ever experienced. I have relived this incident many times and both my gunner and I felt very fortunate to survive a near tragedy.

I have told a few squadron members about this and they seemed somewhat skeptical. FINALLY, at long last, at our 1998 reunion along comes Mr. Clark Herrman, the man who witnessed this from the control tower and he has consented to write his own version of what he saw. Therefore, I will end my story here and let Mr. Herrman write his.

AND NOW THE NAVY'S VIEW
EASTERN ISLAND / MIDWAY ISLAND

by Clark D. Herrman

The year was 1945. Usually during normal operations there were only two Navy men on tower duty in the control tower on Eastern Island during the daylight hours. We consisted of two squadrons on Eastern Island. One squadron were Marines; VMSB 343, the aircraft were Curtis SB2C Hell Divers. The other squadron was PV-1 squadron consisting of five aircraft which were twin engine Long Range Bombers - Naval Aircraft - the other Navy plane was PBY-5A Flying Boat and Commander Demming's SBD Dauntless Dive Bomber which the 2C's replaced. That comprised the full complement based on Eastern Island.

The messengers of the Duty Officers of the respective squadrons would submit next day flight operations. If there was a busy traffic day there would be four operators on duty. One operator was assigned to the radio traffic and one to the visual observance of the planes taxiing or taking off and landing. One of the operators would keep the log. This would record all communications, who said what, when and where. The Senior Petty Officers would supervise and oversee the operations of the other three men.

On the fateful day that we are reminiscing about in this writing, there were twelve SB2C planes taking off for a practice mission. All had taxied to take off position and left the island without incident. The operation consisted of about two or two and a half hours. Upon completion of the mission the pilots were flying in formation approaching the island. The lead plane called in for approaching instruction and the formation broke for landing procedure of single file waiting for their turn to land.

Unfortunately, as fate would have it, the direction of the wind had changed to require us to use the cross runway (or shortest runway) on Eastern Island. Again, the procedure was to land, go as far as the end of that runway, get off the runway onto the apron and hold your position so the planes following you could land. With twelve aircraft on the ground, the situation became crowded. When eight planes were on the ground one of the operators that was watching the landings yelled "LOOK AT THIS!"

In an instant we turned to see a Curtis Hell Diver had made a right hand turn from the duty runway and was heading straight for the tower. (The biggest damn airplane I have ever seen!) At the last minute he leveled off and climbed to clear the tower and the antennas. The Senior man said, "Let's get out of here, he's going to hit us!" We only made it to the roof of the two story administration building, which the tower was mounted on, when the plane passed right over the top of us.

In retrospect, we must give credit to the flying skill of the pilot, "R. D." for maneuvering his aircraft out of a possible deadly situation for all men concerned.

After the danger had passed and the mission was successful, days later we realized that our exiting the tower could have been reminiscent of a Three Stooges or Keystone Cops movie. All four of us scurrying all at one time to the exit door with only one thought in mind, "GETTING THE HELL OUT OF THERE!" On the second try we all made it out the door, down the steps and hit the roof below. We all stood in shock that Reinholdt Deines had missed the tower completely.

It was indeed a great pleasure to meet and shake the hand of this man at the Myrtle Beach reunion this past April 1998. It had been fifty-three years since the happening and I still get chills when I think about that day.

Tradition is that the top ten percent of the class goes into the Marine Corps. That certainly proves that theory to be correct, doesn't it?

NOT A GAMBLER

by Lew "Buck" Buckner

One day while standing in front of the revetment, Sgt. H. C. Harris came riding up in a jeep. He said, "Buck, I'll bet you $20.00 you make Sergeant next month." The best I remember, a corporals pay was about $66.00 a month. Being a real dummy, I didn't realize that H.C. was the guy recommending who would be promoted. Well, needless to say I didn't make Sergeant until almost a year later in Hawaii. I have done some stupid things in my life but this one took the cake.

THE STANDOFF

by Lew "Buck" Buckner

After about eight months on Eastern Island, we moved over to Sand Island. Now I was living in a Quonset hut with a group of guys in the squadron. One day I came out of the hut and rounded the corner, well a Gooney Bird (albatross) had made his take off run and had gotten waist high, he hit me right in the belly knocking the wind out of me and knocking me down. He and I were both angry. He was snapping at me and I was kicking at him. Don't know which of us got the worst of that engagement.

While on Sand, we had a beer party and invited the 6th Defense Marines. We played a few games, but mostly just drank. One contest was a beer drinking contest to see who could drink two or three beers the fastest. The old boy that won was in the 6th Defense. Quite a few years later at Cherry Point, a Master Sergeant joined a squadron I was in. I asked him if he used to be in 6th Defense on Midway and won a beer drinking contest. He said, "Yes". His name was Gunther. We were only together a short while and I went on to someplace else.

WHEELS UP LANDING

by Lew "Buck" Buckner

When we first arrived at Midway Islands, we were stationed on Eastern Island where the planes and the birds weren't the only things that could fly. I lived in an underground hut built into the wall of a horseshoe shaped revetment that the aircraft were kept in. At least two men lived in each revetment, so that one man could be with the airplanes at all times.

In the revetment shared by Dick Velton and myself we had three bunks; one single and one double decker. Martin Lavigne asked Dick and me if he could move into the empty bunk and we agreed that it was OK. Of course we never dreamed that Lavigne laid flat on his back with his mouth open and snored like he did. Fortunately, nature solved our problem. Those little underground huts had plenty of cockroaches about two inches long that could fly.

I was lying there one night unable to sleep because of Happy's snoring when I hear a cockroach fluttering across the room. Well, that thing landed square in Happy's mouth. After a lot of gagging, spitting, and a few choice words, it got quiet and I was able to sleep. Never heard Happy snore again.

One day when a group of us were standing up on top of a revetment watching the planes land, an SBD was making its approach with a Depth Charge hanging underneath. Well, we started talking to each other saying it is about time for him to put his landing gear down. Well, he came closer and closer to the runway and the wheels were still up. Just before he landed we all dived over the revetment bank because we were sure the Depth Charge was going to blow. Believe it or not, he slid down the runway on that Depth Charge until you could see the TNT inside of it and it never went off. Maybe I shouldn't mention this pilot's name, but his initials are Magill*. This must have not gone bad for Mac though, as he went on to retire from the Corps as a Colonel. In fact in 1953 when I was stationed at Opa-Locka, Florida, I ran across Mac who was in another outfit there on the base. I told him I had never been up in a jet airplane, so he checked out a TV-2 two seater aircraft and took me up on my first jet flight. We even landed with the wheels down.

*Colonel James H. Magill

P.S. We only flew the SBD's for dusk and dawn patrol for about two months after arriving on Midway. We then switched entirely to SB2C's.

SICK CALL

by Sam Mottola

I don't know if you fellows remember the "Russian" in your outfit. No matter what job they gave him such as a plumber, carpenter, you name it, and he just was not satisfied. So it was no surprise that he made every sick call, 10 AM and 2 PM each day. He just wanted "out". After a couple of weeks of the Russian making every sick call, I said, "Russian, you know what is wrong with you?"

He said, "No."

I said, "You have bad blood. You notice every time you get a cut or mosquito bite it gets festered up. What you need is a tonic."

He said, "Do you have them things here?"

I said, "Yes."

And he said, "Let me have one."

So I gave him a one ounce glass of Cascara and Mineral Oil. He gulped it down. So I said, "That will cure you."

The next morning about 6 AM I was headed for the chow hall and guess who was coming at the same time? The "Russian", and he started shouting at me, "You genuine son-of-a-bitch, I didn't sleep all night."

I asked, "What happened?"

He said, "I shit seven times last night."

I said, "Come on back and I will stop it for you."

He said to me, "Go to hell, you won't see me anymore," and we didn't.

P.S. I really enjoyed being a pharmacist mate in your outfit. Real bunch of good guys.

A SUBMARINE EXPERIENCE

by Jake Spurlock

The only time I ever went down in a submarine, the damn thing leaked. It was at Midway during WWII. Midway was an advanced submarine repair base. After a period of time in the war zone our subs would "limp" back to Midway, so to speak, for repairs. Meanwhile the crew got a little much-needed R & R, although about the only recreation available on the island was ping-pong, pool, fishing, beer drinking, and watching the antics of the Gooney Birds. Part of our job on the island was to fly out and escort these submarines in to Midway.

I can well remember one sub. I flew out to meet and escort it. It was fifty-four miles out and as soon as I spotted it I noticed there was something different about that sub. It had a red color instead of the usual gray. After I got in closer and got a better look, I could see the reason for the red color. The sub had sustained a tremendous amount of damage from depth charges, and they had knocked off most of the outer gray paint right down to the rust inhibitor paint called "red lead". I could see that practically all of its super-structure was damaged and evidently its navigation equipment was damaged also, because when I was on the radio it called with a request for a heading to Midway. The sub didn't even use the code name "Alcatraz" which we were all very careful to use.

I didn't answer on the radio; I just maneuvered around until I got him between me and Midway and flew low over his deck heading directly toward Midway and waggled my wings. He radioed his thanks and took up the new heading and arrived at Midway with no further incident. I certainly did feel sorry for those guys. I could well imagine the stark terror they felt listening to those depth charges go off around them and wondering whether the next one would be close enough to rip open their ship.

The submarines were repaired by the crew and equipment of a repair ship called a "sub-tender". While we were at Midway another sub-tender took the place of the one that had been there for some months and I found out that a cousin of mine was on board this ship. So one day I visited him and he took me throughout the ship, showed me everything, and we even ate chow on board. He told me something that was very interesting; he said that when they finished repairing a sub it went on a trial run of about two or three hours, and sometimes they took along a passenger or two.

Right then I got a brilliant idea, I thought, but later I revised that estimate. Why not ask permission and go along on one of those trial runs? And I thought I would get another pilot to go along with me--misery loves company. It wasn't easy to find someone who thought the same as I did, but finally a young pilot who had just joined the squadron agreed to go. Even he was luke-warm about the idea. We found the Captain of a sub that was scheduled to go on a trial run next, and asked permission to go aboard. He very readily agreed to let us go along - I think he thought, "Whoever heard of a flyboy wanting to go down in a submarine?" In fact, he seemed a little gleeful about it, which didn't ease our apprehension any at all.

The day soon came, too soon we thought, during which the submarine we were to go on would make its trial run. After shoving off, there was a peaceful, pleasant surface run of about fifteen to twenty minutes, and then it happened. A Klaxon horn blared out, loud and clear, whistles blew, watertight hatches were slammed shut and bolted down. Everybody was on the run or doing something at double-quick time. My partner and I did our best to stay out of everybody's way. We finally took refuge in the crews' Wardroom. Nothing was going on there.

Every dive that a submarine makes is a "crash dive". They try to cut the time down to get ready for the dive as short as possible, which is quite understandable. In seconds we were going down at a rather steep angle; you could tell by the slope of the deck. A sailor's vocabulary has no such word as "floor". It is a "deck" whether it be on a ship at sea or in a house a thousand miles from any water. That house has no floors - they are decks.

We leveled off at 350 feet we found out later. We were in the Wardroom where most of the crew kept their belongings except bedding. It was about 10' x 12' in size with lockers all around that were about ten or twelve inches square and about eighteen inches deep.

Very soon after leveling off we made a startling discovery, at least it was for landlubbers. Just opposite the Wardroom in a passageway there were two or three high pressure leaks, tiny jets of water spurting out into the passageway a couple of feet. You can bet your bottom dollar that my partner and I kept a pretty watchful eye on those leaks.

Nobody offered to guide us around the ship. In fact, very little was said to us. We knew where the torpedo room was, so we finally took our eyes off those leaks and wandered up forward to see that area. We were surprised to find that most of the crew bunked in the torpedo room with the torpedoes and I---DO---MEAN---THAT---LITERALLY! The bunks were arranged in tiers of three high fastened to upright steel stanchions and during the daytime they were folded up to make more room. Space in a submarine is at a premium. As Justin Wilson, the Cajun, would say, "Everything is close---close---CLOSE. Why you couldn't even cuss out a cat without getting fur in your mouth." The occupants of the middle bunks could very easily reach over and put their arms around a torpedo without even stretching. We thought that a bit drastic---having a torpedo for a bunkmate.

We went back to watching "our" leaks and noticed something that surprised us no end. Lots of crew members went right by those leaks but not one of them paid the least bit of attention to them. Why? Suddenly a horrible thought occurred to us. Maybe it was because they knew of some bigger and better leaks somewhere else in the ship that we didn't know about.

Our fears were groundless. The leaks didn't get any bigger. But we were in for one more startling sensation. Just before the sub surfaced the pressure inside the ship was suddenly reduced which caused a thick fog to form throughout the ship. You couldn't see your hand in front of your face, but it quickly dissipated.

My partner and I went ashore with a much, much deeper appreciation of flying and especially of that good air that we breathe, and I for one developed a tremendous admiration for submarine crews.

MAIL CALL RETRIBUTIONS
Midway, Eastern Island 1945

by Jim Love

Revetment 13--Jim Love Plane Captain,
Billy Ingram, Assistant:

All mail and laundry for flight line personnel was dropped at Revetment 13. Pick up was at all party's convenience. This Revetment was approximately the near center to the operations.

John Dolgate, Stanley Harris, and Dick Bowes were in charge of the flight line. Some time during our stay on Eastern Island Sgt. Dolgate drove a jeep into a plane wing and put the blame on someone in this particular revetment. Due to this a lot of resentment and non-trust followed.

On an occasion not long after this episode, mail was delivered to Revetment 13. Billy Ingram and myself began sorting this mail for pickup by each Revetment. About the time we were finishing this task, Dolgate, Bowes, and Harris came by to pick up mail due to them.

During this step several of the packages were cracked open. Dolgate pulled one of the packages open and got candy and cookies, approximately two or three. Some of the other men were present and reported to the man whose package was opened. It was the same man accused of plane damage.

Shortly, this man reported to First Sgt. Lane in the Office. He wanted Dolgate prosecuted for tampering with the mail, this being a Federal offense. Major Gregory was informed. Shortly I was notified to write a complete report on the incident.

All parties concerned were friends of mine. I did not want any one in trouble. For my report I said that after my investigation I have concluded that all parties concerned wanted Dolgate

191

transferred. Harris and Bowes should remain line chiefs. This way no one would lose rank or pay.

Major Gregory called us all in and said that after his investigation, this was his decision. He followed my report and recommendations completely. He did not reveal nor did anyone know I wrote this report. All parties I know were happy.

COMING BACK FROM THE BEACH

by Winton Studt

One of the things we did to pass the time on Midway was to go wading and look for shells and small creatures in the lagoon between the island and the coral reef. When coming back from one such time, something happened that has faded but which I have not completely forgotten.

Another member of VMSB 343, Dick Isreal, and I were walking in the sand along the beach coming from the lagoon back to our quarters. As we plodded along it was relatively quiet except for the sound of the wind and the waves. Gradually we became aware of a drone of an aircraft coming toward us. This plane was one we recognized but did not often see.

This plane was an amphibian, a Grumman Duck. Probably the name "Duck" came from the fact that it could travel on water and on land just like a real duck. However, it did not fly seemingly effortlessly like a duck, but struggled along fairly slowly.

The plane was flying close in along the island clockwise and coming upwind toward us laboriously slow. The unusual slowness was due to it towing a target sock. The intent was to provide gunnery practice for ground defense forces though we were not aware of any firing at the time.

This was kind of an unusual sight and we continued walking and watching. As the plane came more overhead we tilted our heads back so that the plane was not obscured by the brim of our hats.

We also became aware that behind us a flight of SB2C's was returning to base in the normal counter-clockwise direction. Perhaps there were three or six returning planes. I do not remember how many. We had seen such flights before. They were behind us and we had to turn around to see them. We continued to watch the unusual in front of us, the approaching plane, the Grumman Duck.

We tilted our heads back farther to watch the Grumman Duck as it came almost overhead. Suddenly, the SB2C's, which were coming from behind us and had been obscured by our hats, came into view going the opposite direction of the Duck. Almost at once there was a loud crash from colliding aircraft.

It was hard to take in all that was happening. It was bedlam. Planes were swarming in all directions. Planes were falling from the sky. Now the Grumman Duck did look like a duck, a wounded duck. Its wings were folded back and the last part of its flight took only a second or two as it nosed down and took a dive straight down into the lagoon.

Momentum carried wreckage of an SB2C a little farther away from us but it, too, took only a second or two to hit the water. The pilot was Lt. Russel "Buzz" Aiken. Those who were fatalities in this crash probably did not have time to figure out what had happened, or was going to happen to end it for them in their last second or two. Others that were left had time to think about it - for a long time.

Was this something to be accepted as part of the environment with participants involved at random? Or, was there a need to analyze whether something was done wrong, whether something could have been done, or whether something should have been done?

For onlookers, conclusions from such analysis last a lot longer than a second or two, and for anyone feeling responsibility, the conclusions could last a lifetime.

That was a long time ago. Since then, while we might not have been involved in anything with such obvious results, we are continually involved in producing things with more subtle results, some good, maybe some bad. Sooner or later we will all become a statistic ourselves. In the meantime all we can do is to be watchful of what we do, could do, and should do.

DAWN AND DUSK PATROL ON MIDWAY

by Ralph Heidenreich

The dawn and dusk patrols were mandatory since we never knew if a bogie Japanese submarine might be trying to infiltrate our defense station. I also remember the submarine net that was drawn across the harbor entrance to prevent enemy subs from entering. Each time the net was opened, we would have aircraft patrolling overhead looking for silhouettes of submarines in the water, and identified by coded communications.

These islands were our foremost submarine station. That is the reason Japan tried to wrest them from us in the Battle of Midway. If Japan had succeeded in capturing these islands, they would have possessed a forward airfield and submarine base from which to attack Hawaii and the mainland of the United States. Fortunately they lost the Battle of Midway.

The dusk and dawn patrols were designed to observe if any enemy submarines were in the area. The silhouette of a submarine is very discernible in the ocean from the air.

These flights were conducted day by day every morning and night. The dawn patrol would take off before sunrise and the pilots and gunners would receive thirty minutes of night flying entered in red in their logbooks. The dusk patrol was different in that they would take off in late evening and return with some light.

The 6th Defense Marines would begin their work at dusk to defend the islands throughout the night. As part of their training, they would use a J2F Duck Plane to pull a tow sleeve for target practice by the anti-aircraft gunners to gain proficiency. The two sleeves would then be inspected for hits. To this date we do not know if there was a miscommunication between the base and our unit that resulted in the tragedy that occurred.

The VMSB343 dusk patrol was returning to base, having completed their mission, and were making their landing approach when they confronted the J2F pulling the tow sleeve right across their approach pattern. There are always two planes making up these patrols, and the flight leader dove under the sleeve, but the second plane flown by Lt. Buzz Aikens and Radio/Gunner Sgt. M. J. Odette flew directly into the J2F. An explosion occurred and both planes went into the sea. Those of us who observed the accident were in shock. I remember pilots and others running to the tip of the island looking for survivors. A few days later Lt. Aikens' body washed up on shore. Sgt. Odette's body was never recovered.

A military funeral was held dockside, and we all remember the flag draped gurney on the dock while we all stood at attention, showing our respect for one of our own, who would soon be buried at sea.

The loss was with us for a long time, but nonetheless our dawn and dusk patrol continued.

Although the loss of Lt. Aikens and Laney was extremely hard to accept for all of us, it was especially difficult for Lts. Lange, Davis, Holloway, and Inman. All six of these pilots joined VMSB343 at the same time in January 1944. Lts. Lange and Laney flew together while they were stationed at Daytona Beach, Florida, where their flight missions were anti-submarine patrols over the Gulf of Mexico. Josh Laney and Frank Lange were both hospitalized at the same time. While in the hospital, Josh Laney always managed to have a bottle of booze which he shared with Frank Lange. They drove the nursing staff crazy with their wheelchair races up and down the halls. I guess you could say they were a little bit wild.

Lt. Frank Lange took the loss of Lt. Josh Laney very hard when he crashed while on submarine escort at Midway. A search for survivors proved fruitless as the plane was never found, nor was Josh Laney or the Navy Submariner riding in the gunner's seat. This young and excited Sailor had gotten permission from his commanding officer to get his first plane ride. He lost his life while on submarine escort.

Christmas Eve on Midway Islands – 1944

Richard "Dick" Haviland

Lt. Holloway came to the ordnance shack to celebrate Christmas Eve by drinking toasts to the memory of Lt. Aiken who had been killed on patrol a short time before. The whisky had belonged to Lt. Aiken.

During the course of the evening I started a game with Lt. Holloway where I would grab a button on his shirt and ask him if he wanted it. He would say "Yes" and I would yank it off and hand it to him. He thought this was really funny, so before long I had removed all his buttons, bars and wings. I then asked him if he wanted his shirt. He laughed and said, "Yes" , so off came his shirt. What a great guy he was!

He also had the dawn patrol on Christmas morning

THE FIRST MIDNIGHT MASS TO BE HELD ON THIS ISLAND, AND I WAS HERE. WALLY LETENDRE

"Fear not; for, behold, I bring you good tidings of great joy that shall be to all the people:

For, this day is born to you a Saviour who is Christ the Lord, in the city of David."

*St. Luke II, 10 - 11

Midnight Masses
Christmas
1944

Navy 1504 - - Naval Operating Base

High Mass

Celebrant .... Father A. L. Moreau

O Holy Night ....
Kyrie .... Angels Mass
Adeste Fideles ....
Sanctus .... Cum Jubilo Mass
Agnus Die .... Cum Jubilo Mass
Silent Night .... Franz Gruber
Hark! The Herald Angels Sing ...... Mendelssohn

Dowling, T. V.   Choir Director   Giordano, N. A. Organist

Choir Members

Gottcent, J. R.   McPhee, E. V.
Fazio, L. J.   Gzehoviak, H. D.
Pace, D. F.   Schelosky, J. W.
Morgan, G. C.   Blythe, J. R.
Carpenter, J. M.   O' Connor, P. F.
Klein, J. F.   Bagrowski, L. A.
Heithmar, F. J.   Saloman, M. L.
                              Sayegh, E. L.

Low Masses .... 0900 - 1030

Both Chaplains are remembering you and your loved ones in their Holy Masses on Christmas Day.

It is our wish and prayer that the Infant Saviour of the world may bless you abundantly during this Holy Season and throughout the year.

Low Mass

Celebrant .... Father E. P. Manhard. S.J.

Silent Night .... Franz Gruber
Adeste Fideles ....
Angels We Have Heard On High ..... Bishop Chadwick
Hark! The Hearld Angels Sing ...... Mendelssohn

Choir Members

Parent, G. A., Choir Director.	Thelen, J.
Wilson, W. J.	McCosker, B.
Jozsa, M.	Maloney, M.
Basco, J. V.	Tyner, P. W.
Kasovic, P. J.	Idzkowski, E. R.
Tantarelli, J. P.	Muccini, A.
Styanick, E. J.	Mullins, E.

Low Masses .... 0800 - 1030

IN THE BELLY OF THE BEAST

by Walter LeTendre

While we were stationed on Midway, a job order came down to replace all the cables (wires) that operate the plane's rudder and elevators. The cables were attached to the pilot control stick and ran through the narrow fuselage to the tail of the plane. They needed two skinny "volunteers" to crawl on their bellies the length of the plane, dragging the cables with them, along with a light, replace the cables, safety wire, the nut and bolt, and then inch their way backward through the fuselage, and then check the alignment at the controls. I remember that Arthur Denison and I were two of the "volunteers". It was a very hot, sweaty job, with a lot of cut and scratched arms and legs, but we got the job done. I remember "Smitty" Lawrence Smith, our engineering chief, inspected our work and approved it.

OPERATION OLYMPICS

by Robert DeVilliers

I was serving as Sgt. Major of MWSS-2, Marine Fleet Air at Miramar Air Station when in late 1944 orders were received that all male Marines were to be reassigned to the Pacific for staging of Operation Olympic, the USMC invasion of Japan. The operation called for the entire Marine Corps. Women Marine Reserves were to garrison all bases and stations to the maximum extent making as close to 100% of the Marine Corps available for the operation as could be accomplished. Our squadron mission was to provide replacement personnel and material to Pacific units, so it was a huge squadron fluctuating between 2,000 to 4,000 men. We immediately began to disband the squadron and send all members to the Pacific. By early 1945 we had filled all requests for personnel and had dispatched most of the squadron. They had a requirement for a Sgt/Major for Mag-23, so I was designated for that slot and left on 10 February 45 with all the remaining members of the squadron except the CO. When I arrived at Midway I reported to the Sgt/Maj. with the statement, "I'll bet you are glad to see me".

He said, "Why?"

"Because I'm your replacement."

He said, "Hell, what are you talking about, I just got here. I've only been here a week!"

In a not untypical circumstance, the USMC sent TWO replacements for the Mag-23 Sgt/Maj. and he got there before me. I went into the CO's office and he thought VMSB-343 needed a SGT/Maj., so he sent me there. Nope - their new Sgt/Maj. was also already on board. So there I was with no assignment, and MAG-23 didn't know what to do with me because I had too much rank for any open slot they had. I believe only the NCOIC of Transportation and of Supply, plus the Chief of Flight Line, the Chief of

Maintenance and Repair and the Chief of Operations rated six stripes along with the Sgt/Maj., and all those slots were filled. I couldn't have qualified for any of the others anyway. I was advised that MAG-23 contacted Wing HQ about getting rid of me and was told, "find a job for him."

Captain Dan Topping (married to the ice skater Sonja Heinie) was the OIC of Special Services and overdue to be rotated. and therefore was putting heavy pressure on MAG-23 to get away. So, somebody had the inspiration (probably Capt. Topping) and with a little paper shuffling, presto, the slot for Special Services was changed from an OIC to an NCOIC. I found myself NCOIC of Special Services. Capt. Topping left about the next day and I took over. So, every Marine who checked out sports gear got it from my shop. I had a Sgt. and a Cpl. on the staff to keep track of the sports equipment and to maintain the facilities. Every day we raked the ball fields and put in the lines, etc. There was a softball league just starting up, so I became the umpire for the games as I was an impartial non-member of any squadron.

After about a month, a Capt. Frank Klein arrived with orders to relieve Capt. Topping. This created a crisis of course, because that slot no longer rated an OIC, having been changed to accommodate my rank. I know damn well they didn't dare call Wing HQ again, so with some more adroit paper shuffling it was changed back to an OIC slot with a Staff NCO as Assistant OIC. To make it more likely to slip through Wing review, they also designated me as NCOIC of Mail censoring. So that became my two-hatted full time job the balance of my time on Midway.

During May, a ship arrived with Special Services supplies. It had huge boxes (about the size of a washer or dryer) full of Prince Albert Smoking tobacco in tins, thousands upon thousands of tins. Almost none of the Marines wanted to roll their own, as cigs were only five cents a pack at the PX. We filled all of our space with those huge boxes, and then we located a nearby warehouse with space and put boxes upon boxes more in there. We managed to get the Navy to take twenty-five or thirty boxes, but we were stuck with the rest. We did our best to get all the fellows to take this free tobacco of course, but the few pipe fellows would only take so much no matter how we tried, and very few cig smokers took any at all. We tried handing it out at the chow line but gave up on that as everybody refused it. One thing we did that worked, was every time a Marine checked out a basketball, football, tennis racquet, baseball glove, bat, balls, or whatever, we gave him a tin of Prince Albert with it. I have no idea where they threw away all of it.

Normal routine was to sign the sheet when you checked out equipment and bring it back when done. Guys would have favorite ball gloves and insist on that certain one which is understandable. Then if they had a game the next day, or just figured they could get away with it, they would "forget" to turn it back in. So, we didn't make ourselves popular looking them up and demanding the glove back, but shucks, we had to, in order to issue it to another, as our supply was very limited. Well, during June, a ship arrived with lots of new sports gear. All at once we were swamped with it. We quit having the Marine sign for it, and told him to just keep it rather than turn it in. It was kind of like the Prince Albert Tobacco, but not to such an extreme. Suddenly, we were up to our ass in sports equipment. As we were preparing to leave Midway we abandoned all record keeping and urged everyone to take whatever equipment they wanted, and take it with them. Of course, most didn't have room for basketballs, bats, tennis racquets, footballs, etc., but a few did, and many of the rest managed to shove a new baseball glove into their seabag or sea chest along with a few balls. When all of us checked out of Midway, there were still shelves upon shelves of new equipment left behind, and a warehouse of Prince Albert. Naturally, I never cared, and never even wondered what happened to the sports gear or all the Prince Albert, as the USS Colusa took me from Midway and upon arrival at Pearl, from VMSB and MAG-23. I was assigned duty aboard a carrier.

BOXING SMOKERS ON MIDWAY

by Walter Letendre

As part of the Navy's Welfare Department program we had regularly scheduled boxing smokers that was heavily attended by base personnel. Two of the Marines in our Squadron were excellent boxers: Steve Greytak (Welterweight) and Bruno Niedziela (Heavyweight). Steve Greytak had five bouts while on Midway, and his last fight was just before the war ended. Steve fought the semi-final bout, and Bruno fought the main event, and they both won. In his last fight Steve Greytak beat the Navy Pacific Fleet Welterweight champion. Steve won all five of the fights he fought in.

Steve enjoyed sparing with some of his Squadron buddies: Jimmy LaShan, Dave Kohlhas, Frank Lange and others.

The fights were held under the lights.

THE LAST BATTLE ON TURF

25 Cents
In Canada 30 Cents

APRIL
1945

The RING

BUY
UNITED STATES
WAR
BONDS
AND
STAMPS

FREDDIE COCHRANE
World Welter Champ,
Whose Hat Is Back
in the Ring.

The boxing team of naval personnel, Midway Island; is shown above. Men interested in the sport are given expert tutelage by Georgie Abrams, CSp(A), USNR, Long Island, N. Y., himself a contender for the middleweight championship.

Seated, left to right: Jack Heenan, Robert Burnett, Gene Forbes, Robert Bryan, Larry Duran, and Hal Cornette.

Second row, left to right: Robert Streeter, George Tomlinson, Lennie Garcia, Steve Graytak, James Taylor, Gail Gillbreath and Walter Jason.

Standing, left to right: Joe Vozdik, referee; George Abrams, trainer; Comdr. S. H. Ambrustoer, Chief of Staff; Commodore Gail Morgan, Commander of the base; Comdr. Erik Hofman, Executive Officer; Lt. Robert S. Heaman, Welfare Officer; and Wallace Krpan, referee.

WITH THE NAVY *at* MIDWAY ISLAND

These two Marines are telling it to each other in no uncertain terms. Cpl. Gail M. Gillbreath, USMCR, Long Beach, Cal., is shown being told with a left hook to the jaw from Pfc. Steve Graytak, USMCR, Bridgeport, Conn. This was one of the bouts recently conducted as a part of the Navy Welfare Department program at Midway Island. A capacity crowd, including all hands from the Commodore of the base to the most recently arrived boot, was present to witness the fights.

A regular part of the Navy's Welfare Department program is the promotion of boxing smokers. They can be found aboard ship as well as practically every shore station. Shown above at Midway Island is Eugene Forbes, Cmlc, (CB), USNR, Everett, Wash., trading punches with Pfc. Robert Burnett, USMCR, Westona, S. D., Forbes won on a real close decision, which might be attributed to the heavy matting of beard acting as a buffer for his opponent's blows.

THE MEMORIES OF A MARINE

by Joseph "Joe" McIlvain

I do have trouble scribing things in an orderly fashion when it comes to writing. I have always felt that the real memories of the Squadron were the fellows themselves. They were the most decent bunch of fellows that I met, knew, and will forever carry in my thoughts. It was not the great war effort or patriotism, but rather the daily encounters that I remember. Here are a few of mine for whatever they're worth.

Arriving at Parris Island and being addressed by my first name "Joe" really impressed me, thinking how considerate of the D.I. to know my name. It took me all of one day to learn that all boots were addressed "Joe".

The Thanksgiving and Christmas dinners at Midway when the CB's did the cooking, were complete with a turkey dinner, and live music at the mess hall. No reflection on our cooks.

Midway Gunner, Joe Reno, stepped out of the aircraft to assist the plane Captain turn the propeller after the first cartridge failed to start the engine. The pilot started it up, taxied out, and then took off. Joe Reno was left standing at the revetment watching the planes go by.

At Midway, Henry Volk, after a New Years Eve gathering returned to the pack and entertained us with impersonations of everyone from Major Gregory on down. He was from Bay City, Michigan, deceased January '68.

Greenville. The first bugle in the morning was for chow and the second for muster. Since the food was rather sad, several of us would stay in the sack and arise one hour later for the muster bugle. After several warnings, we were of course caught. Lt. Holloway was selected to do the punishment chores, which was a hike, full gear, from about 1700 until the next morning. Corpsman, Bill Drum came along at Doc Hawks request, although he was not one of the miscreants. Several hours into this night trek one member fell into a drainage ditch and poor Bill had to carry the fellow's rifle and pack the balance of the trip. We arrived back at our base just in time to board the trucks to the field and resume the new day's chores. Of course, the food didn't taste too bad after that. Funny, the Marine Corps had a way of making a point.

WATER, WATER EVERYWHERE,
BUT NOT A DROP TO DRINK

by Glenn Kelley

While stationed on Eastern Island, one of two Midway Islands, one of my responsibilities in building maintenance was plumbing. I had no idea why we were moved from Eastern Island to Sand Island, it made no sense. But later we learned the reason was our planes taking off and landing were killing too many Gooney Birds, of which there were thousands. Our leaders had determined that Sand Island could accommodate two squadrons, thus eliminating some of the bird kills on Eastern Island. After we were stationed on Eastern Island, our Officers were given authority to take an abandoned building to convert into an Officers Club. But guess what? They had no fresh water going to the building. The only fresh water on the base came through the Navy water lines that fed Navy facilities. I was asked to try and provide fresh water to the Officers Club.

PFC Glenn Kelley, PFC Bill Pavichavich, and PFC Russell Zurface drew a truck from the motor pool. We took the truck out over where the fresh water lines ran, disabled our truck, and Zurface raised the hood and pretended to have motor problems. I, Glenn Kelley and Bill Pavichavich crawled under the truck with our tools, and pretended to be helping the mechanic, Zurface. In fact, we were splicing into the Navy's water, and later we extended lines from the splice to the Officers Club to provide them with fresh water. You realize they could not drink their bourbon without the water for a mix. Life was suddenly good again.

P.S. Fortunately, the water pressure was very low which enabled us to cut in without drowning ourselves.

SIXTY-TWO KNOT KALMOE

by Wilfred "Wil" Kalmoe

This is a true incident that occurred in the Summer of 1945 while VMSB - 343 was stationed on Midway. The pilots were told that we may start field carrier landings soon, and to get the feel of the plane with the wheels and the flaps down, and maintain altitude. Our planes were SB2C'3's.

One nice day I, Wil Kalmoe the pilot, and my gunner, Dan Reske, were on submarine patrol. I decided to try this carrier approach flying. I put the wheels and flaps down. The air speed started to decrease to 100 knots, then soon down to 90 knots, so I added more throttle. Then the nose of the plane came up with the added power, so I cranked the elevator trim tab forward for nose down. At this time I noticed that I was losing altitude as well as air speed so I added more throttle which brought the nose higher. I then cranked the trim tab some more. A couple more attempts to add power and adjust the trim tab were made, but I was still not maintaining speed or altitude. In fact the air speed was down to 70 knots and the plane was starting to feel like it would stall soon. It did. It vibrated and started to fall off to the left because of the low speed and high power setting. The air speed read 62 knots. I knew I had to get the plane under control or go into the ocean, so I put both hands on the stick and pushed it forward to get the nose down. I heard someone on the radio say, "There he goes". I got the plane headed straight down to gain air speed. I then pulled the lever to raise the wheels so that if I hit the water the plane would not flip over as easily. The air speed increased quickly so I got control and the plane came out of the dive easily with air space between me and the ocean.

I'm sure this was a little unnerving to my gunner so I called him on the intercom and asked, "Are you still with me, Reske?"

He replied, "Yes, but I was half way out".

After that several people called me "62 knot Kalmoe".

Afterward I was thinking of what I should have done to prevent the stall. I should have cranked that elevator trim tab down much more and much faster. You know, we never did practice field carrier landings. I wonder why.

WHEN WE JOINED THE NAVY

by Bernie Gallagher

Rosalie and I attended the 50th Wedding Anniversary of Tom and Alice Gibbons on May 18th at their family parish, St. Gregory the Great. I was fortunate enough to have been in the wedding party that long ago. Rosalie and I enjoyed attending and meeting their family and Tom's brothers and sisters, especially his younger brother Joe who helped us service our short hitch in the Navy.

We were stationed there on Oahu, and I remember Tom saying his brother Joe was coming in on his ship, and should be stationed at Barbers Point. When he did arrive Tom arranged for Joe and a few buddies to spend some liberty time with us at our "Slop Shute." We had a great time and enjoyed the evening with them and they couldn't pay for anything.

A few nights later they invited us over to their place of refreshment. There was Tom, McGlinsky, Duggan, Gordon, Fickling, and myself. Upon arriving at their barracks we walked over to where they serve beer, etc. We were in our Marine fatigues and the Navy guard on duty denied us entrance since only Navy personnel were allowed.

Well, except for Joe Gibbons and his buddies, this may have put a damper on the evening's festivities. We returned to their barracks and figured why don't we just return to our place for refreshments. One sailor, in his whites, walked over to me and said, "You're about my size." The same happened to each of us until each Marine was outfitted with a Navy white uniform.

Once we were suited up in Navy uniforms we returned to their Beer Garden and had an enjoyable evening after passing the guards inspection. I can still remember vividly the guard on duty eyed us suspiciously but didn't say anything.

Thank God we didn't arouse too much suspicion at that time or we'd still be in Portsmouth breaking big rocks into little pebbles.

P.S. To anyone who reads this admission let it be known that the Statute of Limitations has run out!

TIME FOR YOUR IMMUNIZATION SHOTS!

by Bob Devilliers

I enlisted in the Marine Corps in Minneapolis, Minnesota, which was a major Armed Forces induction station. As such it had a medical unit and all the applicants got a pre-enlistment exam. When accepted for enlistment, and qualified to ship to boot camp, they then brought us in for some "shots"! I was totally naive and thought nothing about that until I found that my arm was very sore, and I felt lousy sick during the four day train ride to MCRD, San Diego.

Upon arrival at MCRD, either the second or third day they lined all of us up at the medical center and gave us all the shots. Now I don't know about all of our Platoon, but for me, I got sick as hell and my arm so sore I couldn't use it. I really reacted to the shots. Enough so that I knew I DIDN'T WANT THEM!! Of course, the USMC did not ask for my opinion, and cared less, so in one month we all went in for the follow up or "booster" shot. Once again, they hit me really hard and I now HATED shots. There were quite a few recruits who were the same way, and in fact, a couple even passed out.

After graduation, I went to North Island, and from there to Texas A & M where I joined a Navy Unit and more or less left the Marine Corps while in school. Guess what the Navy medical unit did? Right, they gave all of us a set of shots again, for the "Navy Records". I had the predicted and expected severe reaction getting very ill and with another sore arm for about five days. After graduation from Texas A & M, I came out to San Diego to Camp Kearney and "rejoined" the Marine Corps again. I couldn't believe it, but the medical unit called me in for shots again. I resisted with all the power and strength that a Corporal had, but futile. Naturally I was so sick and with such a sore arm again that I was miserable. When I talk about the sore arm, remember they insisted on giving all shots in the left arm. I would protest that I was left handed so use the other arm, but hell no; EVERYBODY is the same and gets it in the same place. The right handers ate, wrote, and worked with their right arm and the sore left arm was a slight inconvenience, but for us 7% lefthanders, it was absolute misery.

Also the shots they used were "one size fits all". So, while I weighed 120 pounds, I got the same dosage as a guy 240 pounds. I suspect the dosage was set for the average weight of about 175 pounds, so I always felt I was constantly given a double dose while the big guys got half a dose. No wonder I always got sick!

From then on I only had to suffer through the annual booster shots that were required. I always knew when the date approached, and hoped that somehow the medical unit would miss it and fail to call me in. Like hell they did!! And every time I had the strong reaction and very sore arm.

As the war and time progressed, I received overseas orders and as they did with all Marines, the medical unit called me in and gave me my "overseas" shots, plus along with the boosters that are due "soon anyway". I was so miserable on the ship going over to the Pacific I can't describe it. Some of it was probably worse because of sea sickness. If you are sick when you sail, it doesn't take much roll or pitch to get worse. Because of my six stripes, I was bunked in the chief's quarters, and thus allowed to just lay in the bunk and not have to carry on any duties. After arriving in Pearl, I soon was aboard ship enroute to Midway. I arrived with my orders in hand, but NOT my medical records. Procedure was that the USMC and USN trusted you enough to carry your orders and SRB, but NOT your medical records which were confidential and not for your eyes. Those were forwarded under separate cover to your reporting station via mail.

However, when you report to a new duty station the established routine was to report in at the Medical Office. At Midway I was very pleased to meet a Navy Chief Corpsman I had known months before back in the States. This Chief and I were really quite good friends. My medical records had not yet arrived, so he told me to just go about the USMC business.

Some three or four weeks later I got a message that the Chief

Corpsman wanted me to come over. At my first opportunity I chopped chopped over. He hits me with, "SORRY, BUT YOUR MEDICAL RECORDS ARE LOST!! We have to start a new set of records with a full exam and ALL THE REQUIRED SHOTS!!" I begged! I pleaded! I used logic such as, "Everybody knows I have had all the shots during my years in the Marine Corps. Chief - you know that! Hell, I think that at Miramar you gave them to me." I tried cashing on being old friends. No good! I offered to give him my beer ration every week. I could see that he got some sports equipment. I used more logic, "Just wait a couple of weeks and they will come!" So he said OK, he would go talk to the medical Officer and explain it to him.

Cripes, within thirty seconds or so he came back with the Medical Officer who said, "Bullshit, get in here and get it done Marine." Well, you know the predicted result. Sure, I was so sick for the next five days with an arm I couldn't move, that once again I am hardly able to get out of the sack. One improvement, however, was that my buddy the Chief Corpsman did agree to give me the shots in my right arm, so I could function fine with my left arm this time. Eating, brushing teeth, writing, shining shoes, etc., etc., was a snap. If I had known what Marine had carelessly failed to ship out my medical records --- well, the urge to kill.

Some couple of weeks later I got another message the Chief wanted to see me. This time I went reluctantly fearing for the worst. The Chief, (my old buddy) greets me laughing his head off as he tells me my medical records HAVE SHOWED UP!! Worse, he sees they were all complete and I didn't need the shots they gave me, but they would enter them in the records anyway. I was able to rant and rave a little bit and scream "I TOLD YOU SO! Just wait a while and they will show up!!" But I left with the definite feeling I accomplished nothing, and it was me who was 100% loser to the USN.

Sometime later, I fell backwards into a wall, and got a nasty puncture and tear in my shoulder from a nail sticking out of the wall. Everyone said "go over to the medical building and get a tetanus shot".

I said: "Are you crazy??" I never went of course, and the cut healed with no problem. You couldn't get me near them and their shots unless you carried me in unconscious. I had no further business or official contact with the Medical Office although I would see my Chief Corpsman friend regularly. When we left Midway, (I sailed with VMSB-343) my medical records were properly transferred, so I had no more dealings with them. But it left me with an indelible mark of my time on Midway.

Epilogue: Today, 52 years later, medicine has improved dramatically. Shots now are given with dead virus rather than live, and they will usually give it wherever you ask. Also, most are now "sized" according to a patient's weight. I can take all shots now with no pain or reaction at all.

A COUPLE OF REMINISCES
FROM OUR DAYS ON MIDWAY

by Al Vazac

The second week of January, 1945 found me anxiously awaiting news through the Red Cross regarding the birth of my wife's and my first child, due about Christmas time of 1944. Each day found me checking the radio shack - but to no avail.

About that time, Tom McInerney and I were atop a wing of a squadron Hell Diver, making minor repairs inflicted by a Gooney Bird. Out of the radio shack came running R. J. Keefe, with his hands cupped around his mouth, shouting, "Hey guys, Vazac's got a split tail". I turned to Breezy (Tom McInerney) and asked, "What's he talking about?" He promptly replied, "Your wife had a baby girl."

For the record, Barbara Ann was born on December 21, 1944, and I had my first glimpse of her a couple of weeks before Christmas of the next year when I had a month's leave prior to returning to Cherry Point Marine Air Station to be discharged.

A VISIT BY BETTY HUTTON

by Jack Scherer

One of the highlights of our stay on Midway was when Betty Hutton flew in on a military transport to put on a stage show for the Sailors and Marines based there. Her show was put on in one of our hangars. A flat bed trailer was put into service as a stage. Betty Hutton came with a Big Band, and M.C., and three chorus girls. We either sat on wood benches, sat on the floor, or stood in the background. Betty Hutton put on a spectacular show, singing all those wonderful songs popular in the 1940's. At one point one of the chorus girls stood on her hands, spread her legs in a "V" and Betty Hutton said, "That's what you're fighting for!" which got a great roar. The show was a real morale booster.

After the show, the touring group ate in our mess hall along with the Marines. I think we had roast beef and mashed potatoes that day. I have a picture of me leaving the mess hall with Betty. But I didn't even get a kiss.

After the show the touring company flew off to Okinawa, and we were left with our wonderful memories.

GREETINGS!

The Commander of the Naval Operating Base extends Christmas Greetings and Best Wishes for success, health and happiness throughout the New Year to all the personnel on midway, and through them to their families at home.

In this Christmas Season of 1944 the world is being torn with conflict. While there is no doubt of the outcome of the war, this is an appropriate time for us to resolve anew to do our utmost to hasten success, to shorten the war and to save many lives.

Look forward with confidence as you face the New Year. Be not content with any effort less than your best. Make this world and this Base, a better place in which to live.

G. MORGAN

GLENN MILLER MISSING

WASHINGTON, D.C.—The War department announced today that Major Glenn Miller, noted orchestra leader, was missing on a plane flight from London to Paris. Major Miller has been conducting the United States air force band and had been giving concerts for GI's in London.

AT THE MOVIES

NOB THEATER
(Sand Island)

Fri.—"The Lady and the Monster"
    Richard Arlen, Vera Ralston
Sat.—"The Million Dollar Kid"
    Leo Gorcey, Huntz Hall
Sun.—"Gung Ho"
    Randolph Scott
    1200—1430—1800—2000
Movie theater doors will close promptly at show time. No stragglers will be admitted.

SUBMARINE BASE

Fri.—"Lady, Let's Dance"
    Belita, James Ellison
Sat.—"The Lady and the Monster"
    Richard Arlen, Vera Ralston
Sun.—"The Million Dollar Kid"
    Lee Gorcey, Huntz Hall

EASTERN ISLAND

Fri.—"Phantom Lady"
    Ella Raines, Franchot Tone
Sat.—"In Our Time"
    Ida Lupino, Paul Henried
Sun.—"Lady Let's Dance"
    Belita, James Ellison

TAKING PICTURES ON MIDWAY

by Walter LeTendre

Before our squadron was transferred from Ewa, Oahu in Hawaii to Midway Island, we were told we would not be allowed to take any cameras along with us for security reasons. At the time I had a very good 35mm candid camera, and it broke my heart to have to turn it in. I did as I was ordered, but I couldn't picture myself without a camera, so I went out and purchased a cheap Kodak for $3.95 that I was determined to take with me wherever we were shipped. Then if it was confiscated - so what. Once I got to Midway I started taking pictures with the camera and film I had smuggled in. I finally ended up with a bunch of exposed rolls of film, but no place to get them developed. We had thought of that and had also smuggled in some chemicals to develop the film. So, one dark night, Al Vazac, Chuck Luedtke, Al Averbeck and myself made an area of the metalsmith shop light proof and we developed the negatives. I then saved the negatives until we got back to Hawaii in August of 1945 and had them printed. Many of the prints that our guys have in their albums came from those negatives. Most of them turned out pretty good.

MAIL CALL

by Clark Herrman

On Eastern Island we had the newest and the best radio equipment. Any plane that left Hawaii would be on C.W.R.T.* When they were two hundred miles out they'd start sending messages on voice. Using the Morse Code was very time consuming. I could hear them clearly and I would call the base and tell them that they wished to go on voice. I asked if they had any brass or any mail on board. Message came back, "negative brass - 4000 pounds of mail". The three men on the plane were treated like royalty. (They were Army personnel) That evening I received fourteen letters. WoW!!
*C.W.R.T.

Walter L. ___

"The Word"

EDITOR
2ND LT. L.H.VEHON

== VMSB-343 ==
W.E.GREGORY, C.O.

#42

Wednesday,
21 February, 1945.

YOUR PAPER- - -
This paper will appear at or about 1600 daily. It will set
forth the duty assignments of personnel, notices of meetings,
regular and special flight and ground activity schedules, where
practicable, departmental announcements and, above all official
announcements of squadron policy. Other matters of general and
special interest will be included, as well as news flashes and
personal comment.
In order that the publication really be useful, it is requested that department heads use this medium to broadcast
notice of squadron affairs. You may telephone or send a runner
with the item you wish included. Where practicable, all material
should be sent in by 1200, the deadline is 1400.
Everyone is invited to contribute, and the nature of the material submitted is left to the individual. The editors will pass
on its suitability.

SQUADRON DUTY LIST- - -

	Name	Phone
Squadron Duty Officer	Lt. DONOHUE	660
Operations Duty Officer	Lt. BOATRIGHT	660
Tower Duty Officer	Lt. HENRY	603
NCO Watch	S/Sgt DODSON,W.L.	(Report to SgtMaj.
Eastern Is.Security Watch	Corp FICKLING	office at 1500
	Corp GALANTE	on day of duty)
	Pfc IRONS,R.D.	
	Pfc NEUBACHER	

Section Duty Status- - -
L-Sec.2   A-Sec.1   A St.By.-Sec.3   T-Sec.4

SMALL ARMS FIRING- - -
Sec.5 fires .38 cal. today, Thursday, and Friday. This
section is composed of ground officers and gunners. Draw a
weapon from Ordnance and be on the line by 0800.

CHANGE IN SQUADRON MAILING ADDRESS- - -
The official squadron address is now Marine Scout Bombing
Squadron 343, (Not VMSB-343)c/o Fleet Post Office, San Fran-
cisco, California.

(OVER)

A CATASTROPHIC DAY ON THE BEACH

by Frank Lange

It was 1945 and we were stationed on Midway Island. It was a beautiful day, and since I was not scheduled to fly that day I decided to spend some time on the beach. I put on my trunks, put on my sunglasses, and grabbed a book. I also waxed my beautiful nine-inch handlebar mustache with shoe polish. We didn't have mustache wax on Midway - or much of anything else for that matter. I laid out on the beach dreaming of beautiful women and reading my book from 9 AM till about 3:30 PM when I returned to my bunk. I was exhausted and laid down on my bunk and fell asleep. The depth of my sleep may have been due to the bottle of refreshment I took with me. As I remember it was a mixture of Ron Ray Rum and grapefruit juice.

Some of the pilots became concerned because I was gone so long. When they found me in my own bunk suffering from total exhaustion, two pilots nefariously committed a great crime on my body.

Lt.'s R.D.Deines and Tom Inman entered my room and decided they would have some fun. They stood on each side of my bed, Deines (at that time know as Hose Nose) lifted up the left side of my beautiful and irreplaceable lip ornament while Inman (otherwise known as Snuffy) cut that side off.

As soon as I awakened I knew that something was wrong. I could not keep my head from tilting to the right. I looked in a mirror and discovered the disaster. I think I have never been more angry in my whole life, I believe I might have tried to kill the perpetrators had I been able to identify them. I had always wanted to grow a mustache that would curl around in a Turkish fashion; this mustache had almost grown long enough to curl in a circle. The saddest part of the whole situation was that there were no pictures I could show to posterity. I ranted and raved to find the culprits for quite a while, but could not determine who they were. I finally gave in and shaved the remnant of my hair-raising experiment down to the white untanned skin. It was a dastardly sight.

I did not find out until forty-five years later at the Nashville Reunion who the miscreants were. Gayle Haughton hinted that it was he and Deines. It wasn't until eight years later that I received a believable report from the horse's mouth. Lt. Deines admitted that he and Inman were the ones, so much for good buddies.

The moral of this story is, don't grow handlebar mustaches if you intend:

(1 Going to the beach and imbibing an intoxicating beverage.

(2 If you do, lock your bed room door.

(3 Don't trust your buddies.

GETTING IN SHAPE

by Lloyd E. Jefford

In late 1944, after several months of good life on Midway Island, I was getting a little on the heavy side ---267 to be exact!! We had to send to Philadelphia Quartermaster to get uniforms to fit. Bruno Niedziela was getting ready to train for a boxing tournament and talked me into running with him. I lost seventeen pounds in the first week. Dr. Hawks kept an eye on me and I lost 107 pounds in seven months. Never felt better in my life! I've been like a yoyo with weight the last fifty years but still weigh in at 165.

A group of us were on liberty in Tijuana. We ended up on a street wondering where to go. We had heard about a bar the sounded interesting. We called a cab and gave the driver an address. He drove us around the block and dropped us off about fifty feet from where we started. We learned from that one!

MIDWAY NOW AND THEN

By Glen Kelley

The present inhabitants of Midway Islands, the U.S. Fish and Wildlife Services, have major problems with the lack of potable water.

I think I may be able to shed some light on the cause of their problem. While stationed on Midway Islands in 1945 we had an acute problem with a rat infestation. The rats were in our barracks, our chow hall, our hangars; they were everywhere. We're not talking about small rats. We're talking about twelve to sixteen inch roof rats. Dr. Brian Hawks, our Medical Officer, was assigned the additional duties of sanitation and pest control and something had to be done about the rats. Dr. Hawks assigned me, P.F.C. Kelley to be his assistant to eliminate the rat problem. Why Me? Maybe he thought since I worked on building maintenance I would know something about plumbing and lines into buildings. I was the plumber for our unit. When I joined the Marines I never thought I'd be in the role of exterminator to kill rats.

The next thing I knew, Dr. Hawks had us put poisoned bait into the sewer openings and other suspect areas. Keep in mind the ground water was only six feet below the surface. We provided these rats with poisoned food, a mixture of corn meal and molasses that left their mouths dry. They would go down into their holes searching for ground water to slack their thirst. Once there they died, and decomposed into the ground and water, in the process contaminating the water to this day.

I discovered this on one of my recent visits to Midway with the Midway defenders.

P.S. The rat poison we used was arsenic trioxide.

SECTION VI

VMSB 343
POSTWAR
ASSIGNMENTS

RETURN TO PEARL HARBOR - OAHU

by Ralph H. Heidenreich

After our duty at Midway, we were assigned to return to Pearl Harbor. Our Squadron assignment as VMSB-343 was assigned to a new unit that we know as the China Marines who carried the tradition of the squadron to more acclaim and distinction.

On Midway Island they took our administrative staff and squadron association away from us. I was T/Sgt. in charge of operations, next thing I knew, I was Sgt./Major in charge of not only VMSB-343, but fighter squadron VMF-342. I had to close out all the personnel record books for not only our unit, but VMF 342. I worked all night. Loading my gear, throwing it into my locker box, and duffel bag. I proceeded to the converted ship serving as a personnel carrier for troops.

Upon arrival I was informed that I should report to the Captain of the ship. He informed me I had to establish a ship's guard for we were taking eighteen Japanese prisoners to Pearl Harbor. I assigned S/Sgt. Burke Burkeholder as Sgt. of the Guard. Unknown to Burke and I one of the prisoners of war was actually a Korean. He, of course, as we found out later was a prisoner of the Japanese. Totally afraid he was very submissive. We found out if we reached or touched our "45" he would jump up and sing "Yankee Doodle" and dance. Needless to say, when we reached Pearl Harbor he was the most exhausted individual I've ever seen.

Before leaving Midway, loading the prisoners of war was another exercise in enlightenment. A Marine Gunnery Officer, is an enlisted man who has attained the rank of a Marine W/O (Gunner). These officers were a source of years of military experience. When they said jump - you said how high. Men of respect. We attempted to load the POW's blind-folded, putting a foot on a step etc. The

Gunner, frustrated at our actions, came up and said, "Let me show you how to load those SOB's". He took them up the gangplank holding onto their belt and neck and threw them on the ship. Can you imagine the fun our guys had leading the rest of the POW's?

Next thing I know the ship's Chief Petty Officer came up to me and said, "Sgt. you have a problem in the latrine."

I said, "What?" He told me to go see.

Well, as you know, our mail clerk, Cpl. Charlie Franzo, was deathly afraid of flying or riding a sea going vessel. Someone, I wish I knew who, went up to Charlie laying in his bunk while we were tied to dock and said, "Charlie, we're under way." At this time Charlie ran to the latrine vomiting all the way and purged his way between two sailors, doing their business on the sliding seats. Next thing they were pouring out both ends. Then everyone who visited the latrine did the same. When I arrived, this scene was a mess. We finally evacuated everyone. Next thing we knew we were on our way going home.

THE RETURN TRIP FROM HAWAII
AFTER THE WAR

by Walter LeTendre

Once the war was over and we had been returned to Hawaii, the big questions was who is going home first, and how are we going to get them there. Well, of course, the point system was devised, and those with the most points were shipped home first. Some went home on troop ships, some on aircraft carriers, and the less fortunate, like myself were assigned to a D.E. (destroyer escort, The USS Leslie Knox) for the happy trip home. I was part of a group of about 168 Marines who were put aboard this ship in the Fall of l945, and we sailed out of Pearl Harbor for the U.S. We actually outnumbered the sailors who were running the ship.

We hadn't been underway for more than four hours when we started hitting the ground swells. Everyone started to get seasick. The Captain of the ship had thoughtfully asked the ship's cook to prepare a special turkey dinner for us on the first night out as part of the celebration. We were laying all over the topside of the ship, in gun turrets, against bulkheads and along the railings. The railings were great, because you could just roll over and conveniently throw up. Well, only two of our Marine group had the stomach to show up for the big turkey dinner that had been prepared for us.

After they had eaten, the Captain had the two Marines who had their sea legs carry turkey sandwiches up to those on deck who were sick. We were told that if we would eat something we would feel better. Have you ever tried to eat while you're throwing up?? I honestly had trouble shoving tiny crumbs into my mouth to nibble on. Well, I, like just about everyone else stayed sick for two or three days.

One night when the weather got bad, the little D.E. would roll from side to side, then the bow would blow into the waves, then the stern would chew into the water and so it went --up, down, side to side. The Captain told his crew, "Get those dumb ass Marines down below before they all wash overboard." Well, of course, there were no bunks for us, so you would lie wherever you could find a spot. I went down as far into the engine room as I could go, and rolled up on a wood plank flooring between the engines with the heat and the smell of oil.

Well, when you go down to the bottom of the ship, you no longer feel the roll and pitch. In no time I had my sea legs just like everyone else. You can imagine what our group of proud Marines looked like by then. No one had showered or shaved for three or four days. It was sad looking bunch.

Once we got our sea legs back, we started showering, shaving and eating like pigs, and when we finally docked in San Francisco, we marched off that ship just as straight and proud as any Marine group could ever be. But, it was a terrible experience.

REPORTING IN AT OAHU - PEARL HARBOR

August 1945

by Ralph H. Heidenreich

I, as acting S/Major of VMSB-343 and VMF-342 had the duty to supply the Commander S/Major of the 3rd Marine Wing forces with the record books of all of the enlisted men of both units. Having done this, knowing all of us were under quarantine for seventy-two hours, having come from a combat zone, I asked the Command Sgt./Major for liberty passes. Dick Bowles, our NCO, and flight chief, Stanley Harris his assistant, both Master Sergeants (six stripes) and I, wanted to visit Dick Bowles brother who was the commanding officer of the Navy Assembly or repair unit for submarines at Oahu. The Sgt./Major informed me he could not issue passes because we were under quarantine. He said, "All the passes are in my drawer on the right side of my desk, but you cannot have them because of quarantine."

Then he said, "I need a cup of coffee," and invited me to the same, which I refused, and he left his office for a cup of Joe. I knew the purpose of the invitation so I went to the right drawer and evacuated a handful of passes.

Going back to the unit our M/Sgt. Bowles and Harris approached me about passes. I then showed them my rewards. Dick commandeered a jeep and off we went to Navy assembly and repair submarine station. Dick's brother, a Lt. Commander, met us and off to the planned party we went. We had drinks (guess what), food and American Civil Service workers, all female who made us welcome to the outer limits of the mainland.

After a night of fun in which we all got drunk, we went on a checkout cruise of a repaired submarine the next morning. Can you imagine three Marines, hung over on an illegal pass, going on a shakedown cruise on a submarine? Well, that's what we did.

On board, after requesting permission to come aboard, we found ourselves going out to sea. Then the bells started ringing, horns saying W00-W00 and everyone going inside below deck. Next thing we crash-dived down to 180 feet, leveled off, then cruised, checking for leaks etc.

Finally we returned to Oahu, thank God, for this was the most frustrating feeling, the loss of independence, going down to the ocean floor, not knowing what was going on and would we come up again.

When Dick Bowles, Stanley Harris and I put our feet on shore, we thanked everyone for a wonderful time. We three thanked each other, for we had the forsight to be Marines, not "submariners".

MY GREATEST WAR EXPERIENCE

by Frank J. Lange and Frances Lange

There I sat in the bar of the Wilton Hotel in Long Beach, California, at 5:00 PM Christmas Eve 1945, minding my own business enjoying a reunion with my seaman brother after two years separation. We were waiting for the hotel to assign us a room. I was truly not interested in any of the ladies there since I already had a date for later in the evening. She did show up with her mother, but she left when I told her I was with the girl I was going to marry. Is it possible mama misinterpreted the innocence of my intentions?

Three lovely Army Nurses sat down at the end of the bar. I found out later they had just docked that morning and unloaded 1,100 wounded from hospitals in the Philippines. Their Army Hospital ship was the ACADIA, a converted Caribbean cruise ship. They were also waiting for rooms. Did I say that I was not interested? That does not mean that I, like any good Marine was not prepared for any eventuality. I had a sprig of mistletoe just bursting with need to be utilized.

Utilize I did, I went up and kissed all three Nurses and asked them to come to our table. They politely declined, probably mistaking me for a lecherous Marine womanizer. I went back to our table and thought about those three lovely ladies, but especially the little Irish one. I have no idea how I knew she was Irish. Finally, after five minutes or so of deep thought, I told my brother that I was going to kiss the little Irish one again. KISS HER AGAIN I DID, no mistletoe! Upon my return to our table, I told my brother I was going to marry that little lady. Well, it certainly was not productive telling him, so I returned to the scene of my enchantment, asked her name, (Frances Casey), and told her that I was going to marry her. She, of course, said I was nuts. From that point I started calling her "PAT", not because she was Irish, but rather because she looked so pattable and I wanted all of that pattability for myself. I still like to pat.

Never the less, we did celebrate Christmas Eve together in the company of several thousand Sailors and Marines, and many of the nurses and other medical personnel from her ship. The streets of Long Beach were filled with caroling military people, not many of which were sober. About 2:00 AM Frances went to bed, in spite of anything I could say, with her lady friends.

Early in the evening I met one unhappy Sailor, who made Paul Bunyon look like Mickey Mouse. He introduced himself by saying, "I don't like Marines." After careful and speedy consideration I decided he was entitled to his opinion and departed intact. Later in the wee hours of the morning, both of us were more spirited than we had been earlier. I made a mistake and was knocked down a flight of stairs.

Thinking to take advantage of my injuries, mostly pride, I called Frances and told her I was mortally wounded and would she come and minister to my injuries. She laughed and told me to sober up and go to bed. However, she did agree to meet me for breakfast.

She and her ship were to leave port January 4, 1946 to return to the Philippines and Okinawa to pick up more wounded. This left us only ten days to get to know each other. As a fill-in job while waiting separation, I was assigned shore patrol duty in Laguna Beach every other night. This meant that we only had five dates and I had to report in each morning. About the third night I stayed past the last bus and had to walk eleven miles. No woman is worth that, or is she? As anyone can see I returned for more. The lady just kept saying no!

Through the auspices of the Red Cross I was able to follow her ship and learn her date and port of return. We had not been able to contact each other at anytime during her voyage. Our letters caught up with us several months later.

She arrived in San Francisco on the afternoon of February 26, 1946, just two months and two days after we met. However, the port authorities held the ship in the harbor until the next morning, the 27th.

Like a lamb led to slaughter I was waiting on the dock for her to disembark with a bunch of roses, an engagement and a wedding ring. But, I had no real wedding plans, except to explore the mind of this wonderful woman. As I was putting the ring on her finger, a photographer asked us if we would like to have our pictures in Life Magazine. He offered to pay for the whole wedding and a reception, as well as arrange everything. We declined. Had I known how much it was going to cost I might have accepted.

Not realizing the complexities of getting married, I assumed all we had to do was go to the license bureau, find a JP, and it was done. Oh ye of simple minds and hot pants, how wrong can one man be. It was my intent to get married that day, come hell or high water. Fortunately, the folks at the license bureau were very helpful. They called the blood testing office and expedited our blood testing and sent me to see a Judge of the California Supreme Court who happened to be in a nearby office. He emphatically stated that he would not wait after 4:45 o'clock. In addition, we would need a best man who would also act as a witness. That almost stumped me. Still being very much in a mind-exploring mood, I spied two Marine officers walking in our direction, a captain and a lieutenant. They consented to help me out after I explained that there would be a reception at the ballroom of the Mark Hopkins Hotel, and there would be several beautiful nurses attending. A further inducement was that Les Brown and his Band of Renown would be playing there.

We returned to the license bureau accompanied by the Marines and a nurse about 4:30. As soon as I saw the paperwork I knew we were not going to make the appointment with the Judge. However, there were two Marines eager to do battle to protect our wedding plans and their appointments with a flock of nurses. They said they would hold the Judge until we could get there no matter what it took. I was always afraid to ask how they did it, but hold him they did. I will forever be in their debt. We all then went to the room in the Mark Hopkins Hotel I had rented for two nights for the exorbitant price of $10.00 per night. After everyone freshened up we all retired to the ballroom. Being in an expansive mood I suggested that if they had a friend or two please invite them. I thought two or three of each. **"Oh ye of simple mind"** again. Most of the nurses from her ship showed up and it looked like a battalion of Marines. We went to bed about midnight, but the party continued. When I got the bill I almost had a heart attack, almost $900.00 in 1946 dollars.

Poor Frances, her wedding night must have made her worry about what the future held for her when she found herself married to a man who wouldn't let her sleep with him. Yes, after being satisfied with her mind and other things I went to sleep. When I woke up in the morning she was sitting in a chair beside the bed. She said I rolled over and knocked her out of bed and would not let her back in. I apologized by saying I had never had a strange woman in my bed before. Needless to say she forgave me, thank God. I will never know if she believed me or not.

This tale ends with our fiftieth wedding anniversary in San Francisco at the Mark Hopkins Hotel. We were registered there for two nights at $190.00 per night (inflation). However, since we had spent our original honeymoon there, the hotel installed us in the bridal suite on the top floor at no extra charge. There was a party for us at the "Top of the Mark" with fifty gold balloons and dinner with a beautiful cake in a private dining room. The next day we were remarried in a Cathedral nearby. I am not sure that this one was legal since I did not get a license. This was all arranged and paid for by our son Frank, supported by Dan. Twenty-five friends from California and Florida helped us celebrate.

As we approach our 53rd anniversary, I thank God for a mutual love that has grown greater every year.

REMINISCING: MY LAST DAYS AS A MARINE

By Walter LeTendre

Number One:

When we came home from our overseas tour of duty on Midway Islands, we were given thirty-day furloughs. My furlough ended the day before New Years Day, and I was back in Cherry Point for the beginning of January. The first time I was in Cherry Point in 1944 I was housed in a nice new red brick barracks. This time, since the war had ended, the barracks were closed and out of service. We were put up in small tents on the lots right next to the barracks. Being as it was January, it got very cold at night and we couldn't understand why we couldn't be in the brick barracks. After three days of freezing I had had enough, and I and a couple of buddies broke open a window on the barracks, crawled in and slept on the bare bedsprings. At least we were warm. In the morning we'd climb back out, and go back into our tents. I kept it up until I was discharged.

P.S. Now Shirley and I sleep without blankets.

Number Two:

While stationed at Cherry Point in January 1946 we frequently were given liberty to go into town. We had been issued new, wool, winter greens which we hated. Our regular wool greens had been taken away from us when we were shipped overseas, since we had no use for them in the Pacific.

A "sharp" Marine used to shave his wool uniform to make the cloth thinner and thinner, and when pressed it looked like wool gabardine. Really sharp. The new outfits they issued us made us look like "Boots" all over again. We also hated the new wool overseas caps we were issued, for the same reasons, so we'd go to the Army/Navy stores in town and buy the hard finished gabardine caps that were officer's issue.

Well, on one of my liberty days I was passing through the main gate and I was stopped by the PFC Guard who said I was out of uniform because of the officer's cap I was wearing. I was furious. I thought to myself, here I am a Staff Sergeant, back from a tour of overseas duty and this Private, probably just out of Boot Camp, is telling me what I can and cannot do. I said to him, "Well I'll go back to my barracks, change caps, put this one under my coat, and put it back on when I get outside." At that he called the Officer of the Day, and related the story to him. The Officer of the Day said, "Liberty is denied, and you are on three days restriction!" Every day I had to sweep and mop the offices.

That day I learned a valuable lesson: authority is authority. Since then, if I'm stopped by a traffic cop for suspicion of speeding or some kind of offense, I show respect and answer "Yes Sir" or "No Sir". I found this is the best course, in any confrontation with someone with more authority.   Be civil - - be polite.

Number Three:

When the day came for my discharge from the Marine Corps in Cherry Point it was February 3, 1946. I was given $200 and travel clearance back home (to Milwaukee). I told them I first had to stop in Mount Vernon, New York on my way, which was approved. I didn't tell my parents or my girl friend that was my plan. I caught my train in Rocky Mount, North Carolina and went straight to Mount Vernon to visit my good buddy, Al Vazac, and his lovely wife, Evelyn, and their new baby daughter, Barbara. (That's how tight we were). After a few days of visiting in New York, I finally headed west for Milwaukee - - and the rest of my life, wearing my gold Ruptured Duck on my lapel - - a symbol of my Honorary Discharge.

P.S. We've gotten together with the Vazacs every year since then.

THE OLD GUNNY

By Lewis D. "Buck" Buckner

Like the rest of the guys in the VMSB 343 I was ready to get out as soon as possible after the end of WWII, but I got stuck in Ewa, Hawaii for over two months. I was then sent back to Cherry Point, put in VMF 914, an F4U Squadron for a couple of months.

I was finally discharged and went home to Clarksville, Tennessee, and back to work for B.F. Goodrich. After a couple of months B.F.G. went on strike. They stayed on strike for a month or so. We went back to work and about six months later they went on strike again.

Being fed up with strikes I decided to go back in the Marine Corps. Well I had been discharged as a Sergeant, but all the Corps would offer me was Corporal. I went over to the Army Air Force and they offered me Sergeant. With the globe and anchor in both eyes, I just could not go into the air force, for which I kicked myself several times after that. I would go aboard an Air Force base and see them living one or two men to a room in an air conditioned barracks. We were living eight or ten men to a tent on the same airfield, most of the time walking in mud and dust blown in your eyes.

When I went back in I went to Turner Field at Quantico, Virginia. It is only about forty miles from Washington DC. At that time Washington was filled with pretty white women. Oh how it has changed.

In early 1947 the Marine Corps had an Air Field in Shenyang, China, and were asking for volunteers to go there. Well several of us volunteered to go, but by the time we reached Hawaii the Communists had overrun Shenyang, and we were stuck in Hawaii for the next couple of years. I know all of you are saying that must have been great, but let me tell you it wasn't. Very few tourists were coming to Hawaii then, and there were at least ten military men to every single woman. To top that off the Royal Hawaiian Hotel watched everyone with a good haircut like a hawk. I remember one time I went into the hotel bar and saw a young lady sitting at a table by herself, and I walked over and asked her could I join her. She said O.K., but before I could take my seat, two bouncers grabbed me and started out with me. The young lady's father must have been in the "head" because he returned just as they grabbed me. He wanted to know what was going on. They told him this serviceman is bothering our guest. Well this old gentleman said, "This serviceman happens to be my guest." Needless to say I felt ten feet tall.

I stayed in Hawaii until October 1949, at which time the Marine Corps closed Ewa. We came back to Edenton, North Carolina, were there only a few months, when our whole MAG 15 group went on maneuvers to Puerto Rico. I think at that time I was in VMF 322, a F4U Corsair Squadron. Needless to say while we were in Puerto Rico the USMC closed Edenton, so we returned to Cherry Point.

While we were in Puerto Rico my old buddy C. B. Whitacre, who I had been with since the days at Quantico, decided to catch a bus into San Juan for liberty. We got a hotel room and put on a fresh set of khaki uniforms. I went into the bathroom and there was a fixture in there I had never seen before. It looked something like a commode, but was shaped something like a coke bottle. It had some knobs on one end of it, and in between them was some word in Spanish. It was Dushe or something like that. Well I wanted to see what would happen if I turned those knobs, so I bent over it an proceeded to turn them. A stream of water came up out of the middle of that thing that just about drowned me. Luckily, I had another set of khaki's.

We were in Puerto Rico about three months, and returned to Cherry Point. I was transferred to VMF 211 which was getting ready to go on a Mediterranean Cruise. The six months we were over there we made a lot of good liberty ports like France, Italy, Spain, Turkey, Beirut, Lebanon, Tripoli, Libya, Algiers, and

Algeria. Algiers might not sound like such a good liberty port, as you don't dare fool with Arab women, but at this time there were a million and a half French people living in and around Algiers. Some of the most beautiful young girls I have ever seen that were working for the Yankee Dollar.

Got back to Cherry Point about the first of November 1950. Well I had left my brand new 1950 Mercury with a telephone operator in Rocky Mount. We were married November 18, 1950. Always told everyone I had to marry her to get my car back.

After returning to duty at Cherry Point I was transferred to Squadron VMF 122 which was getting ready for a Mediterranean cruise. We went aboard the Coral Sea for a shake down cruise. After we had been on it less than a week and had cracked up four airplanes, the Captain of the ship stopped us from flying and said we were not ready for a shake down cruise. Lt. Col. Marshall was our C.O. and one of the meanest officers I have ever seen; one that only a mother could love. Cecil Field, Florida was an unused Navy airfield, so we went down there for two months of night and day practicing carrier landings. One of the men came up with the idea that you can drive a horse to water but you can't make him drink, but Col. Marshall knew better than that. All you have to do is push his head in the water and suck on his rear end.

When we left Cecil Field we were ready for carrier duty, so we boarded the USS Midway and away we went back to the Mediterranean for another six months. I also made an Arctic Cruise on the USS Sicily. We were in the Labrador Sea and that area for a couple of months. It snowed so hard that we only got a couple of days flying done, but during that time our planes were supposed to drop some live bombs on an uninhabited island. It just so happened the island they dropped them on has Eskimos living on it. No one was hurt, but needless to say we didn't get a good report out of that.

All together I operated off about half a dozen aircraft carriers. I was in VMF 314 in Opalaka, Florida when we boarded the USS Palau for a trip to Japan. We went through the Panama Canal where even a small carrier just can skim through. In fact it tore up several of the life rafts that hang on the sides of small carriers. We had liberty at Panama City on our side and Balboa on the other. From there we sailed up the coast to San Diego for our last look at people with round eyes for the next sixteen months.

All together I spent three tours of duty in Japan. The first one at Naval Air Station, Asugi, not far from Yokohama and Tokyo, and the next at the Marine Corps Air Station, Qwakuni. Qwakuni is still a Marine Corps Air Station located not far south of Hiroshima. The second tour of duty in Japan I had a motorcycle and used to go up to Hiroshima a lot. Since that is where we dropped the A Bomb a lot of people don't particularly like Americans, but you could still walk all over town by yourself at midnight or after and no one would bother you. In fact on my last tour of duty I used to stay in the Shinto Temple when I would go to Hiroshima. The Priest and three generations of his family lived there.

For at least twenty-five years the money in Japan remained at 360 Yen for a dollar. I shipped home dinnerware, glassware, a hand carved portable bar of teak wood, and many other things that were bought at real good prices. In fact the staff NCO's had house boys that worked six days a week for about 800 yen a week.

I guess you could say liberty in Japan was about the best of anyplace I have ever been. The beer and the food were cheap about every place except Tokyo. There are lots of cabarets in Japan and there are just about always more hostesses than there are customers. Most of these hostesses were very pretty young women (Josana). I don't know but I've been told that you could get a short time for 100 yen or stay all night for 300 yen. Just about all the cabarets had rooms either upstairs or in the back. Of course, if you wanted to you could rent a place that was fully equipped with Josan and all for about $50.00 a month.

The staff NCO Club at Qwakuni had something going on almost every night and all day Saturday and Sunday. There was a good floor show at least once a week, bingo was played twice a week and a lot of movies were shown, so we didn't go to the local movie house often.

I rode my motorcycle everywhere I went. One night I parked it in front of the Staff Club and went in for a few sociable drinks. Well that thing must have sneaked in and had a few of its own. About midnight I decided to leave the base. There was a sharp curve about half way to the gate, and that thing laid down with me at about forty miles an hour. A heavy jacket saved my upper body, but a pair of pants just won't take a lot of sliding under a motorcycle. Needless to say I had some pretty bad skin burns.

On my last tour in Japan things were heating up pretty good in Vietnam. Our Squadron, VMA 225, got orders to Chu Lai, Vietnam. At that time there was no airfield there, but lucky me was chosen to take eighty men down to get ready to bring in the first airplanes. I don't know what they had against W. O. Snyder, but he was our officer in charge. We loaded an LSI with all our equipment and set sail for the unknown.

The Marine Grunts had already secured the area when we arrived and the Sea Bees had started grading with a Marine guard riding on every piece of equipment. The area was one big sand bar. The sand went back about two miles to where the mountains began.

We set up our tents and as soon as the Sea Bee's had 3,000 feet of matting down and enough space to park six airplanes, our first six planes came in. We had to catch them with Morise Gear just like aboard carriers, and launch them with a Jato bottle fastened on each side of the fuselage. They were dropping bombs on the V.C. in sight of the airfield the first day of arrival.

I had already put in for retirement a couple of months before I left Japan, but if you are a career Marine the Corps can extend your service, so that is my reason for being in Vietnam. It was by far the worst duty I had in my twenty-three years in the Corps.

When I left Vietnam I flew into San Francisco. Couldn't get a plane out of there until the next day, so I put on my uniform and went downtown. This was in 1965 and I knew nothing about what was going on in the States. I soon found out I wasn't a hero for being in Vietnam, but was the scum of the earth.

After a thirty day leave I was sent to the Navy Air Station, Olathe, Kansas where I would be discharged at the end of the year extension that had been put on my enlistment.

We had an eighty-man detachment at Olathe and a dozen F8U aircraft that the Reserves came in to fly every other weekend. Well, I was assigned Line Chief, and the first Saturday the Reserves came in, I pointed out about five of them and told them to go get a haircut. About thirty minutes later I got a call from my CO, Lt. Col. Lynch, one of the best men you would ever want to know. He said, "Buck come down to the office. I want to talk to you." I went down to the office. He told me to sit down. Then he said, "I agree with you those clowns need a hair cut, but they are civilians and you can't order them to get a hair cut." I said that after all these years in the regular Marines it may be hard to put up with them. He said, "If you don't want to, you don't have to." We had Mondays and Tuesdays off the weekends the Reserves came in. He said, "Go pick out four or five men and bring them in on Monday and Tuesday instead of working on the weekends." So that ended my dealings with the Reserves.

I know this story has gone on too long. So, to make a long story short I was discharged April 24, 1966. The Fort Levenworth Army band played for the parade, and passed in review in my honor, and I lived happily ever after.

EMEMY ATTACK

By Jordan Italia

VMF 312 – 1945 OKINAWA
AWASI AIRFIELD, BUCKNER BAY – V.J. DAY

A few days earlier we were alerted for a gas attack. We were issued gas masks and were going through practices that evening. We went back to our tents and thought nothing of it. All of a sudden the ships in the harbor were letting go with everything. The sky was lit up like it was an invasion. I said to myself, here it comes, the invasion of Okinawa. I grabbed everything I had: one rifle, two 45's, one sub machine gun, one carbine, and all the ammo.

Our tent was pitched on the side of a hill so I ran under the floor of the tent, with all the guns and ammo and I said to myself, "I'm ready."

Everything was in total confusion. It took quite a while before the message reached us. As the word came along, guys were shouting everywhere. Some guys were being shot, but the word came along, "The War Was Over". Hurray, it's over.
END OF WAR

SECTION VII

CHINA

ADDITIONAL HISTORY OF VMSB 343

FROM AUGUST 1945 TO APRIL OF 1946

by Leonard J. Haney

Shortly after the war ended in August 1945, personnel of VMSB 231 were transported to VMSB 343 at Ewa Marine Air Station in Hawaii. VMSB 231 was sent back to the States on paper and I believe that the VMSB 343 personnel who had served on Midway were transferred back to the States for reassignment.

VMSB 343 reformed, then boarded the USS Arneb (AKA 56) and sailed to Okinawa. Upon entering Buckner Bay, Okinawa the ship was advised to turn around and head for the open sea due to a severe typhoon headed in that direction. Typhoon Louise struck on October 6, 9, & 10, 1945 with winds estimated at 150 MPH and 60 Ft. waves. The Arneb was able to make the open seas where many others did not. We were later informed that only the many thousands of gallons of aviation gasoline in the holds of the ship prevented a disaster (along with almost 270 ships that were sunk, grounded, or damaged beyond repair.)*

After riding out the typhoon the Arneb sailed up the Yangtze River toward Shanghai, where the Japanese managed to cut loose all the mines in the river, forcing the Arneb to retreat to the open sea. The ship then headed for the port of Tsingtao on the Shantung Penninsula where VMSB 343 docked, and we unloaded the cargo of gasoline and other supplies.

VMSB 343 was quartered at a Japanese airfield and in a former German school. This field was located in a neutral area between the Communist Army and the Chinese Nationalist Army, and more often than not they chose to shell each other, firing over our heads. The Communist ground forces often fired their rifles and machine guns at our planes but we were forbidden to fire back.

In April of 1946 many members of VMSB were rotated back to the States for discharge aboard the USS Randall.

*"Top Secret", Davis, James Martin,
Ranger Publications 1986, pp.22-23

POSTWAR REDEPLOYMENT

VMSB 343 in CHINA

As a preliminary in the planning for the Kyushu invasion, 1st MAW headquarters was scheduled to move from Bouganville to join its three groups at Zamboanga. This movement had begun before the war ended, and on 15 August elements of the Wing started arriving in the Philippines. On 21 September MAG's 12, 24, 25, and 32, along with Wing headquarters and other units, began moving north from Mindanao. Attached to III Phib-Corps, they spent two weeks on Okinawa, moved thence to Tientsin, Peiping, and Tsingtao. On 1 November Louis Woods took command from "Sheriff" Larkin, who had relieved Ralph Mitchel on 10 August.

Mag-32's tactical squadrons arrived at Tsingtao 16 October, five days after the Corps. MAG-24 sent two night-fighter squadrons and two air-warning squadrons to Peiping; MAG-12's flight echelon joined up 25 October. Two squadrons of MAG-25 furnished the only kind of reliable transport in China where the war against Japan had long since given way to the civil war between Nationalists and Communists.

The 1st MAW planes began flying show-of-strength patrols on 1 November, and they were frequently fired upon from the ground. There were no casualties until 8 December, when 6 of a 12-plane flight of SB2C-5's of VMSB-343 were lost in a snowstorm near Communist-controlled Laichow. Only 2 of the 12 flyers survived and only eight bodies were recovered. Villagers provided 48 ceremonial bearers to carry the coffins of the dead flyers to trucks and jeeps which got through; this was in the days when Chinese Communists still wrote touching mottoes about their friends, the Americans. "May the friendship of America and China increase!" was inscribed on a ceremonial arch in the village square; a reward of 3,000,000 yuan paid for recovery of the bodies was returned.

ITINERARY TEMPORARY AVIATION DUTY
TSINGTAO TO OKINAWA VIA SHANGHAI
AND RETURN

Lv.	Tsingtao, China	27May46	0830
Arrive	Shanghai, China	27May46	1130
Lv.	Shanghai, China	28May46	0930
Arrive	Okinawa, Shima	28May46	1330
Lv.	Okinawa, Shima	29May46	0830
Arrive	Shanghai, China	29May46	1130
Lv.	Shanghai, China	29May46	1330
Arrive	Tsingtao, China	29May46	1530

I certify that:

At Shanghai, China, subsistance and quarters were
furnished.
At Okinawa, Shima, quarters were furnished, but
subsistance was not.

Donald C. Bangerter
Paul W. Dougherty.
1st Lt. USMCR

31 August 1943
Third Marine Air Wing
Marine Air Group Thirty-Four
VMSB-343   3 SBD-4, 4 SBD-5
(Formed 1 August at Atlantic Field)

1 January 1946
MAG-32 Tsingtao
AWS-11   VMSB -343

Victory and Occupation

History of U. S. Marine Corps
Operation in World War II

by Benis M. Frank & Henry I. Shaw, Jr.

Volume V

Excerpts from: Historical Branch, G-3 Division, Headquarters, U. S. Marine Corps

An Extended Stay

The search and reconnaissance missions requested by General Shepherd in October evolved into a daily patrol routine that gave the Marines at Tsingtao an excellent picture of Communist activity in eastern Shantung and kept them informed of the progress of Japanese units moving toward the repatriation port. One search pattern was flown over the mountains of Shantung Peninsula to Chefoo with a return leg that paralleled the northern coast and turned south at Yehhsien to follow the main cross-peninsula road into Tsingtao. A second route took the planes up the railroad as far as Changtien before turning south and west through mountain valleys to the road and rail junction at Taian; from Taian pilots followed the tracks through Tsinan and all the way home to Tsankou. The third route covered by regular aerial patrol ran south to the mountain chain that bordered the coast before turning north through tortuous defiles to Weihsien and the favorite railroad return route.

The importance of the railroads indicated by the attention given them in the MAG-32 patrol schedule was emphasized on 2 November when a semi-weekly rail reconnaissance over the whole length of the Tsingtao-Tsinan-Tientsin rail net was directed. The two-seater bombers returned to Tsangkou Field across the Gulf of Chihli reporting on junk traffic that passed beneath them.

The hazardous nature of winter flying over mountainous terrain was vividly emphasized by an accident that occurred on 8 December. A major portion of each MAG-32 squadron flew to Tientsin that day to take part in an aerial show of strength on the anniversary of Pearl Harbor. The show went off without a hitch, but on the return flight to Tsingtao the planes ran into one of the season's first snow storms over Shantung Peninsula. Each squadron was proceeding independently, and the planes of VMTB-134 and VMSB-343 climbed above the storm to come in. The scout-bombers of VMSB-343, attempting to go under the tempest, were caught up in its blinding snow swirls. Only six pilots managed to bring their planes home safely; six others crashed into the mountain slopes near Pingtu in the center of the peninsula.

As soon as it became evident that the VMSB-343 craft were down, intensive efforts were made to locate them. Virtually every plane in MAG-32 and VMO-6 had a turn at the search, but it was three days before Chinese civilians brought word of the location of the crash and pilots confirmed the fact. Communist villagers had rescued the only two survivors, one of whom was injured. The communists of Shantung Peninsula also held two other Marine airmen at this time, the crew of a photo reconnaissance plane which crash-landed on 11 December on the shore near Penglai. Leaflets were dropped in both wreck areas offering rewards for the return of the living and the dead.

The photo plane at Penglai was part of a flight of three from VMD-254 on Okinawa which had tried to fly around a heavy weather front and reach Tsankou Field. All three planes were forced down, one by propeller and engine trouble and the other two by empty fuel tanks. Both crew members of the second plane died in a water landing near Weihaiwei, but the crewmen of the third craft, which went down on the beach near Jungchen, escaped unscratched and were picked up by OYs of VMO-6 on 13 December. On the 15th, the VMD-254 plane crew from the Penglai crash and the uninjured survivor of the mass accident at Pingtu were released by the Communists. **Recovery parties of the 6th Division picked up these men, and also drove north on 24 December to accept the remains of the VMSB-343 flyers killed on 8 December. The injured survivor of this crash was returned to Tsingtao on Christmas Day.** Through all the negotiations attending the recovery of these Marines, the Communist villagers had been most cooperative, refusing the proffered rewards, and treating well the men they rescued.

By prior arrangement with the Communists, an attempt was made to recover the photo plane down near Jungchen. The 6th Division organized a task force built around Company F of the 29th Marines with appropriate air and ground attachments to handle the job of getting the plane airborne again. Traveling to Jungchen on the 17th on board an LST, the recovery force found the plane could not take off because of soft ground. The aircraft was stripped of usable parts and the carcass burned. The same fate met the wreck of the plane down at Penglai. In both instances, the cooperation of the local villagers was exemplary. For whatever reason the Communist harassment of the Marines in Shantung faded a bit after the crashes of December. The respite unfortunately proved to be temporary.

The sporadic ground fire that met American air patrols was a severe trial to pilots who had to stand the sniping. General Rockey attempted to establish a set of conditions under which this anti-aircraft fire could be returned, and on 6 December he issued combat instructions. The flyers could shoot back if the source was unmistakable, if the fire from the ground was in some volume, if the target was in the open and easily defined, and if innocent people were not endangered. With permission to fire hedged by these qualifications and the possibility of open warfare always resting on their decision, the Marine pilots remained discreet but frustrated. While in General Wood's opinion the individual pilot should have been given considerably more freedom of action, no Marine in China, regardless of his position, had anything resembling a free hand in conducting operations. The orders from General Rocky were an accurate reflection of the policy directives that reached him from higher headquarters.

Certainly, the directive most difficult to comply with was the admonition to avoid support of the Nationalist armies in the civil war. The very presence of the Marines in North China, holding open the major ports of entry, the coal mines, and the railroads, was an incalculably strong military asset to the Central Government, and the fact that the U. S. had provided a good part of the arms of the troops scheduled to take it, Battery E of 2/15, platoons from the tank and motor transport battalions, and detachments of engineers and ordinance men. The new rail guard unit left Tsingtao on 6 November and arrived at the coal port the following day, reporting to the 1st Division for orders. On the 9th, when all its supplies and equipment were unloaded, 1/29 moved to Peitaiho to set up its command post. Operationally attached to the 7th Marines, the battalion from Tsingtao was soon deeply involved in the mettlesome routine of guarding the Chinese railway.

General Shepherd realized that one of his major problems in Tsingtao was keeping his men occupied. So long as the Communists posed no serious threat to the city and the repatriation process ran smoothly, there was a good chance that combat troops might lose efficiency. Idleness, even that of a relative nature, can be a curse to a military organization geared to operate at full capacity. In order to maintain unit standards of discipline, appearance, and performance, Shepherd instituted a six-week training program on 12 November which laid emphasis on a review of basic military subjects. The division commander also directed that each unit schedule at least ten classroom hours a week studying academic and vocational subjects, to be held concurrently with the military training schedule.

Among the officers and men in the wing squadrons at Tsankou Field there was equal emphasis and interest in an educational improvement program. Work schedules were arranged to encourage study, but heavy flights commitments of MAG-25 and MAG-32 ate into the time available for training not directly connected with operations. By the end of October, Tsankou had developed into the wing's busiest and most important base in China. Command of the field and its complement rested with General Johnson, the assistant wing commander, who reported to General Woods at Tientsin for orders except where the defense of Tsingtao was concerned. General Rockey had altered the original command setup to give General Shepherd operational control of both ground and air units in a defensive situation.

As a result of the wide separation of major elements of III Corps in North China, Marine transports flew an extensive schedule of personnel and cargo flights connecting Tsingtao, Tientsin, Peiping, and Shanghai. In order to make maximum use of the planes available, MAG-25 operated VMR-152 and-153 as one squadron. The transport pilots and crewmen frequently returned to Pacific Island bases, particularly Okinawa, to pick up cargo from the vast supply dumps assembled to support the invasion of Japan. The demand for cold weather gear was constant and pressing, and most of that which found its way to the men manning rail outposts and windswept flight lines arrived at Tsingtao and points north in the transports of Marine Aircraft Group 25.

While most transport flights kept well above the range of Communist small arms, the scout and torpedo bombers of MAG-32 frequently landed with bullet holes in their fuselages. Chance alone prevented some riflemen or machine gunner from bringing down one of the planes; the near misses were frequent.

CHINA STORIES

By Harold Heinrichs

While we were stationed at MAB on Ewa, Hawaii, we received orders from headquarters, 3rd MAW, FMF, c/o F.P.O. San Francisco, California dated August 28, 1945, to report to VMSB 343, 3rd MAW FMF, c/o F.P.O., San Francisco, California.

Twenty four of us w/757 Spec, 1 @ 769 and 5 @ 769E SPEC., boarded an AKA, Arneb for Tsingtao, China to report to the C.O. of VMSB 343. Our quarters was a hold amidships on cots and sleeping bags. (I have a set of orders w/name, rank, serial No. and spec. in my possession signed by D. H. Davis, and J. C. Adams.)

The trip was uneventful until we came into the harbor at Guam. They wouldn't let us drop anchor, as a monster hurricane was almost upon us. We went back out to sea and rode it out, heading for China. Many ships were lost in that storm. They put extra men on watch, and we were told to keep a lookout for Japanese mines that storms might break loose. I was in one of the mid-ship gun turrets and the waves were as high as the ship's bridge, when the watch in the forecastle gave the alarm of a mine on the port side, which happened to be exactly where I was stationed.

A huge wave came up about even with me and I spotted a large black object riding the top of the wave. It was eight or ten feet in diameter with six projections protruding in all directions, and they were moving. This was a giant sea turtle which had given us all a major scare. A few days later we arrived in China safe and sound, Oct. 12, 1945.

How We Got From Los Negros to Ewa, Hawaii

August 1945 -- Type of Machine, R5C-1 – No. of Machine, 39557

Pilot: 1st Lt. Lapan – Passengers: Heinrichs

DATE	DURATION OF FLIGHT	REMARKS
23 Friday	5.7 hrs	Los Negros - Guadalcanal
23 Friday	3.6 hrs	Guadalcanal-Espiritu Santo
24 Saturday	3.4 hrs	Espiritu Santo-Nandi Fijis
	DATE LINE	
25 Saturday	4.6 hrs	Nandi Fijis – Tutuila Samoa
26 Sunday	4.4 hrs	Tutuila Samoa – Canton
27 Monday	5.2 hrs	Canton – Palmyra
27 Monday	6.1 hrs	Palmyra – Ewa Oahu

*See above paragraphs for journey from Ewa to Tsingtao.

On Christmas Day 1945 we had a huge dinner. They had even prepared a menu for us. We had Roast Turkey, mashed potatoes, and all the trimmings, that was prepared in a field kitchen (out of doors of course) and in front of the large brick building that would soon be our mess hall until the time we left.
We left Tsingtao Air Base on schedule to fly cover over a ceremony in remembrance of Pearl Harbor Day, to be held in Tientsin, China, and I understood we were to refuel there and fly back home.

When we were flying north we climbed to around 10,000 feet to clear a cloud cover over the shantung peninsula. When we arrived in Tientsin, they apparently had canceled the ceremony, and as they estimated we would have enough fuel to return to Tsingtao without refueling, we were told to do so.

From the radio conversation, the flight leader thought we could conserve fuel by flying under the cloud cover. We went over the water in formation at a fairly low altitude when we flew into a heavy snowfall, and Lt. Ballew asked permission to leave formation to try to get above the clouds. It was snowing so hard we could not see the ends of our wingtips at times. Permission was granted and at this time my pilot, Lt. Ballew, instructed me to leave my radio on intercom so if he needed to tell me anything it would avoid confusion. We were climbing steadily and at around 8,000 feet we broke into an opening in the clouds, and directly below us was the top of the mountain. My intercom came on and my pilot asked if I was all right. I assured him I was, and he said that just before we broke into the clearing he had ordered me to bail out, and had opened his canopy to do the same when he noticed my canopy was closed. He closed his again and we broke into the clearing.

We climbed to around 13,000 feet to clear the clouds and get a bearing to our airbase. There were no clouds over Tsingtao and we were informed we had about two hours of fuel left.

After suddenly finding the VMSB 343 reunion association, around March 1, 1999, my name and phone number were in the next association newsletter. I received a phone call from a person who was a radio gunner during the same flight. Needless to say we talked quite a while, and in the course of our conversation he mentioned that as they were climbing his radio came alive with someone saying, "Bail out!", then immediately canceling that order. Thinking about this later, I knew I was on intercom as ordered, hence unable to hear his broadcast. This matches my experience of my pilot telling me to bail out. Did he key the broadcast switch instead of the intercom? If so, it probably saved my life (as well as his own), since I would surely have hit that mountain before my parachute would have opened. I can only speculate.

I don't remember the proper sequence of some of the things we saw and did, but we did see China at ground level.

When we arrived sixteen or eighteen of us were loaded into an open 6 x 6 and taken to the Jap air base. Enroute we came across a squad of Jap soldiers who had caught a dog. They had built a fire, and were roasting the dog, hair and all. I didn't eat much supper that evening.

The air base was six or eight miles inland and they dropped us off at a barracks where some of us found some abandoned Japanese officers wooden foot lockers or trunks. We put these to good use, and I still have mine. They were well built trunks with cast iron handles on each end, and excellent hasp with padlock eye. Inside are a large bottom compartment and two trays. Overall dimensions sixteen inches wide by thirty inches long by twenty inches high.

The Red Chinese Army was a ways off when we arrived and we were allowed to go out into the surrounding towns, which several of us did. We would come to a small town, and a lot of people would greet us in a friendly way. The town Mayor would invite us to drink hot tea with him. We had been told that if your cup was allowed to sit empty, it meant you had overstayed your welcome. We always left with a full cup on the table and an invitation to come back.

On one occasion Mike Hammel, Steward, and I found an old tintype photo shop in one of the towns, and we posed for a picture. It would be a while before it would be developed so we almost forgot about it. Then Mike Hammel was one of the gunners killed on that fateful flight of December 8th over Teintsin and I climbed over the back wall of the base and retrieved that picture. I sent Mike's family one of the prints, I still have my print, and have had it reproduced.

We had a good ready-room on the flight line and we built wall lockers for our gear. We purchased a thirty-cup coffee maker and hot plate at the PX. We also hired a local man who we called "Louie" as our full time "No. 1 Boy". He would purchase fresh eggs for us from farmers who he knew. We paid him $5 a week and he kept the ready room clean, made coffee, etc. Bacon came from our mess hall in square tins. Louie said if we would like he would take us rabbit hunting. Six or eight of us went to the quartermaster and checked out 12 gauge pump shotguns and ammo. A good time was had by all. J. K. Bradley and one other buddy both got a rabbit. Louie and his wife had fresh rabbit for supper. Louie purchased a new bicycle and got married again while we were there. His first wife had been killed during the war. He was a good friend, and he hated to see us leave.

We also went on liberty in Tsingtao. We rode the rick-a-shaws all over town. We saw sights like St. John's Cathedral, Buddhist and Shinto shrines, public bathhouses, sampans, charcoal burning trucks, Chinese funerals, fire drills, and much, much more.

One of my favorite places to go was the Asia Hotel, with bar and restaurant. This had been an international hotel before the Japanese invasion. It was a three or four story structure with fine dining rooms, a bar, and well dressed waitresses. The owner was friendly, and a gentleman by the name of Hinter Lee spent a lot of time there acting as an interpreter. He was a middle aged Chinese gentleman who had worked in the Post Office before the war. One night he invited me to bring all my friends in and he would honor us with a seven course dinner. We finally settled on six Marines, Hinter Lee, the head waitress, and the owner. We had a real seven course dinner with chop sticks and silverware. There were three drink glasses in back of our dinner plates, with vodka, brandy, and liqueur. These were not allowed to sit empty, and many toasts were made in the course of our banquet. In the wee hours of the morning, there were rick-a-shaws to take us to our bus. What a night!

THE CASANOVA CAFÉ

The owner, a Filipino, was named Roxas. It was rumored that he had killed a man in the Philippines, and had wound up here, opening his own business.

Three of our 343 Marines, Blanche, Dulina, and Hammell owned and operated the Blanche-Dulina-Hammell, Inc., acting as purchasing agents. When Dulina was due to ship out for the U.S.A., it took three shore patrol men to put him on board that ship.

The Red Chinese Army kept getting closer and security was really tightened up, so we didn't get into the country toward the end of our stay.

Flying with Lt. Crain on a sector search one day, we were flying at around 8,000 feet. I observed a column of troops on the road we were flying over. It looked about a mile long and several abreast. (Note: we had had some heavy rain for several days and the ditches were full of water and the fields were very muddy.) I called my pilot and reported what I was observing. He asked me where they were, and I told him we were passing over them on the road below. He told me to fasten my seat belt as we were going to have a closer

252

look. We were heading west and he looped the plane over and down, and when we straightened up we were heading east about fifty feet above the road. It was pandemonium as we approached the troops (who were later identified as Red Chinese) and I could see soldiers in the ditches, mules with Howitzers going across the muddy fields, and we climbed up and went back to the base.

I never had any first hand knowledge of the repercussions, but I heard that we had machined gunned them, etc. The facts came out that our cannons were spiked, there was no machine guns in the rear cockpit, all the fire power we had were two Smith & Wesson revolvers and we hadn't taken them out of their holsters. I never heard any more about this. To wind this down, while the main squadron left the first part of April, twelve pilots and twelve radio-gunners were left to fly our planes to Okinawa. On May 27, 1946 we flew from Tsingtao to Shanghai to Okinawa where we flew into Awasi Field, and left our planes. We were flown in a R4D-5 to Yonabaru Field where we stayed in tent city and slept in our sleeping bags. The mosquitoes were as large as buzzards and they had a field day feeding on us. (and no nets!)

To finish the story, that night we found a slop-chute where we could carry out beer. I purchased a case of Coors and packed it in my duffel bag to take back. Well we boarded our R4D-5 the next morning and took off for Shanghai. About halfway there one engine started acting up. The pilot assured us the R4D could fly fine on one engine, but we might need to lighten the plane of excess weight. I promptly broke out my case of Coors Beer, and we all had a can of beer, and then popped the empties out the vent. This must have been enough as we arrived safely in Shanghai. They reconnected something on the engine and we proceeded to Tsingtao.

On June 8, 1946 @ 0700 we departed Tsingtao, China aboard U.S.S. General H. W. Butner. We stopped in Shanghai to finish loading and arrived at Treasure Island, San Francisco, California, U.S.A. on June 24, 1946 where I received my honorable discharge from the Marine Corps.

ADDITIONAL HISTORY OF VMSB 343
FROM AUGUST 1945 TO APRIL 1946

by Robert Sherrod

Shortly after the war ended in August 1945, personnel of VMSB 231 were transferred to VMSB 343 at Ewa Marine Air station in Hawaii. VMSB 231 was sent back to the States on paper and I believe that the VMSB 343 personnel who had served on Midway were transferred back to the States for reassignment.

VMSB 343 reformed then boarded the USS Arneb (AKA 56) and sailed to Okinawa. Upon entering Buckner Bay, Okinawa the ship was advised to turn around and head for the open sea due to a severe typhoon headed in that direction. Typhoon Louise struck on October 8,9, & 10, 1945 with winds estimated at 150 mph and 60 ft. waves. The Arneb was able to make the open seas where many others did not. We were later informed that only the many thousands of gallons of aviation gasoline in the holds of the ship prevented a disaster (along with almost 270 ships that were sunk, grounded, or damaged beyond repair).*

After riding out the typhoon the Arneb sailed up the Yangtze River towards Shanghai where the Japanese managed to cut loose all the mines in the river, forcing the Arneb to retreat to the open sea.

The ship then headed for the port of Tsingtao on the Shantung Peninsula where VMSB 343 docked and we unloaded the cargo of gasoline and other supplies.

VMSB 343 was quartered at a Japanese airfield and in a former German school. This field was located in a neutral area between the Communist army and the Chinese Nationalist army and more often than not they chose to shell each other firing over our heads. The Communist ground forces often fired their rifles and machine guns at our planes but we were forbidden to fire back.

In April of 1946 many members of VMSB 343 were rotated back to the states for discharge aboard the USS Randall.
*Top Secret -- - - Davis, James Martin, Ranger Publications 19986 pp. 22-23.

Disaster struck the squadron on 8 December 1945, shortly after it participated in a mass parade formation over Tientsin. On the return trip to their base, six of the twelve planes were downed in a snowstorm. Several days later Chinese civilians had reported the location of five of the wrecked planes south of Laichow. Reports came in on 15 December, that two survivors were being cared for by the Communists at Ping Tu, and several days later Second Lieutenant Robert E.Blount and First Lieutenant Raymond B. Wordehoff were returned by the Communists. A military funeral for eight pilots and gunners whose remains were recovered was held on 28 December. On 31 January 1946 the missing pilots and gunners were transferred to the POW and Missing Persons Detachment, HCMC.

Pilots lost were:

1st Lt. William Noser, USMCR

2nd Lt. Leroy K. Sheldon, USMCR

Gunners lost were:

Sgt. Staacey J. Hammell, USMC

SSgt William E. Hickman, USMC (SS)

SSgt. Michael A. Carnival, USMCR

On 16 May 1946, various personnel were transferred to MAG-25, 1st MAW, FMF, while others were transferred to Service and Maintenance Squadron 32 (SMS-32), Mag-32, 1st MAW, FMF. The historical summary for May 1946 shows 21 officers and 57 enlisted transferred while 128 officers and men remained with the unit. The squadron embarked on board the USS General J. C. Breckinridge (APA-176) for return to the United Sates and arrived at San Francisco on 2 June 1946, joining Marine Air, West Coast (MAWC) from the lst MAW, FMF. During the period 18 May – 10 June, the squadron was attached to Headquarters Squadron, MAG-32, with Major W. F. Cornell assigned additional duties as the squadron commander.

The squadron was deactivated on 10 June 1946.

As of October 1967, the squadron was entitled to have the World War II Victory Streamer, the China Service Streamer (China, Oct. 1945-May 1946), and the National Defense Service Streamers attached to its colors.

Commanding Officers of VMSB 343

Major Walter E. Gregory	1 Aug 43 – 2 Aug 45
Major Harold G. Schlendering	3 Aug 45 – 17 Aug 45
Major Perry H. Aliff	18 Aug 45 - 30 Aug 45
Major Jack Cosley	31 Aug 45 – 10 Jan 46
Major Louis R. Buff – Acting	7 Jan 46 – 10 Jan 46
	11 Jan 46 – 16 May 46
Major W. F. Cornell	18 May 46 – 10 Jun 46

1ST MARINE AIR WING (MAW) MARINE AIR GROUP 32
MAG (32)
MARINE SCOUT BOMBERS VMSB 343

By Chet Hurd

Robert Sherrod's account of Dec. 8, 1945 is sketchy. I was one of the fortunate twelve who made it to the base safely that day. Ten of my friends did not.

Japan had surrendered in September, 1945, and the Marines were in China for two purposes; to transport Japanese soldiers back to Japan, and to provide a "show of strength" in support of Chian Kai Shek's Nationalist government. The Chinese Communists controlled the countryside, but not the major cities. By late 1949, after American forces had left the area, China came under Communist control.

On December 8, 1945, my twelve plane squadron, VMSB 343, was part of a show of strength flight over Tientsin 300 miles north of Tsingtao. The date was chosen to commemorate Pearl Harbor Day, December 7, in the U.S. Our round-trip flight from Tsingtao (now spelled Quingdao) was to be approximately four hours. I logged 4.7.

In the fly-over parade there were to be:

50 F4U's

7 F7F's

20 SB2C's

18 TBF's

Our flight formed up and left for Tientsin at approximately 8 A.M. The fly-over was to be at noon. Enroute, we flew at a very cold 8,000 feet altitude The.weather was partly cloudy. Even with fleece lined boots, my feet were cold!

On our return leg, we dropped to the warmer air at less than 1,000 feet About half way back, we encountered a dense snowstorm which we thought would be brief. It wasn't. We could not raise Tsingtao by radio and our vision was limited to our cockpit interior. Flying blind is not only unnerving – it is scary.

The flight leader's voice came over the headphones. He favored trying to go "under" the storm, but gave each pilot the freedom of choice.

My pilot was Lt. Bill Harper. "What do you think, Chet?" he asked.

"Upstairs sounds best to me," I replied.

"I vote the same," he said. His choice saved our lives.

We began climbing to 8,000 feet, still flying blind. I asked the Lord for a little help. He gave no audible response but guided our path.

Our 1942 map of Shantung Province showed hills and mountains near Tsingtao. These ranged in height from 300 feet to the Tai Shan range of 5,048 feet. Tai Shan was a centuries old sacred mountain which had 6,300 stone steps leading to its summit. It lay 80 miles NNW of Tsingtao. Eighty miles due north of Tsingtao were lower mountains with heights from 300 feet to over 2,000 feet. One such mountain, between Laichow and Pingtu, rose to 2,428 feet. We learned later that it was in this area that six of our planes struck a mountain at approximately 2,000 feet altitude. Four pilots and six radio-gunners were lost. Two pilots survived and were later retuned to base.

We continued SSE for about twenty minutes, then "Lo & Behold", we broke into a bowl of clear blue sky of about two miles diameter. Another SB2C of our flight was circling in the clearing. A third plane emerged from the clouds – upside down! I never learned the name of the pilot but he certainly gave credence to the effects of vertigo!

Within a short time we had a fix on the beam at Tsingtao. With our course set, we returned to the base.

It took two days of Sector Search patrols to locate the crash site. After another eight days of negotiating with the Chinese Communists, eight bodies were returned to Tsingtao, where they were interred on December 28, 1945.

There were no dry eyes when the bugle sounded Taps.

FINAL INTERMENT OF TEN MEMBERS OF VMSB-343 FROM TSINGTAO, CHINA

1948 – Remains of the following five Marines returned to the United States for burial at Ft. Scott National Cemetary, Fort Scott, Kansas:

S/Sgt Michael A.Carnival, USMCR
Sgt Stacy J. Hammell, USMC
S/Sgt William E. Hickman USMC
1st/Lt William Noser USMCR
2nd/Lt Leroy K. Sheldon USMCR

The following were intered as follows:

Sgt Frederick B. Campagna USMCR – Private burial 1947,
Mt. St. Mary's Cemetary, Flushing NY
2nd Lt Herbert R. Kruger USMCR – Private burial 1947
Resurrection Cemetary, Chicago IL
2nd Lt Kenneth V. Leeper USMCR – Private burial 1947
Wiscotta Cemetary, Redfield IA
S/Sgt Robert V. Luna USMCR – Private burial 1947
City Cemetary, Okmulgee OK
S/Sgt William R. St. Pierre, USMCR – Private burial 1948
St. Joseph Cemetary, Rutland VT

Source: Dept. of the Navy, Headquarters: United States. Marine Corps, Marine Corps Historical Center, 1254 Charles Morris St. S.E., Washington Navy Yard, DC 203745040

A SAD DAY IN TSINGTAO
DECEMBER 8, 1945

By Bill Harper

Herewith is a story of the disastrous flight of VMSB 343 from Tsingtao, China on December 8, 1945. In China, December 8 is the same as December 7 in the U.S.

Twelve SB2C-5's and twelve TBF's took off at 8 a.m. with the base commander leading. We were heading to Tientsin, and carried fifty-gallon wing tanks since we were not to land at Tientsin but make a round trip

We climbed to 8,000 feet to get over a storm north of our field. About an hour later arriving at Tientsin, we rendezvoused with twelve Corsairs from Bejing. After the rendezvous, we flew on a heading of 90 degrees for about twenty minutes, then turned around to a heading of 270 degrees to the shoreline.

At that time, the base commander relieved the Corsairs, and ordered the TBF's and the SB2C's to return to Tsingtao independently, by squadron.

I was flying on the extreme right flank of the formation. We were in a diamond shape. Our flight leader pointed his nose down to gain speed over the TBF's and so beat them back to the base. We were cruising at 200 knots.

About an hour later, we crossed the northern coast of the Shantung peninsula, but were heading into the back of the earlier storm. Since we were on a descending flight path we flew under the trailing edge of the storm. Then we encountered snow at about 450 feet over the terrain when we made landfall. The snow was forcing us lower. So at about 300 feet, someone yelled over the radio, "Let's get the hell out of here."

The flight leader pulled up and turned left, followed by nine planes. My roommate, Bo Bryant was flying on his left. We started to climb, but my leader started to spiral to the right into me. Since we were in the clouds, it was hard to fly straight.

My leader had not been through instrument refresher course in over a year. After straightening out on to 90 degrees, but still climbing, he went into another spiral. My roommate and I separated from him by about fifty feet, but still in formation. My leader then poured the coal to it and started to climb at a faster rate. I held my climb to 300 feet per minute, so as to conserve fuel for the long climb. After about thirty minutes I broke out at 10,000 feet but there was no one in sight. We were instructed to call Tsingtao homer for direction. After a long count, the homer directed me to the base. Then, my roommate broke out, and joined up with me on this heading.

After about twenty minutes, we were the first two to land, even ahead of the TBF's. We just couldn't believe that no other planes from our squadron had landed. Finally, after about fifteen minutes, my leader landed. We were the only 2C's that returned from the flight. This meant that nine 2C's were missing. The next day an inquiry was held by the Commanding General. Each one of the surviving pilots was questioned about the events of the flight. I told him where we crossed the coast before turning away from the formation.

The following day, we flew search flights over that route, but didn't see anything. Again, the next day, we repeated the search, and again nothing.

Finally, on the fourth day a native from the place where one of the missing pilots landed in a parachute drop, arrived at the base with the information where he could be found.

The 1st Marine Division, which was quartered in the city of Tsingtao sent several craft around to the northern shore, and rescued two pilots. They also found eight more bodies, and brought them back for burial. Only one pilot returned to the squadron, but he later was sent back to the States because he had injured his leg on the tail of the plane when he jumped.

His report led us to believe that the clouds were responsible for the other planes to become disoriented. The mountains north of the base were only about 300 feet high, but evidently the leader didn't pull up soon enough. Since we didn't hear any further calls after my leader's turn, it is felt that these nine planes ran into these mountains which were hidden in the falling snow.

The eight bodies brought back by the Division were laid to rest in the Tsingtao cemetery. For some reason, the squadron was not notified of the ceremony, so no one attended. The Skipper and Exec were relieved and replaced by a Major Babb who proceeded to snap the whip.

THE LOSS OF SIX SB2C-5'S DECEMBER 8, 1945
AS ENTERED IN MY LOG BOOK
BY PILOT, 1ST LT. WILLIAM BALLEW

by Harold Heinrichs

DATE TYPE OF NUMBER OF DURATION CHARACTER PILOT PASSANGER REMARKS

MACHINE MACHINE   OF FLIGHT OF FLIGHT

| 8 | SB2C5 | 83247 | 5.0 | K | BALLEW HEINRICHS |

PARADE COVER TO TIENTSIN LOST 6 ON RETURN

| 9 | SB2C5 | 83247 | 3.0 | J | BALLEW HEINRICHS |

SEARCH FOR PLANES

| 13 | SB-2C5 | 83289 | 1.5 | J | BALLEW HEINRICHS |

SEARCH FOR 3 SB2C5'S

MEMORIES of CHINA

by Chet Hurd

On Friday, October 12, 1945, the USS Arneb dropped anchor at 4 p.m. in Kiachow Bay, Tsingtao, China. The red tiled roofs of the city looked impressive. The concrete and brick buildings were well lighted by electricity. The port had an unpleasant smell and guard duty was assigned. I was given a Thompson sub-machine gun. I had no occasion to use it. The crated supplies and rations were transported by truck to the airfield, where they were stacked in the open. My assignment was changed from riding shotgun on trucks, to foot patrol around the supply dump. As a result, I was one of the first eighteen on the base

When off watch, we checked the empty buildings for souvenirs. I acquired an excellent locker box, two parade helmets, and two tennis racquets. I still retain Marine gear in the locker box. The tennis racquets no longer give service.

Off loading required four days. By October 17th, all gear was ashore. While waiting for the mess hall to be set up we served ourselves K-Rations from tins. On October 22nd, the mess hall began service and foodstuff was moved indoors from the supply dump. During that five-day period, while crates of C-Rations were under guard in the open, there was frequent pilfering of the crates for the bacon, candy, cigarettes, and toilet paper they contained. The guard detail was doubled, the loss increased. No culprits were apprehended.

A movie projection booth was built of wood along the West wall of the mess hall, and movies began showing by October 30, 1945. On April 8, 1946, the movie was, "A Guy, A Gal, & A Pal". The movie was not too hot, but before the second showing at 9:30 p.m., the mess hall was! A fire began in the projection booth and the mess hall was consumed, leaving only a brick shell. This was one of four destructive fires on the base. Three other fires preceeded the loss of the mess hall in 1946. MAG 25 lost their Quartermaster building, January 30, 1946; the parachute loft of VMSB 244 burned on February 8, 1946; then on March 1946, AG 25 had a $70,000 loss when their radio shop/parachute loft building was burned.

Cultural differences between the Orient and the United States became evident very early, during the off loading. On the road from the docks to the base, one could see women washing clothes in a roadside ditch, while unwashed children played nearby. A few yards upstream an unconcerned male would relieve himself in the same stream. Other parts of town were not so squalid.

When Germany controlled Tsingtao, during the 1920's to mid '30's, attractive homes of brick and concrete were built for the wealthy. These were in the hills behind the beach area and were in stark contrast with the living quarters of the average Chinese family.

The Edgewater Beach Hotel, located at the shoreline, was used as Officer quarters for the 6th Marine Division during 1945-46. The hotel was still serving the tourist trade in 1983. An international Conference on Oceanographic Technology was held in Tsingtao, June 1983. The enclosed postcards were sent me by a colleague who attended the conference in 1983.

Transportation within Tsingtao was mainly by foot or by rickshaw. Small, wiry Chinese would pull the two-wheeled rickshaws at a slow trot through the narrow streets. Most streets were but narrow lanes, not wide enough to accommodate the few charcoal burning and smoke belching taxis. The rickshaws were more dependable. Frequently, young boys would jog alongside a rickshaw and encourage the Marine rider to come visit his sister.

Radio/Gunners of VMSB343 were quartered in one story brick buildings on the base. Some of the pilots were also quartered on the base. Others were located at a BOQ outside the perimeter of the base. These buildings were well constructed, but lacked inside heads and showers. My room #14, held ten cots and we had adequate space. Showers were installed in our building, by January 23, 1946, and we no longer had to use the communal bathhouse.

The bathhouse was on a slight rise, fifty yards from our barracks. The traditional Japanese family bathes as a family – all in the same bath water – and apparently the same custom was observed by Japanese soldiers. Scuttlebutt had it, that the Tsingtao base was used for R & R for Japanese Officers. I have no documentation for that. The bathhouse was medium sized, and of brick, with many large windows to provide light. The bath pool was circular, like a wading pool, and held waist deep water heated by a coal-fired boiler. The boiler was stoked by a Japanese who was guarded by a Chinese soldier. The tiled pool was approximately twenty feet in diameter. Early bathers got clean water. Late bathers were not so fortunate.

Another oddity to us as Americans was the Japanese style of latrine. Their head was a separate building, also of brick, which was fifteen feet long by ten feet wide. Their appointments were of enamel and tile, but no toilets! In place of our customary seat to sit on, there were only enamel basins at floor level, designed to squat over. By October 19, 1945, the carpenters had converted crates into seats for these latrines. This served until more customary outhouses were built.

On October 17th I reported home that at least four of us had obtained samurai swords from a Chinese Captain in charge of confiscated weapons. My pilot at that time was Jack Mimnaugh, who had heard of the possibility. (Mimnaugh later transferred to TBF's.) He loaned me a 2nd Lieutenants bar, to observe protocol, and we made a visit to the Chinese Captain. We made what conversation we could, gave him four packs of Camel cigs, and came away with a sword apiece! At that time, we knew of only two others who had gotten swords –Mimnaugh's roommate and the Squadron doctor.

On October 19, 1945 the officials who were to officiate in the formal surrender ceremonies of October 26th deplaned at the field. The entourage included a Chinese General and a Japanese Admiral. Brigadeer General Clemens represented the U.S. The party spent very little time at the field before leaving for town.

Crewmembers of VMSB244 arrived from the Philippines on October 19, 1945. We learned that there was to be two dive bomber squadrons, VMSB343 and VMSB244, plus one TBF Squadron at the field. With a regiment of 22nd Marines and two Service Squadrons, there would be some 5,000 personnel on the base. By October 22nd the aircraft for these squadrons were on the field. On October 24th seventy F4U's landed at Tsingtao, enroute to Tientsin and Peiping.

The official ceremony for the Japanese surrender of the base took place on October 25, 1945. In the fly-over parade, VMSB343 and VMSB242 put thirty-six SB2C's in the air, accompanied by twenty-one TBF's. It was our first squadron flight in China – Mimnaugh was my pilot. (See Chinese Newspaper enclosed.).

During our first three weeks at Tsingtao, the paper currency in use was the yuan notes issued by the Federal Reserve Bank (FRB) of China. The exchange rate for these notes was 3,000 to one dollar U.S. currency. To stabilize the currency, new bank notes were issued in November '45 from the Chinese National Bank (SNC) in Chunking. The new rate of exchange was to be 2,000 to 1.

The base Colonel informs us on the 24th of October that Japanese soldiers had been rearmed to guard the base perimeter against the Chinese Communists who occupied the hill area five miles out. Within two weeks we learn that a battalion of 6th Marines had assumed this responsibility.

Beginning November 1, 1945 Radio Gunners with rates below Sgt. Were assigned to mess duty. I was so assigned. I did not learn until November 21st that I had been made Sgt. on August 18, 1945!

Chinese workmen were allowed on the base to perform odd jobs. Their presence created a minor problem around the mess hall garbage cans. Eager to retrieve anything edible, the Chinese would gather near the exit to gather discarded food, which they would put into any small containers they could find. It became necessary to post a guard at the exit to avoid congestion.

The mess hall entrée for November 12, 1945 was fresh shrimp. I noted this date because I spent the entire morning cleaning shrimp! Had I any vote in the manner, I would have been flying! However, I did not have to clean the turkey for the Thanksgiving meal, November 29th. That menu is enclosed.

Our first mail call in China was on November 14th. On that same date, 28,000 Chinese troops arrived to strengthen the force around the airfield.

MAG 25 was aboard by November 16, 1945.

During our early patrol flights over the area, our planes were subject to small arms fire from the Chinese Communists. A few planes received small puncture holes, but none were seriously damaged. The Base Commander threatened to bomb the village area near where the ground fire had come; we never did. Ground fire was only a threat when we were flathatting over the countryside.

Mess duty for me ended on November 30, 1945, but two of my friends from VMSB244 were not so fortunate —they were assigned an additional month! All Radio/Gunners in VMSB244 below the rate of Staff Sgt. were reassigned to the Spec. Number for General Duty (521). Jack Jensen and Bob Runyan were displeased! Later Bob Runyan was given an assignment more suited to his artistic talent. He was selected to paint murals on the walls of the NCO club. His illustrations of the female form rivaled that of Esquire's Petty. Much later, 1960, Runyan had received international acclaim for his work as a Graphic Designer and Art Director. The Olympic Committee of 1984 selected Runyan's Stars-In-Motion design as the official Olympic Symbol for 1984.

Electricity in the barracks was unreliable during December of 1945. Any night activity in the barracks was lighted by candle or lantern. By January '46 dependable service was restored.

Stateside beer became available in the slop-chute by December 5, 1945. In addition to Iron City brew, we could spend our two per day ration on Schlitz, Blatz, Pabst, or Budweiser. These could be augmented by a few bottles of the local Tsingtao beer obtained at "The Wall". Local beer had risen in price from five cents per bottle in October to thirty-five cents per bottle in December.

"The Wall" was of brick, ten feet high, and flanked both sides of the Main Gate entrance. Marines would sit atop the wall and bargain with Chinese peddlers below. At this open air flea market, one could buy eggs, chickens, wristwatches, postcards, trinkets, and Tsingtao beer. "The Wall" was a popular place to shop during October and November, but lost some of its charm by December when regular liberty sections had been set up.

VMSB343 lost a total of seven SB2C's in China. Six of those on December 8, 1945 (December 7, 1945 in U.S.) on the return from the Tientsin air parade. You have several reports, and recollections about that flight in the snow storm. I sent you my recollection last Spring. The 7th SB2CX which was lost, went down in Kiachow Bay on May 3, 1946. The Radio/Gunner on that plane was Crook. I do not know who the pilot was.(Capt.Wilcox) Crook's pilot's engine conked out, and they pancaked in the Bay and were picked up by Chinese fishermen. Neither pilot nor gunner were injured.

Here is a brief chronology for December 1945:

12-9-45 (Sun) Sector search hops begun, seeking downed planes

12-10 (Mon) Air crews from December 8th hop, report to Gen. Johnson,

Assistant Wing Commander.

Pilots make written reports. Gunners not questioned.

12-12 (Wed) No word of planes.

12-13-45 Full greens issued. I took mine to a tailor in town. Later a Squadron

picture was taken, per the copy of enclosed. Picture date???

12-14-45 We know little about what happened to missing planes.

12-17 We learn that two pilots survived – Lt. Bob Blount and 1st Lt. Ray

Wordenhoff; ten were lost, four pilots and six Radio/Gunners. On this date we

had very heavy snow with strong winds – some rudders were damaged by the

wind.

12-18-45 Water pipes frozen – ice in the Bay.

12-22-45 Payday! We were paid in $5 bills. I had 35!

12-24-45 For Christmas Eve our pilots played Santa and brought us gifts of a

basket with peanuts, sardines, cigs, and beer.

12-28-45 Funeral for the eight bodies returned. Interment in the Tsingtao International Cemetery. Two bodies were never recovered. Also, on this date, Russ Moore received a package at Mail call. It had been mailed on September 18, 1943!

12-31-45 Lights were back on in the barracks. The Red Cross opens a canteen across the road from the barracks. Still cold weather – ice remains in the Bay and canteens freeze.

1-3-46 VMSB244 cuts all flight orders for Radio/Gunners with rates less than Staff Sgt. VMSB343 will retain twenty-four Radio/Gunners.

1-7 In an afternoon Alert Drill, 343 put four planes up in eight minutes.

1-13 Bob Blount visits me.

1-22 Showers were completed in our barracks.

1-30 Mag 25 Quartermaster building burns at 7:30 a.m.

2-8 Mag 25 Parachute loft Quonset hut burns

2-19 I have a hop over the Commie port of Cheefoo, with Dwight Deay as pilot.

2-21 We receive a blue and white tin button from Chang Kai Shek with the promise of a better one later. I received the better one in August, 1987! All who served in China qualify. See letter with address enclosed.

3-2 Gen. Wedemeyer visited the base in the morning, VMSB343 sent up a twelve plane escort for his R4D's arrival. The morning escort was uneventful – the afternoon departure escort, Bill discovered that the protective sleeve was still on the pitot tube! After a hot landing, and removal of the sleeve, we were again airborne – but playing catch up! We neared our flight a few miles out, as they were making a climbing, starboard turn, on their approach to join up with the Generals R4D. Bill had the throttle in, to make the join up. By the time we had leveled off, to join, we were carrying a load of several knots more than our Major's lead plane. Our assigned slot was on the Major's starboard side, and to port of the General's R4D. We glided through that slot, smooth as silk, and led the parade! Smoke came from our headphones and the air turned blue from the

Major's comments. We dropped out and returned to base early. I was fortunate to talk with Bill, in April 1999. We made plans to meet during the Summer. That is now postponed until he and I can meet later, at some air-speed class in the sky. He was a friend.

3-10-46 On this Sunday ten of us went rabbit hunting in the hills around Tsingtao. Our houseboy, Louie, was our guide. We checked out shotguns from the Rec. Dept. Willie Dawe had a 36" barrel, full choke shotgun. The rest of us had riot guns with trapload of eight chilled shot. We left the base at 7:30 a.m. and tramped the hills until 4:30 p.m. Three of our party, Willie Dawe, Harry Henirichs, and Les Sheplor bagged one rabbit each. The rest of us bagged only tired feet! Enroute back, we stopped at Louie's small village and left the game with his family. Louie's village was of adobe and the huts had dirt floors. His mother sat before a small hearth of charcoal embers, stirring a blackened pot containing vegetables. Her feet were bound and appeared to be about four inches long, an ancient custom designed to prevent wives from running away from home. She was very happy to get the rabbits. At a widened space between the huts was the "honey dippers" mound of dung, to be used for fertilizer in the overworked soil of China.

3-13-46 We get word to not fly over the Commie port of Cheefoo. 175 miles across the Lao-Tiehshan Channel was Port Arthur, a Communist port of the Soviets. This port was named Port Arthur /Darien in 1946. It is now named Luta.

3-17 High point men begin leaving for the States. Chaplain Pat Paterson will soon leave for the States. He will be replaced by D. D. Wilkinson as Chaplain.

3-19 Enroute from Peiping, F4U's of Fighter Squadron 541 land at Tsingtao to refuel, and then on to Okinawa. Mag 25 loses $70,000 worth of equipment when their Radio/Parachute Loft building burns.

3-29 Squadron party in town – Menu enclosed.

4-4 My last hop with Bill Harper – he will ship out soon. We pull a three day RON in Tientsin. I am able to visit with a Cousin who is in the 3rd Marine Division stationed there.

4-6 Our barracks are nearly empty – 75% of Squadron has shipped for home with the thirty-five point men. (I have 29!)

4-8 Mess Hall burns.

4-14 On this Sunday, a Chinese pilot retracts too early on takedoff and pancakes an R4D.

4-15 General Farrell to inspect the base on Tuesday (4-16) and General Woods to inspect on Wednesday. (4-17)

4-16 I have a hop to Tientsin, and return with Croninger as pilot.

From 4-17 to 4-29 little was happening; 177 left in the Squadron, and rain caused flights to be scratched.

5-1-46 With Sims as pilot I have a Ground Control air hop.

5-3 With Capt. Wilcox, we make strafing runs on ships in the harbor. One plane, with Crook as Gunner, conks out and pancakes in the Bay. Neither Crook nor pilot was injured. I do not know the pilot's name.

5-5 VMSB244 is packing gear to move out. I ask to be removed from flight list.

5-8 Harry Heinrichs won at Bingo at the Red Cross and gave me his chicken dinner prize ticket. I am to fly with Captain Wilcox (5-13) to ferry planes to Okinawa. I ask him to delete me and he does. Only the 3rd Brigade remains, of the 6th Marine Division.

5-12 Last liberty to be granted.

5-13 Those not on ferrying duty will board ship USS Breckinridge on Saturday, May 18th.

6-5 After a brief stop at San Francisco, we have arrived at a nearly empty base, Mirimar, San Diego.

6-21-46 Received discharge and travel pay. Headed for Kansas!

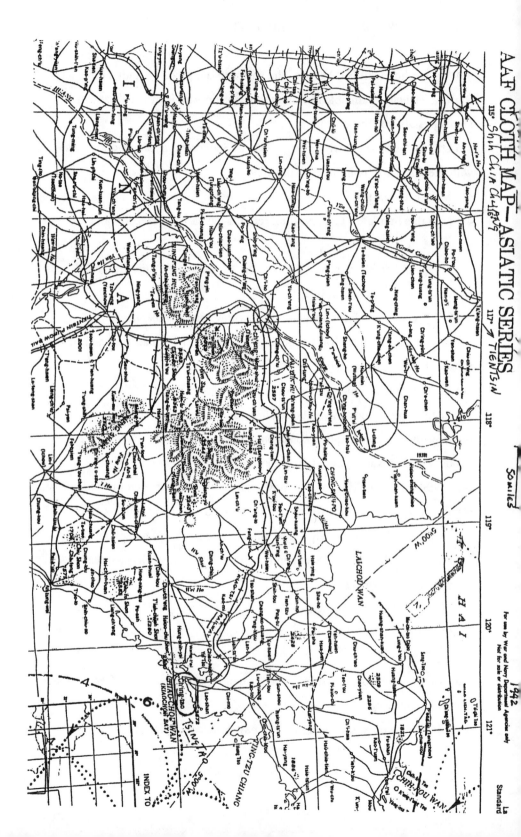

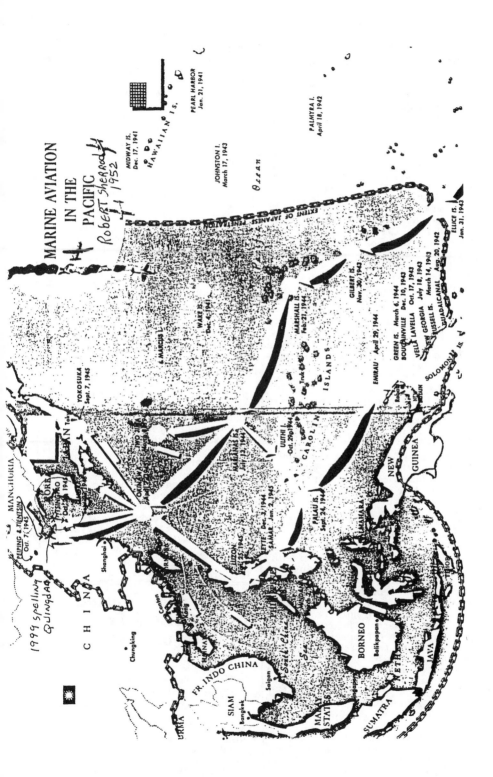

MARINE AVIATION
IN THE
PACIFIC
Robert Sherrod
1952

MANCHURIA

1999 spelling
Quingdao

CHINA

PEIPING & TIENTSIN
Oct. 7, 1945

TSINGTAO
Oct. 1945

Chungking

Shanghai

Canton

JAPAN

Tokyo

YOKOSUKA
Sept. 7, 1945

OKINAWA

IWO JIMA

MARCUS I.

WAKE IS.
Dec. 4, 1941

MIDWAY IS.
Dec. 17, 1941

HAWAIIAN IS.

PEARL HARBOR
Jan. 21, 1941

PALMYRA I.
April 18, 1942

JOHNSTON I.
March 17, 1943

Ocean

EXTENT OF JAPANESE PENETRATION

FORMOSA

LUZON

LEYTE Dec. 3, 1944
SAMAR Jan. 2, 1945

FR. INDO CHINA

Saigon

SIAM

Bangkok

BURMA

MALAY STATES

SUMATRA

BORNEO

Balikpapan

JAVA

NETH

Celebes

Sea

PALAU IS.
Sept. 24, 1944

UITHI I.
Oct. 29, 1944

CAROLINE ISLANDS

Truk Is.

MARIANAS IS.
July 13, 1944

MARSHALL IS.
Feb. 21, 1944

GILBERT IS.
Nov. 30, 1943

EMIRAU   April 29, 1944

GREEN IS.   March 6, 1944
BOUGAINVILLE   Dec. 10, 1943
VELLA LAVELLA   Oct. 17, 1943
NEW GEORGIA   July 18, 1943
RUSSELL IS.   March 14, 1943
GUADALCANAL   Aug. 20, 1942

SOLOMON IS.

NEW GUINEA

NEW BRITAIN

Rabaul

ELLICE IS.
Jan. 31, 1943

Cherryvale Marine Gets "Off the Track" In Tour of China

The following is taken from a letter received by Mr. and Mrs. C. A. Hurd from their son, Sgt. Chester Hurd, who is with the United States marine corps in Tsingtao, China. The letter was dated Jan. 11:

I'm sorry I haven't written sooner but I've been on a sort of disorganized tour of China. Last Tuesday I had a Tientsin search hop in a four-plane section, following the railway up to Tientsin, but somewhere along the line we got off the track (literally) and were lost! The weather was good, with only a little haze, but after we'd been up for four hours and running low on gas—70 gallons—I began to think we'd have to set down in the boondocks when we sighted a small air strip at the foot of some mountains. We circled and saw only Nip planes on the strip, but with no radio contacts with our bases, and not knowing where we were, we had to land—taking a chance the field was not in Communist's hands.

As soon as we cut our engines a group of Japs and Chinese gathered around and we wondered if we were to be interned by the Reds. Presently a Chinese officer arrived who spoke English, and we were relieved to learn they were friendly to Americans. He said he could supply us with 150 gallons of 100 octane gas—enough to reach Peiping, only an hour away by air. Peiping? That was definitely off our intended course, but such was the case. It was four in the afternoon by then, and as their method of refueling was very slow (all done manually) we decided to ron tuere (remain over night). The name of the town was Shih Chia Chuang and wasn't even on our maps, but a good sized city nevertheless. The truth is, we were not only off our own course, but so far off the territory we were in wasn't even on our maps! The Chinese officer told us we chose the best field cause only five miles away was a Communist-held air strip! But without that question for a burden we headed for Shih Chia Chunag!

The driver of our truck took us to a cafe and we ordered supper. What a town—no swabbies! In fact, no Americans! But soon in rushed a Catholic missionary to welcome us. He was a Dutchman, spoke very good English and was bubbling over with enthusiasm at our arrival. He told us there had been only one other American there, an army colonel, and the people had spread the word throughout the town that we were there so he came to see us. After we ate, we went to his church to meet his associates, a Frenchman (who spoke no English but gave us some French tobacco because I could say "merci beauceaup" which I think means "thanks" in French); a Chinese doctor who spoke good English, and a Chinese priest who spoke only Chinese.

The Dutchman told us the town had been bombed by the Americans and as souvenirs we had some bomb fragments. He also had been in a concentration camp for two years while the Japs were in power, and as gratefully as he expressed himself made me feel almost humble—he was so thankful to us. Anyhow, after talking for quite some time, in came the mayor to pay his respects and offer his services and before we left for the field that night he gave us three cartons of Chinese cigs (we were completely out, all eight of us), a basket of pears and a basket of grapes. In every other sentence they all apologized for being unable to do more for us. They were really nice.

That night we slept in some Nip quarters as the facilities at the base were poor compared to our living standards. The personnel at the base consisted of Chinese officers and Nip enlisted men. However, I did sleep that night and the next morning (Wednesday) we went into town for breakfast. The mayor and some gent with the title of "sub general" had planned a sort of banquet for us. We ate at the same cafe as the preceding night, and what a

Cherryvale Marine Gets "Off the Track" In Tour of China

(Continued from Page 1)

meal! First, we had a plate of cold cuts, next a bowl of soup, followed by an egg omelet. Then they brought us a steak and French fries (and at this point, I was stuffing myself) After we finished that, fried chicken and rice were served, and remember, many cups of tea between each course. After that meal I was really full. As it was after nine when we finished eating (we were in a hurry to get back into the air) we rushed back to the field to be off.

We took the Chinese doctor and the Dutchman along to see our planes and they were as excited as children. Well, it developed that only two planes would start—Nick Blache's and mine, so we two took off, gave the field a buzz and headed for Peiping. When we arrived there we informed "Operations" of the location of the town and they sent a transport down with a starter and heater. My pilot went back with the R40 and Nick, his pilot and I went into Peiping.

What a change from Tsingtao! Trolleys, clean streets, worth-while merchandise, and European hotels with baths! We got a room in the Peiping hotel for 60 cents apiece and had a nice bath and then Nick and I went out to shop. We had only an hour to look around as it was 5:00 p. m. then, but I found time enough to buy some bracelets made of filigree silver which I think are very nice. The differences between Tsingtao and Peiping are beyond even comparing. Anyhow, the other two planes came in and the next morning we planned to leave, but the colonel advised us not to leave there until he arrived with an R40 to escort us back. I guess he figured we'd get lost again, but we did as he directed and so here I am, safe and sound. And that's where I've been these past three days. I hope you weren't worried about me. I'm alright, except my beard is pretty long right now.

Lt. Blount came in to see me the next day after we got back. We didn't know each other but knew the same kids in Independence.

I was just thinking of something that might be interesting to you that I haven't mentioned before and that is that the Chinese cannot understand how we drink cold water! They drink only hot water, and it baffles them that we drink it cold. Screwy, isn't it? But so is China.

CHINA – ADDENDUM

by Chet Hurd

On one occasion, I attended a Chinese opera performance in Tsingtao. I believe it was an opera because the performers wore ornate costumes and there was a semblance of musical sound. The sound, however, seemed to be produced by striking various gongs, while stage hands jostled tin cans in barrels and slapped flat sticks together. The audience was either involved, or inattentive, for they were quite noisy. Perhaps that is why the musical sounds were high-pitched twangs and bangs, with a frequent crashing of cymbals. I learned no tune to whistle.

The Chinese utilize every possible planting space. Small terraced plots of ground appeared as steps going up the hillsides. Outside of the cities of Shantung Province, it was very rare to see a tree of any sort; wood of any kind was an expensive commodity.

In Tsingtao, the Catholic Church (pix enclosed) and a Buddhist Temple gave evidence of past missionary work. However, I saw no evidence that Taoism was popular. For most Chinese, Confucianism was the guide for political and social living.

The Confucian concept of devotion to family and ancestor worship was visible at burial locations around Tsingtao. From the air, one could see row after row of mounds of soil, some much larger than others. These were the older graves, made larger from the custom of depositing a spade of soil each year on an ancestor's grave. The larger the mound, the older the grave.

1999 Airfare to Tsingtao, via Korean Airlines leaving Kansas City, Missouri: $1099.

RE-ASSIGNED TO VMSB 343

By Robert Hellen

After Japan surrendered we were on Majuro Island in the Marshall chain. I was, or still am, a radio gunner in the SBD's & SB2C's. Of course, everyone was thinking of going home!! At roll call one morning all flight personnel were ordered to report to Tsingtao, China by fastest possible means. Getting flights going west was quite a chore. I, NCO in charge of Gunners, had to break up our group into several small ones to facilitate the transportation.

I guess after several weeks a portion of us arrived at our destination. We flew patrols from Tsingtao, to Tientsen and Peking. We lost six planes and crews (SB2C's). They crashed into nearby mountains on a return patrol in a blinding snowstorm. I have some pictures of burial in Tsingtao, cemetery.

My story was a week or two later. On a routine patrol to Peiping, three of us (a section), with Lt. Delano and myself as section leader, and our wing-men (names elude me now) were lost and running low on fuel. Darkness was coming on fast. We had all decided to pick a spot and do a wheels up landing in order to stay close to each other. In those days the Communists weren't too friendly!!

We were preparing for our landing when one of us sighted a short landing strip. On approaching we noted two or three Jap Zeros on the strip!! Delano decided we would go in first and the other two would circle and see what happened. I mentioned to Lt. Delano, "I hope they know the war is over!!"

We landed and a cloud of sand and dust was something else. There must have been two to three inches of dust and sand on the strip. I got out on wing and directed Lt. Delano to a small building where the Zeros were parked. We came to a stop and about thirty or forty troops, waving and brandishing rifles came rushing toward us. I figured this is it, and Lt. and I with one 38 and a 45.

Lt. Delano and I got out and meantime the other two planes were circling. An officer approached and he spoke pretty good English. "You need gas?" It turned out they were Chinese troops. We signaled the other planes to land. We were put up in Chinese officers quarters (a padded mat on the floor). That evening a French Catholic Priest from a mission came and invited us to dine with him at the mission. We accepted and were treated royally by Nuns and Priest, and a Chinese Bishop!!

The next day the priest, who spoke French, English, Chinese, and Japanese, the Nuns and the Bishop all came to see us off. We had used radio at Air Strip to contact Peiping, who in turn called our base at Tsingtao. The CO of our base came up in a DC-3 to guide us home. I'm sure there was some ass-chewing given those pilots.

I often wondered about this episode and if any of those involved are still with us.

MY CHINA EXPERIENCE

By Don Lipsi

In your request for news of China Marines I will try not to be redundant. VMSB 231 *Ace of Spades", upon returning to Hawaii for Operation Olympic obtained all new equipment and upon the termination of the war most of us were transferred to 343. As the first echelon we boarded the AKA 56 USS Arneb at Pearl Harbor in September 1945 and sailed to Bruckner Bay, Okinawa. Upon arrival we were ordered back out to sea along with the entire Pacific Fleet due to Typhoon Louise, a very severe and destructive storm where the ship was more under water than on it. It was a very frightening experience. After the storm abated we sailed up the Yangtze River for the city of Shanghai, when the Japanese decided to cut the mines loose in the river. We quickly turned around and headed back out to sea. As I recall the Marines were itching to use the mines as target practice but, the ship's captain only permitted the sailors to shoot. Needless to say no one single mine was hit. We then headed to the port city of Tsingtao where we disembarked and were taken by the trucks of the sixth Marines to the nearby airfield where we were quartered in an old German schoolhouse that had served as quarters for Japanese officers.

I recall the many Chinese applauding us and of them standing at the end of our runway cheering as each plane took off or landed. At that time the weather was quite warm and many of our communications men were followed by the Chinese. When the Marines took off their dungaree jackets and shirts, the Chinese, who have little or no body hair, were amazed at the amount of hair we had on our chests and out of curiosity would touch our hairy chests.

We were ordered to spike our 20 mm cannons and ordered not

to fire back at the Chinese Communists who often fired at our aircraft in the air and at us on the ground.

On December 7, 1945 many of our planes took part in a victory celebration flyover at Peking and on the return trip back to Tsingtao, flew into a severe snow squall where we lost seven planes and their crews. I will never forget that incident for I was scheduled to fly as gunner when I was bumped off the flight for someone else.

My most vivid memory of China is the poverty and hunger of its people. After the last of us emptied our mess kits into the garbage cans the Chinese were allowed to take all they wanted of the leftover garbage and they usually took it all. Also, since there is little or no fertilizer in China they would often wait to clean out our slit trenches, jumping in with bare feet and a large bucket to fill their carts. Is it any wonder why we were forbidden to eat the fruit and vegetables of the region?

We celebrated Thanksgiving with a turkey dinner, and Christmas with an excellent dinner (no seconds) and several parties. In February we helped the Chinese celebrate their little New Years and a week later their big New Years.

I along with many members of 343 were rotated back to the States for discharge in March of 1946, but 343 continued to stay in China with our replacements until later in the year.

A RUDE AWAKENING

By Don Lipsi

While stationed in Tsingtao at airfield #1, we were restricted from going into a neighboring village that was put off-limits due to Communist Control. At night we usually climbed over the wall surrounding the air base and walked to the village for a little R&R. One evening while walking to the village, an MP jeep on patrol was observed coming down the road and we immediately dispersed, diving into the bushes alongside the road. It was my unfortunate situation to land hands down into a still warm do-do from a recent Chinamen. Well, I had to maintain a position hands down with my nose about one inch from that do-do until the MP jeep was safely out of sight. When the all clear sound came, I smelled so bad they would not let me walk with them until we got to town where I could clean up. I learned not to dive into the bushes that day.

CHINESE HUNTING PARTY

By Doug Charles

Our squadron had been transferred to Hawaii, and in July 1945 we were getting new planes, new shoes, new clothing, new equipment, and the US Vac Shots. The scuttlebutt was that our squadron was going into Japan as part of a carrier task force. They dropped "the bomb" and everyone thought they would be going home. But we were wrong.

Everyone was loaded on a victory ship, The USS Arneb, and we were headed for China. Enroute we ran into the tail end of a monsoon or typhoon near Okinawa and we were in danger of being sunk. Through skillful maneuvering of our ship by the Captain, we survived, although many ships were sunk. We landed in Tsingtao on the Shantun Peninsula. Our squadron was the first Americans seen in this area for a very long time. We were transported in open semi-trailers and the Chinese had hung flags across the roads on cords. Because the trucks were so high, the cords were hitting us in the face. We got to the abandoned Japanese airfield where we were to be stationed. There was an abandoned Japanese air school and a former German school. A lot of scavenged Zeros were sitting on the airstrip.

The troops were put up in a large ranch-type house, which I think was the former German school. We put up bunks and potbelly stoves to keep warm since it was very cold. This was probably late October. There was a lot of disease going around. We were located in a neutral area located between the Nationalist Army and the Communist Army. They would shell each other, lobbing shells over our position, but none of us were ever hurt.

We set up a big warehouse, cleaned it up, repairing it in the process. Then we put up a lot of women's pictures on the walls.

We also got hold of a lot of beer that was sold at five cents a can. We set out GI cans for empties, so we could party.

Then someone devised a game we would play called "Numbers". You would sit around tables, and one person would call out numbers. 1,2,3 - - you hit the bottom of the table. Call out 4 – you hit the top of the table, then 5,6,7 – under, 8 on top. The numbers keep going up in increments of 4. If you miss you had to chug-a-lug a beer, stand up on your seat and then throw the empty into an empty GI can. If you missed the GI can you had to chug-a-lug another beer.

This was done to keep us on Base. This big warehouse was about a mile from the main base. From time to time they'd find one of our guys half-frozen along the way back.

Inside another building the Japs had a huge pool 40' x 40'. Their custom was to soap themselves down and submerge themselves in the pool. The Marines wouldn't do that, so they just poured a bucket of water on their head to rinse off. They learned not to take their clothes along. It took us almost a month to figure out the power house to be able to supply warm water.

There was a thirteen-year old Chinese boy who wanted some food. He had nothing but rags, and was filthy. The parachute rigger sewed him some clothes out of old dungarees, and the kid started living with us, to keep the fire going and clean the barracks. One day we noticed something missing, and we accused the kid of stealing. We warned him, gave him a toothbrush and made him clean up. Unfortunately, we caught him stealing again and we had to kick him out.

We were assigned to do reconnaissance flights using F4U Corsairs, which meant all the gunners were transferred. Then we went back to using SB2C's and mechanics became gunners on those flights.

After a while boredom set in, and a group of us decided to go hunting. We took a weapons carrier one Sunday morning, and we had our M-I's and Carbines, and a few of us had 45's. In the group was a Second Lieutenant, a Warrant Officer, and some NCO's. We drove into a little town at about 5 a.m., circled around and found ourselves facing a boarded up end of town. We turned to back up and found ourselves surrounded by fifteen to twenty rough looking guys with rifles. They put the rifles on our throats, but our Second Lieutenant said to play it cool. We thought it was the end. We tried to explain what we were doing, but since our ability to speak Chinese was lousy, we didn't accomplish much. After two or three hours a Chinamen came up and said "Americanisk", obviously Russian. One of our Marines, Mike, spoke Russian and he talked to the man to explain we were there to hunt rabbits, and not to hurt anyone. He also said our men back at the base knew where we were. They finally let us go, and our hunting expedition was over. We drove straight back to our Base.

When we got back we found they were warming up the planes to go look for us. The Major called us all in to chew us out, individually. He said we could have easily caused an international incident, and he should bust us all. Fortunately, he didn't. We had all learned a lesson.

SECTION VIII

THE ORIGIN
& HISTORY

OF

VMSB 343
REUNION
ASSOCIATION

ORIGIN AND FOUNDING OF VMSB 343
REUNION ASSOCIATION

by Ralph Heidenreich

Early in July 1986 I received a telephone call at my home in Greenville, North Carolina.

"Hello, is Ralph Heidenreich there?"

"Yes, this is Ralph."

"Glen Kelley here, a VMSB 343 Marine!"

"Hi, Glen, what brings you to Greenville?"

"I have a daughter living here and I want to contact former VMSB 343 members and get a reunion started. I called T/Sgt. Bill Wells and he told me you lived here also. He said he thought you would probably be interested."

Glen and I agreed to meet at the Ramada Inn for lunch. He expressed to me his desire to have a reunion in Greenville over the Labor Day weekend. Of course, I was not receptive to this idea, it being July and Labor Day the first of September!! As I explained to Glen, I felt sure everyone had probably already made plans for this upcoming holiday. I also pointed out that we had no names, mailing addresses of former members, and even if we did, who would be responsible for room reservations, etc. for such an undertaking? We both agreed that the time element was against us at this time, but we would try later to accomplish a reunion next year. We said our goodbyes and parted.

The next thing I know, I receive a telephone call from Charlie Franzo in Reno, Nevada. Charlie was a former member of VMSB 343 and was our mail clerk. I was advised that he and Glen Kelley had put together a reunion in Reno for the early part of March 1987. Of course I asked who all was coming, and was advised there would be former members present and my presence was desired.

For the next month Charlie and I were in constant contact. I did not want to incur all the expense a trip to Reno, Nevada from Greenville, North Carolina would entail unless I was sure others would be present. Finally, Evelyn and I decided we would go for it. Early in March 1987 we flew to Reno to meet with former buddies of mine.

We arrived in Reno and went to Karl's Casino and hotel where the reunion was to take place. There we were met by Charlie and Dottie Franzo, Eddie & Libby Galante, Bill and Dena Gregory, Norman Brown, Steve and Gene Greytak, Willie Kalmoe, Glen Kelley, Donald and Doris LeMar, Walter and Shirley LeTendre, Chuck and Peg Luedtke, Tom and Barbara McInerney, John Sandefur, Joe and Glorie Swenarski, Al and Evy Vazac, Alex Anderson, John and Carol Jacobs, "Bo" and Mary McCann, Jack Milarch and Sam Motolla!

What a reunion Charlie and Dotty put on!! The arrangements at Karl's, the meals and gambling, but most of all reuniting with buddies we had not seen in over forty years! What a time that was!! The "icing on the cake" was Gene Greytak, Steve's brother. Gene is a Pope John Paul III look-a-like. With permission from the Vatican, Gene dons his robes and comes in to talk to us. As you can well imagine, all of us nearly dropped dead when he walked in. Although Gene had been with us all the time, when he walked in that night no one realized it was Gene we were looking at! He was an absolute "dead-ringer". After all of us recovered from the shock and realized it was Gene, we talked him into strolling through Karl's Casino with all of us trailing along behind. What an experience!! Gene blessed everyone as he passed by. One lady pulling a twenty-five cent slot looked up, saw Gene, fell to her knees and made the sign of the cross, kissed his ring, and immediately jumped up and pulled the handle for the next spin of the wheel. It was absolutely hilarious!!! That stroll through that casino was really something else. We all laughed so hard the tears were rolling down our cheeks. What a night!!!

At the business meeting, before the "Pope's" visit, we agreed the next reunion would be held in Greenville, North Carolina, where VMSB 343 was stationed. All I can say about that was we had very strong feelings about returning to Greenville. Evelyn and I agreed to act as Chairman for this event even though no funds were available, no roster, but a great big desire to go forward for our next reunion. Before I agreed to chair this event, I asked Evelyn if she were "game" even though we knew it was going to cost us upwards of $1,000. She said, "Let's go for it!"

We returned to Greenville, and for the rest of 1987 and into 1988 it was on!! Evelyn had one time locating former members. She would be fed information from others, and be off. When I would come home from work I would find a most excited wife telling me who she had found, what they talked about, and as a result of one conversation, being given information about someone else who she had called, etc. etc. I wondered what in the world my telephone bill was going to be like each month!!!

After all the searching in the dark to put on a reunion - the "how-to's" and "what-to's", etc. in April 1988 we put it on. We had sixty-eight Marines and their ladies in attendance. The highlight of this venture was seeing former buddies come in who had not seen each other in over forty years, and the excitement of reuniting. It was a very moving and exhilarating experience!!!! What a time we had!!! It was worth every bit of the time and effort it took to accomplish this undertaking. At our banquet and dance on the last night, "Hap" Simpson and Gayle Haughton took up a collection, and with this money, Evelyn and I came out on a break-even basis.

The 1989 Reunion was held in Milwaukee, Wisconsin with Wally LeTendre as Chairman. It was at this reunion we appointed a chairman to work on constitution and by-laws, and Evelyn was appointed as secretary-treasurer. In 1990 the reunion was held in Nashville, TN. It was there we adopted our constitution and by-laws recommended by the committee of Walter "Bill" Gregory, Ralph Heidenreich, and Walter LeTendre, chairman.

So here we are today preparing to return again to Nashville, TN for our thirteenth reunion with Harold Gore again chairing it with Leonard Haney, co-chairman. Every reunion gets better and each of us looks forward to the upcoming reunion and seeing our dear friends again. It is like a family reunion once a year. We continue to go forward and will do so until the last one stands.   As we Marines, as well as our ladies always say, Semper Fi.

MARINE REUNION

News Bulletin

It will be a homecoming of sorts for former members of Marine Scout Bombing Squadron 343 late next month when they arrive in Greenville for a reunion.

Gregory's Gorillas VMSB 343 was stationed at Pitt-Greenville Airport, then Marine Corps Auxiliary Air Facility, Greenville, from December 4, 1943 until July 15, 1944. Ralph Heidenreich of Greenville, hopes fifty or more of the former squadron members will attend the April 18-22 reunion.

Heidenreich, chairman of the reunion, first came to Greenville as a member of the squadron, as did Billy Wells. The squadron was commissioned in August 1943 at the Marine Corps Auxiliary Air Facility, Atlantic, under the command of Maj. W. E. Gregory. The 225 men and fifty officers that moved to Greenville in December 1943 were the first large contingent of Marines to be stationed at the airport during World War II. The City-County airport, leased to the Navy department, was used for final flight training before shipment overseas.

The squadron left Greenville for Miramar, California, then, in August 1944 sailed for Ewa, Hawaii. It moved to Sand Island in April 1945. VMSB 343 moved again in September and October 1945 to Tsingtao, China.

Heidenreich said twenty former squadron members gathered in Reno, Nevada last March for a reunion. This year's reunion, Heidenreich said, will include a bus trip to the Cherry Point Marine Corps Air Station and to Atlantic Field and Morehead City. Heidenreich said any area residents who have memorabilia relating to the squadron's stay in Greenville, or have addresses for any VMSB 343 members, are asked to call him at 759-8030.

MOM SAVAGE

by Ralph Heidenreich

Mom Savage, known to all WWII servicemen who visited the Women's Club, also USO, in Greenville NORTH CAROLINA has become a legend in the annals of WWII. Mom Savage was the inspiration of the whole affair. My wife Evelyn, her sisters, Thelma and Sarah, were Junior Hostesses at the club. You know, young, good-looking females who would serve coffee, tea, and delicacies to the service personnel.

Mom's personality, education, and stature in life, which many of us never knew, exalted her to a plane none could challenge. She was always, "Mom".

When we had our first reunion in Greenville North Carolina (our second reunion, the first reunion was in Reno, Nevada with twenty members attending) it was a must for Mom Savage to attend. She called us all, regardless of age, "her boys". What a great lady. She, at age eighty-five plus, was escorted by her son, Stewart Savage, to the banquet. He told me his mother was very excited to see some of her many sons from WWII who came home safe.

If you will read her obituary, you will realize Mom Savage was an institution in herself. Her devotion to helping others, through the USO (Women's Club), teaching, and many other aspects of her life, her love for humanity NEVER extinguished. She was a Mom to everyone.

I, fortunately, had the great pleasure and experience to know Mom Savage. She made the USO, to all of us who visited, a home away from home. God Bless you, Mom Savage.

Semper Fi

MARINE AIR REUNION ... Lt. Col. Walter E. Gregory, USMC retired, chats with Elizabeth Savage and Ralph Heidenreich at a dinner Thursday that ended a reunion of Marine Scout Bombing Squadron 343 here this week. Gregory was commander of VMSB-343 when the squadrom moved to Pitt-Greenville Airport in 1943 to complete its training before being assigned to the Pacific. Heidenreich, of Greenville, was chairman of the reunion, while Mrs. Savage, known as "Mom" to many of the squadron members, was a hostess at the USO, housed in the Women's Club building then at the intersection of Third and Greene Streets. Over 30 percent of the squadron's 250 enlisted men and 50 officers attended the reunion. Brigadier General James M. Mead, Eastern area USMC commanding general from the Marine Corps Air Station at Cherry Point, was guest speaker for the banquet. "What is it that's different," about Marines, Gregory said. "Love ... that's what. They fight because of the Marine beside him ... the legacy of love." (Reflector Staff Photo)

THE CHRONICALS OF MILARCH

By Jack Milarch

Forty-five years after the stationing of Gregory's Gorillas in Greenville, North Carolina, the "Old" Veterans of VMSB 343 winged and motored their way back to the formation and training sight of the former Marine Air Corps Dive Bomber Squadron.

Quite a surprise to reacquaint with those eighteen to twenty-year old fellows who have now joined the senior citizen – social security set. About seventy former "officers and men" homed in on their memories of World War II, some with their Greenville sweethearts turned wives and one whose wife turned him back to his Greenville sweetheart.

There were those with limps and gimps. Most had slowed down a bit, but the old spirit and sparkle returned as they talked of those "bygone" experiences. The picture albums helped as we often heard, "that was me" and "do you remember?" as the members dove into the treasure chest of memories with both joy and sadness.

For Louise and I, the "getting there" and "coming home" was also a memorable experience that will add to our own treasure chest of memories. We may never again experience the beauty of the season as we did during the most profuse display of Spring's splendor in North Carolina and the Virginias! My memories of the Carolina springs were reinforced with this trip.

Getting to Ashville located at the end of the Smoky Mountain National Park and the southern end of the Blue Ridge National Park, would have been, in itself, a delightful experience. From Knoxville one soon trades the expressways of convenience for the byways of beauty starting at the entrance of Smoky Mountain National Park. It is truly an experience in driving coupled with the excitement of sights. Each new view is a panorama of spectacular proportions. Ashville itself is a beautiful city and we remarked that it may be a place one would want to check out for retirement. Evidently others thought this same way at the end of the last century when the Vanderbilts established the Biltmore estates at Ashville. The one-day tour we afforded ourselves was a spectacular Sunday experience. For a few dollars we were privileged to see the opulence of life for the wealthy in this memorial of an American estate equal to, and modeled after, the estates of the wealthy English Barons of yesteryear.

On Monday, rain, drizzles and fog discouraged further driving on the Blue Ridge Parkway road and we headed east on I-40. Louise would have liked to visit some of the furniture showrooms in Highpoint, but a cocktail party scheduled for the evening in Greenville kept our travels from any further sight-seeing excursions that day. As we traveled toward Greenville, I witnessed flashes of recollection: the flat farmland, the stately pine trees, the tobacco drying sheds. There were still some skeletons of homes, occupied by the poor – sitting on stones for foundations – no window shades or curtains and the only furniture one would see was a rocker on the front porch occupied by a black mother surrounded by children and a dog or two under the house. Fortunately, those sights have disappeared and the evidence of fine homes and buildings are present today. The appearance of the depression that was still present during the war has been replaced by the eco-comforts of the 80's.

Most of us who drove through Wilson commented on the beauty of Azaleas and Dogwood and the explosion of color bursting from every yard and wood lot. Greenville was a surprise. I don't think I like it better, with everything scattered to the outskirts, but the amenities of progress are there, while the downtown business area, as we remember it, resembled a ghost town. None of the stores and business places we knew are occupied.

I couldn't find the free city pool, or the skating rink. The corner drug store is empty as well as the department store next door where I could buy fifteen cents worth of jelly beans on Saturday mornings, and at my request, the attendant would pick out all the black ones. The Proctor Hotel is closed as is the Greek restaurant across the street. Oh what beautiful steaks I would select from the cooler, what beautiful people.

The theater is closed. I wonder when they played "Dixie" for the last time before the show began. Also the bowling alley where "ten pins" were in vogue rather than bowling.

The Carolina Grill, where I learned of the delectable flavor of fried oysters, still has a sign but the business is gone. I'll bet the deep-fried aroma still permeates the inside of that building. And so it goes. We can't turn back the clock.

Evelyn and Ralph Heidenreich; these two need a special place in the storehouse of memories we took home. Their efforts and interests made it all possible. They surely walked the extra mile to make our reunion a happy and memorable event. The many pictures taken will keep these memories alive.

The trip to Cherry Point and the "new Marine Corps" did not reflect what our Marine Corps was like. The location is the same but few men are seen. The hangars exist but the planes near them are foreign to me and some fly "funny". They need no runway for the take-off! They hover and even back up in mid air! Somebody called them Harrier Jets. I called them fascinating.

Atlantic field was also foreign to me. I was never stationed there, thank goodness, but some of the squadron members enjoyed the visit. The field is also a relic of wartime.

The only sad incident to our trip was to Harold Schatschneider. Harold suffered a heart attack on the last day. Fortunately, the modern Greenville-Pitt Hospital was located directly behind the Holiday Inn Motel, bringing emergency care promptly, and the staff of the capable and caring specialists treated Harold to minimize the pain and continued damage. Last word was that Harold was doing well.

Early Friday morning, Louise and I were on our way again, this time heading South and East to Moorhead City and Cedar Island to catch the Ferry bound for Ocracoke Island and the outer banks. The outer banks are an interesting phenomena of our eastern seaboard consisting of a narrow strip of land many miles along the Atlantic Ocean. The one road threads its way between the water and occasionally one will find a town or resort complex; endless beaches to play on and they report fishing is terrific. The salvage business at one time was the second enterprise as merchant ships were blown to their graveyards during storms – at times with a misplaced lantern to guide the ships to their demise.

Roanoke Island, "Elizabethan Gardens" and the "Lost Colony" (just across from the bridge from Nags Head) where the most delicious sea foods were served on the whole trip. Glad we spent some time there – wished we could have stayed longer.

Kitty Hawk, Kill Devil Island, and the Wilbur and Orville Wright Memorial, just a stone's throw away from Nags Head, was a worthwhile intermission. Interesting to learn that the dunes that now impede our view for the entire length of 120 miles along the outer banks were man-made.

We leave the outer banks and soon attempt to thread through the tunnels and bridges of Norfolk, Portsmouth, New Port, and Hampton. What a tangle of misdirection. We were glad to find Williamsburg and settle into a motel on the complex for the night. A couple of cocktails and a delicious dinner dispelled the nerves.

Our tour of Williamsburg was limited only by our stamina – a delightful place where more time is needed to digest the early American culture and habit of living. A truly historical museum of our American past. I commend the Rockefellers and their foresight to restore Williamsburg for what it is worth to us and our future generations.

Back to Norfolk and we enter the Chesapeake Bay bridge and tunnel complex, a 20 mile marvel of a man-made ribbon across the lower Chesapeake Bay. I don't know if the waves were intentionally designed in the road, but my soft riding Oldsmobile just about made me seasick at 50 M.P.H.

We entered the Delmarva Peninsula and marveled at the many large beautifully maintained country homes. What in the world would a family do with such large homes unless there were fifteen to twenty kids to fill up all the rooms? It is the only place in the U.S.A. where I have seen such a display in a rural area.

Ocean City, Maryland and its ugly complex of high-rises and motels has changed from my last visit, twenty-five years ago. The boardwalk and quaint shops are still fascinating and the beach is beautiful. I don't think I would care to be there in the summer months.

On to Annapolis and a quick drive among the buildings of the Naval Academy and on to Washington, D.C. after a stop at Popeye's for a newly discovered delicacy of Creole beans and rice. Their coffee is also great. We arrived at my sister Edith's and her husband Al's home in time to view the gardens before cocktails and dinner. Edith is always the perfect hostess and Al's stories are interesting and enjoyable. One of particular merit depicts the inflation of Washington, DC. Their home is one of several built by a contractor. All are on the same floor plan and of brick veneer. Al paid $34,000 in the early fifties, a price similar to what others paid for theirs. Last fall the house next door sold for $250,000.00. Al states his house is now worth $300,000.00. What a story!

The next morning finds us plying the banks of the Potomac until we find a chain bridge, then to Hwy. 50, and across Virginia. We enjoyed the quaint towns along the way, the rolling grassy hills amid white fences and horse farms. From West Virginia on to Ohio the road is an exercise in driving – up, down, around and around until you're sure you've scrubbed all of the rubber off of the tires.

The Ohio river changed the highway, the terrain, and the driving as we entered Ohio. By then, we were anxious to get home, check the, mail, and mow the grass. Ohio and Indiana were familiar routes and the end of an interesting, enjoyable, and memorable trip.

P.S. I was "awarded" a ticket in Brown County, Ohio for traveling an anxious 66 m.p.h. in a 55 m.p.h. zone. No points, no court appearances, just send in $35.00 please. As we used to say in the Marine Corps. "Up your gigi," Ohio.

"POW" IN MOBILE, ALABAMA

By Ralph Heidenreich

After many years of separation from our friends of VMSB 343 we found each other at our first reunion at Reno Nevada 1987. The second reunion was held at Greenville, North Carolina (our home stations) and we had a great reunion. Can you imagine the excitement of Marines who served together in 1943 through 1946 getting together again after forty years, after not seeing each other for any of those years. What a joy of life. No one can imagine the feelings we felt when we saw each other after all those years of separation.

Our VMSB 343 association grew through the years by getting old addresses of our buddies and today we have a mailing list of approximately 250. We wrote a Constitution & By-Laws and formed VMSB 343 Reunion Association in Nashville, Tennessee in 1990. Since then we have developed the best reunion association in existence. We voted to have a yearly reunion, so through the years this is what we did. Our ninth reunion was held in Mobile, Alabama. Evelyn, myself, Wally and Shirley LeTendre, Frank and Dorothy Pnyg went in early as the crash crew to set up for the reunion. Frank Lange was to bring the alcohol spirits from Florida so we were assigned the duty of getting all the fixings for the hospitality room. Wally, Frank, and myself went to Sam's Club to buy what we needed, such as mixers, potato chips, etc. – only to find out we could not buy two liter bottles of coke, 7-up, Sprite, etc. because they were considered wholesalers and they could not sell it. We then went to a super discount store where we purchased all the chasers. Frank, Wally, and I purged the aisles selecting our merchandise, selecting twelve two-liter bottles of Sprite which had a fifty-five cent discount on the next purchase. In the check-out line Wally told the cashier we were only staying for five days, so we needed to cash in these coupons now. He asked me if I had a knife, and I supplied one. He methodically cut off seven discount coupons, but on the eighth he cut too deeply into the two liter bottle and it exploded. He was covered with Sprite, his glasses dripping, the cashier dripping, her check-out counter wet all over. I was in front of him covered with Sprite as well as Frank who was behind. All the people in the check-out line (ten check-out counters) plus everyone else stopped and wondered what was happening. The "POW" sounded like a gunshot and everyone stopped in their tracks. Frank was laughing and so was I. Wally being quite embarrassed looked to me and said, "It's not funny".

I then said, "Wally, everyone's laughing".

He then looked around, saw everyone laughing, then smiled himself.

The young lady cashier, totally confused, gave us discount on all twelve bottles when Wally said we must get another two-liter Sprite to replace the defective bottle. We received a replacement and pushed our cart full of purchases to the car, leaving behind the excitement of "POW".

WHAT A REUNION
by Ralph H. Heidenreich

In 1988 around the first of May while we were having our second reunion in Greenville, North Carolina. We had our hospitality room located in a large room at the Greenville Holiday Inn. After a busy day of fun-making, everyone left the hospitality room except Skipper Bill Gregory, Glenn Kelley, our bartender, and myself. Glenn had tended bar through a busy day, drinking all his mistakes as well as other drinks of his own.

Bill, Glenn and myself sat in a triangle in the middle of the room. Bill and I had a one on one conversation going, not noticing Glenn at all. Suddenly we heard a loud thump, looked and there laid Glenn on the floor next to the chair he was sitting on, still asleep or whatever. We got him up and decided we better call it a night - for the time was 2:45 AM.

That sure was a good VMSB-343 hospitality room party.

FRIENDSHIP

By Ralph H. Heidenreich

What is friendship – I can tell you What. "But"--
it's when you go to a VMSB 343 Reunion and see again your
Marine buddies you served with fifty-five years ago shake hands
and hug. (Yes I said hugged each other.) It's the greatest feeling
you ever experienced. The next greatest is when you can hug and
say hello to their wives who support our reunions as their reunions,
for they are as much a part of the reunion association as we are.

We are extremely proud of our association, but mostly for the
support and love our wives give to this association. Without this
love and affection we could not have achieved the VMSB 343 we
now have.

May god bless us all, so that we can have many more reunions
together.

Semper Fi

IN LOVING MEMORY OF "BETTY"

March 28, 1999
by George Bobb

March 1943: I was a twenty-two year old Marine and an "Old Salt" (three years in the Corps with the Big Naval Air SEA Battle for Guadalcanal, November 13, 14, 15, 1942 behind me), when I found myself and fellow air crewmen from VMSB 131 (First Marine Torpedo Squadron) on R&R in Sydney, Australia.

The very first night there, as I walked toward a dance hall with a buddy, a beautiful young Australian girl in a white dress caught my eye. She was a vision of loveliness walking toward me, and a lady in every sense of the word, as time would prove.

My heart skipped a beat as I greeted her and her friend. She introduced herself as Betty and friend, Elsie. The conversation went well and I invited her and Elsie to accompany us to a squadron party being held at Bancrofts, the best nightclub in Sydney. As she accepted the invitation my heart was pounding.

We arrived and found Bob Woolfe, now living in West Los Angeles, Gorden Miller, Norman Pearson, Tex Zimlich and others already there. We had a wonderful time drinking and dancing the night away. That night, while dancing with Betty I heard the song "White Christmas" for the very first time and it was our song night after night.

During the course of the evening I learned her name was Elizabeth Margaret Wighton, that her mother was deceased, that she shared an apartment (a Flat as she would say) with her older sister Joyce and Aunt Sandra. Her father was a Mining Engineer working in Western Australia, and she was employed as a secretary for Overland, a car manufacturer. I met Joyce and Sandra the next day.

Later, after seeing a photo album, I found out she Figure Skated, that she was a Semi-Finalist in a Beauty Contest, in a Scarlet O'Hara LOOK ALIKE contest and that she modeled.

The group partied for seven unforgettable nights and each night when the party ended I would take her home, kiss her goodnight and return to my hotel room where I would dream about tomorrow night.

I was in the first group that flew into Sydney and scheduled to fly out on the eighth day. The second and third groups would leave the next two succeeding days. The morning I was to leave, I grabbed my bag, hailed a cab and headed for the airport. Enroute I was thinking of Betty – that I was headed back to the Canal and that I might never see her again.

I gave the cab driver her address and arrived at her Flat just as she was leaving for work. She told me to go inside and wait. Both Sandra and Joyce were there and they made me feel quite at home. That night Betty and I went to the club and had another wonderful time. When the evening ended I took her home and spent the rest of the night sleeping on a sofa.

The next morning I caught the SCAT plane for Espiritu Santo, a stripped down DC-3, bucket seats along each side. Several of us ended up in the back lying down on the baggage, half asleep and half awake. I was in a state of reverie, listening to those two big Pratt Whitney engines playing White Christmas all the way back to Espirtu Santo.

Tony Bennet left his heart in San Francisco; I left mine in Sydney, Australia.

Arriving at VMSB 131's camp site I was surprised to see all the top NCO's on area clean up detail. I found out that some one had HI-JACKED an ADMIRAL'S CASE OF SCOTCH from one of the transit TBF'S our squadron was servicing. Minutes later I found myself on the same detail for missing the first plane out of Sydney. It was worth it.

During our first tour, November 12, 1942 thru February 18, 1943, the squadron lost eleven men as a result of anti aircraft fire and Zero attacks while engaging the enemy combat vessels off New Georgia.

March 19, 1943, a few weeks after R & R in Sydney, Norman Pearson and Capt. Stiles were killed in the crash of an SNJ at Espiritu Santo. Twelve more would lose their lives, including Gorden Miller and Tex Zimlich April 8, 1943 after encountering a violent thunderstorm on a night bombing run from Henderson Field to Bougainville. The squadron was relieved at the end of April.

I returned to Cherry Point, was assigned to VMSB 343, a new dive bombing squadron. September 1944 we left the West Coast for Midway via Ewa where we acquired new SB2C-3's. Midway was a sub base and our mission was to fly Frontier Sea Patrols, escort subs in and out, and to fly sub cover during sea trails prior to their returning to combat.

Before leaving Ewa I sent Betty an Hawaiian Hulu Skirt from Honolulu. Betty and I continued to exchange letters, and early 1945 I received a letter accepting my proposal and some official papers to be filed through channels. The papers would allow her to obtain a passport and transportation. I filed them via the C.O. and sent her the fare.

The war ended August 1945 and I again found myself back at Cherry Point with two years and four months left to complete my second four-year enlistment. The letters kept coming, but the long wait for the one that would give me a departure and an arrival date continued until Oct. 1946.

Each one of her letters had become a MILESTONE along the road to a lasting reunion (San Francisco, November 14, 1946) and a marriage (Moorestown, New Jersey, December 7, 1946) that would end, only when GOD called her.

Betty and I celebrated our first week together, March 1943, in the company of fellow Marines, and our last formal night out, November 7, 1998 in the company of fellow Marines. We attended the 223rd Marine Corps Birthday ball as Guests of Marine Aircraft Group 49, Naval Air Station, Willow Grove, Pennsylvania who hosted the affair.

There we met Sgt. Maj. Dave D. Horvath and his lovely wife Karen. Dave is one who cannot sit still when the music is playing. When Karen needed a rest he grabbed Betty and had her hopping around the floor like a schoolgirl. She had a great time. Dave, upon finding out that she was from Australia, said that he had spent six months there and that he had an Australian Flag for her.

December 5, 1998 I attended the VMA-131 Deactivation Ceremony at Willow grove and it was there, that Dave gave me her flag. The flag was displayed at her viewing.

She was a wonderful wife, companion and devoted loving mother of four, grandmother of six. Her talents were many: an excellent cook, housekeeper, decorator, and seamstress – she made her own wedding dress in Australia while waiting to come over.

Never one to sit around, she became a sales representative for Dutch Maid, Fuller Brush, and finally, a local Real Estate Brokerage Firm. She was forced to leave after a triple by-pass operation June 7, 1993. As soon as she regained her strength, she volunteered her services to Kennedy Memorial Hospital twice a week and made doll clothes for our four granddaughters' American Girl Dolls.

She suffered a stroke February 8, 1999 and passed away at 6:26 PM, March 1, 1999.

She is sadly missed by her husband, children, grandchildren and the many friends she made along the way.

Loving Husband,
George Bobb

In Loving Memory of

FERNER L. BURKHOLDER

Date of Birth
August 16, 1923

Date of Death
February 17, 1996

Services
Wednesday, February 21, 1996
11:00 am
Gaut-Bacha Funeral Home, Inc.

Officiating
Rev. Wesley V. Myers

Interment
Shirey Cemetery

Arrangements By
Gaut-Bacha Funeral Home, Inc.
Pleasant Unity, Pa.

Ferner Lohr Burkholder M/Sgt –E8 Retired

Tours of Duty Jan 9, 1948 – Sept 30, 1966
              Oct 9, 1942 - Feb 4, 1946

Active duty

Maintenance Control 2.5 years M/Sgt E8
Quality Control   3.5 years M/Sgt E7
Aircraft Mechanic
Aircraft Flight Crew Chief

Last duty was at MCAS Quantico, VA consisting of Maintenance Control Chief and Quality Control Chief. These duties required supervision of approximately 50 lower rated enlisted personnel and 10 senior NCOs.

History
    First tour:
        Trained in North and South Carolina and Florida.
        Served aboard Saratoga on submarine patrol between Midway Island and home base.
        Saw action at Tarawa, Iwo Jima and Okinawa
        Awarded 3 Battle Stars

    Reenlisted
        1948 to 1952   Quantico, VA
        1952 to 1953   Japan
        1953 to 1959   Cherry Point, NC
        1959 to 1960   MCAF Iwakum, Japan
        1960 to 1966   SOES, MCAS, Quantico, VA

Schools

        Aviation Maintenance School A   March 1943 to Aug 1943
        Aviation Maintenance School B   Sept 1951 to Jan 1952
        Fairchild A/C Factory School   May 1953
        Wright Patterson A/C Engine School   Aug 1953
        A/C Logs and Records School   Aug 1960
        A/C Material Maintenance Management   July 1966

Retired to inactive after 22 years active duty

A LUCKY FIND AND A MIRACLE

by Walter LeTendre

The Following story is about Paul Swenarski, the son of Joseph Swenarski, who was a prop specialist with VMSB 343. It is a story of how Paul Swenarski's Dog Tags were blown off his body during an enemy attack while he was serving in Vietnam.

There are currently three Marines in the Swenarski family, Grandpa Joe Swenarski, his son Paul Swenarski, and Joe's grandson, Paul.

After more than 30 years, veteran has dog tags returned in the mail

By MITCH MAERSCH
Daily News Staff

Swenarski

For Vietnam veteran Paul Swenarski, finding his dog tags was better late than never.

Swenarski received his lost tags in the mail Sept. 8 of this year. The tags were lost May 10, 1968 in Vietnam and had been missing ever since.

"It was weird," Swenarski said of holding his dog tags for the first time in 30 years. "I never expected to see them again. It's something you don't want to lose."

The U.S. Marine private had his Second Battalion Thirteenth Marines First Marine Division camp attacked early in the morning by a North Vietnamese army, according to a citation by the U.S. Marine Corps.

The citation explained the camp was attacked with grenades, mortars, B-40 rockets and automated weapons. Swenarski provided cover fire for his companion with a 30-caliber machine gun fire.

Even after being wounded, Swenarski retrieved grenades and threw them back, and expended more than 20 magazines with his M-16 rifle. He was awarded a Bronze Star for his heroic actions, and the Purple Heart for being wounded.

"They got blown off, basically," said Swenarski, a former West Bend resident who now lives in Fredonia. "I got hit, lost the dog

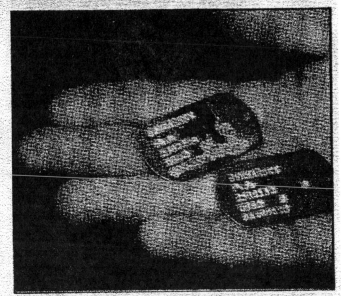

Mitch Maersch/Daily News Staff
Paul Swenarski holds his recently found dog tags. The tags were lost in Vietnam for 30 years. The tags still have mud stains and black marks from electrical tape.

tags. Basically, they spent 30 years sitting in the mud until these guys found them."

Team Commander Major Ken Royalty of the 51st Joint Task Force, Camp Smith, Hawaii, found the tags in Ngok Tavak in the Quang Tin Province.

Debbie Swenarski, Paul's wife, got a call from Tim Brown of the Disabled American Veterans in Dallas, Texas, early in September.

"They called me at two in the afternoon and I was freaking out,"

she said. "They said we have his dog tags and I said you can't, they're in Vietnam. They said 'Yeah, we were there.'

"He said it was one of the most remote places he's been to for recovery."

"They were so pleased they found the dog tags from a live guy," Paul Swenarski said. "They found all kinds of things. The major is going to keep in touch with me."

Please see **TAGS**/A6

Tags: 30 years later, man receives his dog tags

A wire communications specialist, Swenarski used electrical tape to tie his tags together to prevent jingling. He kept his can opener in between them. The troops were fed C-rations at the time.

While Swenarski was wounded, he was still one of the lucky ones.

"Of the 42 (Marines) we had 12 killed and 24 wounded," he said. "I was on the last helicopter to get out.

"We also had a platoon of Arvin (South Vietnamese Army) with us for protection and a platoon of

Chinese Mercenaries with us headed by an Australian captain. He was very instrumental in getting some of the guys out ... spotting all the booby traps, setting them off."

Swenarski spent a total of six weeks in Vietnam, then a year and a half in hospitals to take care of his wounds. He was in a hospital in Guam for the first two months, then at Great Lakes (just north of Chicago) for 14 more.

"He has over 100 pieces of shrap-

nel left in his body," Debbie Swenarski said. "He can't go through an airport detector — it beeps."

Paul Swenarski is a second generation member of the U.S. Marines. His son, Paul of West Bend, enlisted on Sept. 20, 1988, exactly 32 years to the day after dad enlisted.

Paul Sr. has been a systems technician for Ameritech for the past 26 years. He and Debbie celebrated their 29th wedding anniversary Sept. 13.

JOINT TASK FORCE - FULL ACCOUNTING
BOX 64044
CAMP H. M. SMITH, HAWAII 96861-4044

4 Sept 98

Dear Sir

It is an honor to present you with your Dog Tags found at the battle site of Ngok Tavak during the 51st JFA. During my EOD survey of the site a Vietnamese official found them laying close to the 4.2 mortar position. As I am sure you are aware, a recovery element is currently excavating the site and have already found remains.

Ken Royalty
MAJ. IN
Team Commander

SECTION IX

A FINAL PERSPECTIVE

A FINAL PERSPECTIVE

by Walter Letendre, Compiling Editor

When I look in the mirror each morning, I don't see the seventy-six year old man whose graying hairline is receding more and more each day, whose waistline has grown from twenty-nine inches to thirty-eight inches, whose aching right knee slows his progress, and whose acid reflux needs regular medicinal treatment. What do I see? I see a twenty year old marine recruit with a crew-cut and sun-tanned face standing at attention in front of his D.I. (Drill Instructor) in boot camp. The D.I. barks: "Stand up straight!" "Suck in that gut!" "Square back those shoulders!" "Tuck in that chin!" "Get your hands out of your pockets!"
I still hear his voice, and that's the me I want to see looking back at me from the mirror. Someone who was taught that it's important to keep in shape and look after your buddies.

What I learned in the Marine Corps has had a positive effect on everything I have done in my life since I volunteered to sign up with the Marines: in my professional career; in my family; in my church; my relationships with others; and ultimately now with those of us in V.M.S.B. Reunion Association. Having found one another again after more than forty years, and the joy and happiness that brings us proved the D.I. was right. Semper Fi.

Another Perspective
On the occasion of our Fiftieth Wedding Anniversary on July 5, 1997, our son, Dan, expressed his own interpretation of the Marine Corps' influence on my life – and his life, too:
"How to do just about anything the Marine way: … My dad had a way of showing us how to do anything the way they did it in the Marines. I was amazed at how many things the Marines did. I

always thought they just fought the bad guys. I did not realize that they also made beds, folded socks, put up storms, washed cars, shined shoes, brushed teeth, cut the grass, did the dishes, peeled potatoes, the list goes on and on. It always started with, 'This is how we did it in the Marines', which usually meant that you were doing it all wrong and needed to start over. I can't even imagine what it's like at those Marine Corps reunions, but I'll bet that everything is done the Marine way there."

"Hair. This too was done the Marine way. My father only knew one style of cut -- the crew cut, and I just want to say that not only was I paying attention (which was hard because you usually had two or three brothers sitting in front of you trying to make you laugh while you got your hair cut), but I learned how to give the haircut. If you'll look at my sons you can see I am now a third degree blackbelt in crew-cutting."

And this is what our son, Wally, had to say: "I remember when my parents would get us ready for a day long invasion of Beaulah Beach. It was much like a military operation. Dad was the drill sergeant, keeping us all in line, making sure we were all equipped with the proper gear and in the personnel carrier on time.

"Mom was the supply officer, getting all the necessary food, drink and hardware neatly packed with a speed and precision that would have impressed General Schwartzkopf.

"Upon arrival at the lake, we'd secure our zone and set up camp. We would then storm the beach. I should mention that there were six boys and two girls in our family, so it closely resembled leading a platoon into action."

Walter LeTendre

INDEX

BATTLE ZONES
Bougainville – 23,88,90
Coral Sea -- 81
Guadalcanal – 22,75,77,79,82,84,137,249,296
Midway – 22,32,33,34,52,54,55,71,74,75,120,139,149,150,153,161,
   163,164,165-220,221,231,235,240,254
Okinawa – 3,214,228,239,240,242,245,247,253,254,271,272,276,279
Pearl Harbor – 3,31,35,51,52,80,86,162,166,221,223,225,244,249,
   257,276
Solomon Islands – 77,82
Tulage Harbor -- 89
Vietnam – 237,299

BETTY HUTTON – 214,214a

CASANOVA CAFÉ -- 252
CHINESE COMMUNISTS – 233,242,244,245,246,255,257,259,267,268,
   274,277
CHINESE NATIONALISTS – 242
CHRISTMAS ON MIDWAY 1944 – 196a-d
CITIES: China Occupation – maps and news articles - 272a-d
Laichow – 242,255,
Peiping – 242,247,267,271,274,275
Shantung – 240,243,244,245,249,254,258,260,273
Tsingtao – 10,11,240,242,243-251,253,254,257-262,264-271,273-279,285
Tientsin – 242,243,247,249,255,257,258,260,263,267,269,272

EASTERN CAROLINA TEACHERS COLLEGE (ECTC) – 31,94e,141

GOONEY BIRDS – 120,165,166a-i, 170,187,204
GREENVILLE, NC RESIDENTS
Barber, Mr. N. H. 100,118, 119
Brown, Mrs. J. Keif   97
Clark, Mr. 110,115
Hearne, Mr.   146
Moore, Sarah   97
Perkins family   122
Pollard, Elizabeth   98
Savage, Margaret   100
Savage, "Mom"   286
Savage, Stewart   286
Tew, Father Maurice   113
Tournage family   109, 146

PHOTO DIRECTORY

SECTION III

ABREVIATIONS FOR MILITARY RANK

MARINE CORPS

Gen.	General
Lt. Gen.	Lieutenant General
Maj. Gen.	Major General
Brig. Gen.	Brigadeer General
Col.	Colonel
Lt. Col.	Lieutenant Colonel
Maj.	Major
Capt.	Captain
1st Lt.	First Lieutenant
2nd Lt.	Second Lieutenant
C.M.G.	Chief Marine Gunner
M.G.	Marine Gunner

NAVY

Adm.	Admiral
V.Adm.	Vice Admiral
R. Adm.	Rear Admiral
Com.	Commodore (obsolete)
Capt.	Captain
Comdr.	Commander
Lt. Comdr.	Lieutenant Commander
Lt.	Lieutenant
Ens.	Ensign
C.W.O.	Chief Warrant Officer
W.O.	Warrant Officer

Friends Made, Moments Shared, Memories for Life:
An Oral History of World War II

One of a kind book written and compiled by the reunited veterans of a World War II Marine bombing squadron—VMSB-343.

"Not all Marines got into combat in World War II yet their service and sacrifice was just as real as those that did. Their experiences are just as worthy of remembrance too. This book makes this point abundantly clear. It is the product of the Reunion Association of Marine Scout Bombing Squadron 343 (Gregory's Gorillas) and it traces the history of VMSB-343 through the "recounting of human experiences held alive in hearts and memories"(ii) of former members.

"VMSB-343 was commissioned on 1 August 1943, trained on the East Coast and deployed to Midway Island flying Curtiss SB2C-3 'Helldivers' in October 1944, long after the war had moved westward toward Japan. Ironically, it entered a more hostile environment after the war when it deployed to Tsingtao, China. As is characteristic when using oral history, the human experience is told in these memoirs which provides readers with an important and interesting look at squadron life in World War II. Details often overlooked in more "official" histories come out, such as first impressions of the Marine Corps, off-duty activities, interaction with civilians in Greenville, North Carolina and China, the hazards of operational flying and poignant memories of friends lost in accidents. A good many, in fact, most of the memoirs are from former *enlisted* Marines, therefore, the book presents an aspect of World War II Marine aviation often forgotten or overlooked—the experiences of the gunners, mechanics and crewmen in Marine squadrons. Also included is a great collection of photographs, newspaper clippings and official documents that help tell the story of VMSB-343.

"The Reunion Association of VMSB-343 is to be commended for undertaking this project. Maybe more veterans' organizations will follow their example. By so doing we can preserve the priceless heritage of Marine aviation and learn more about what the day to day life of Marines was like at the same time."

Fred Allison, Washington Naval Yard, Marine Corps Oral Historian, Marine Corps Aviation Assn. Yellow Sheet, Quantico VA

Comments, Thanks, & Words of Praise for "Friends Made, Moments Shared, Memories for Life: An Oral History of World War II"

"Thank you, thank you. You have no idea of the pleasure I had in reading 'Friends Made, Moments Shared, Memories for Life."
                              Col. Russel Janson, Orange CA

"I loved reading "Friends Made, Moments Shared, Memories for Life". War is a scary word, however, the book shed a natural and truthful light on how each individual felt and dealt with the war through their own eyes, spoken from their minds and hearts. It covered fears, fun, facts, romance, dedication to each other and our country. It felt so real. Over all, it put a new perspective for me on the war. I've read it twice and I know I will read it again and share its inspiration with others."   Ginny Rinka, New Berlin WI

"I don't believe you guys. This book is incredible, stupendous. Any ink left in your pens? How much shoe leather did you wear out? Thanks for the memories."   Edward A. Galante, West Palm Beach CA

"This book is wonderful. What perfect timing. My husband, Jefford, has really gone down hill healthwise. It was such a pleasure to see him fondle the book with tears. God Bless You"
                              Libby Jeffords, Gulf Shores AL

"I enjoyed the book immensely. Brings back many fond memories."
                              T/Sgt Jim Love, Winter Haven FL

"I'm not reading the book at one sitting. I'm savoring it page by page and enjoying every moment."   Len Haney, Nashville TN

"The book is wonderful. I get very emotional reading it, and I will treasure it all my life."   Polly Beckham, Satuma AL